Universal Orlando

The Ultimate Guide To The
Ultimate Theme Park Adventure

Kelly Monaghan

Universal Orlando

The Ultimate Guide To The

Ultimate Theme Park Adventure

Published by
The Intrepid Traveler
P.O. Box 531
Branford, CT 06405
http://www.intrepidtraveler.com

Copyright © 2003 by Kelly Monaghan
Third Edition
Printed in Canada
Cover design by Foster & Foster
Maps designed by Evora Schier
Library of Congress Card Number: 2001099730
ISBN: 1-887140-42-5

Publisher's Cataloguing in Publication Data. Prepared by Sanford Berman.
    Monaghan, Kelly.
    Universal Orlando: the ultimate guide to the ultimate theme park adventure.
Branford, CT: Intrepid Traveler, copyright 2003.
    Revised and updated edition of Universal Studios Escape (2000).
    Includes five maps.
    PARTIAL CONTENTS: Universal Studios Florida. -Islands of Adventure. Seuss Landing. Lost Continent. Jurassic Park. Toon Lagoon. -CityWalk. -Resort Hotels.
    1. Universal Orlando--Description and travel--Guidebooks. 2. Theme parks--Orlando region, Florida--Guidebooks. 3. Hotels--Orlando region, Florida--Guidebooks. I. Title. II. Intrepid Traveler.
    917.5924

Trademarks, Etc.

Other Books by Kelly Monaghan

The Other Orlando:
What To Do When You've
Done Disney & Universal

Fly Cheap!

Home-Based Travel Agent:
How To Succeed In Your Own
Travel Marketing Business

The Travel Agent's Complete Desk Reference
(co-author)

Choosing A Host Agency

Air Courier Bargains:
How To Travel World-Wide For Next To Nothing

Air Travel's Bargain Basement

Table of Contents

List of Maps

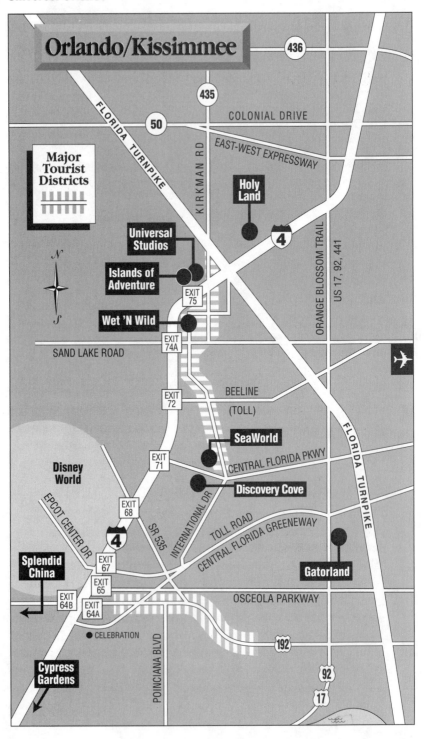

Orlando/Kissimmee

Major Tourist Districts

436

435

50

COLONIAL DRIVE

KIRKMAN RD

EAST-WEST EXPRESSWAY

FLORIDA TURNPIKE

Holy Land

Universal Studios

Islands of Adventure

4

EXIT 75

ORANGE BLOSSOM TRAIL

US 17, 92, 441

Wet 'N Wild

EXIT 74A

SAND LAKE ROAD

EXIT 72

BEELINE

(TOLL)

SeaWorld

EXIT 71

CENTRAL FLORIDA PKWY

FLORIDA TURNPIKE

Disney World

Discovery Cove

INTERNATIONAL DR

EXIT 68

EPCOT CENTER DR

4

SR 535

TOLL ROAD

CENTRAL FLORIDA GREENEWAY

Gatorland

Splendid China

EXIT 67

EXIT 65

EXIT 64B

EXIT 64A

OSCEOLA PARKWAY

CELEBRATION

POINCIANA BLVD

192

Cypress Gardens

92

17

CHAPTER ONE:

Planning Your Escape

Move over, Mickey! Universal Orlando is here and Orlando will never be the same.

First came the Mouse. Walt Disney World, that is, which opened near Orlando in 1971 as a new, improved version of California's Disneyland. With the luxury of 43 square miles in which to expand, the new park quickly eclipsed its West Coast namesake. Three more theme parks followed the Magic Kingdom — EPCOT, Disney-MGM Studios, and Animal Kingdom. For good measure, Disney threw in a couple of water parks, a slew of themed resorts, and a sprawling entertainment district.

In 1990, Universal Studios opened Universal Studios Florida. Like Disney World it was an outpost of a California original. It quickly became Orlando's number-two attraction but it was just one theme park to Disney's many and seemed doomed to perpetual also-ran status.

That all changed in 1999 when Universal Studios Florida almost literally exploded and, in the process, was renamed Universal Orlando. For the first time, Walt Disney World had competition worthy of the name and Orlando had its second multi-park, multi-resort, multi-activity, all-in-one, never-need-to-leave-the-property vacation destination. But Universal Orlando is no mere copycat operation. It represents a new departure in theme park and resort destinations that is very shrewdly positioned in the marketplace to build its own following and capitalize on any decline of the Disney brand. It is sure to capture the imagination of new generations of vacationers who are seeking a different kind of theme park experience as they enter the new millennium.

Just What Is 'Universal Orlando'?

Universal Orlando bears a superficial resemblance to Disney World in that it is a multi-park, multi-resort vacation destination. But whereas Disney sprawls over a vast area, Universal Orlando is comfortably compact, allowing its guests to spend less time getting around and more time enjoying themselves. And while Disney World harkens back to an earlier time, Universal is very much of the moment, with an eye to the future.

There are two theme parks here. The original movie-studio-themed **Universal Studios Florida** (USF) is still going strong. It continues to add new thrills using the very latest in technology. Almost literally next door is **Islands of Adventure** (IOA), an attraction that takes the whole notion of "theme park" to the next level, with awesome rides and fine dining.

CityWalk is an entertainment and restaurant complex that lies between the theme parks. This is very much an adult experience, although several restaurants will also appeal to the younger set. CityWalk recognizes the ethnic diversity of America in a way that is new to theme park entertainment. It also sets a new standard for luxury, with an ultra-gourmet restaurant. And CityWalk rocks. It boasts the world's largest Hard Rock Cafe and Hard Rock Live, a performance space that hosts some of pop music's biggest names.

The clearest signal that Universal intends to go mano-a-mano with the Mouse is the proliferation of themed, on-property resort hotels. **Portofino Bay Hotel** has set its sights on becoming Orlando's first five-star hotel. This ultra-luxury property is a photographic reproduction of that favorite destination of the international jet set, Portofino, Italy. Here you can unwind in the splendor of high-tech suites and dine in a world-class restaurant before catching a complimentary motor launch to the theme parks. More casual is the **Hard Rock Hotel**, which radiates a hip California sensibility and is just steps away from the front gate to Universal Studios Florida. The **Royal Pacific Resort** evokes the romance of far-off Bali, just minutes away from the theme parks by foot or boat. Two additional properties are planned but they do not yet have names, let alone projected completion dates.

Just a stone's throw away is **Wet 'n Wild**, a water park which Universal now owns. It has not been officially rolled into the "Universal Orlando" brand, but it is included in some ticket options and is well worth a visit. In addition to the hundreds of acres on which Universal Orlando sits, Universal owns more land nearby, fueling rumors of yet more future expansion.

Universal Orlando is a family destination. But, unlike some parks we could name, Universal seems to recognize that "families" come in all sorts of different packages. Parents with little ones will find this an almost ideal place for their kids. And yet families with teenagers will not have to worry about

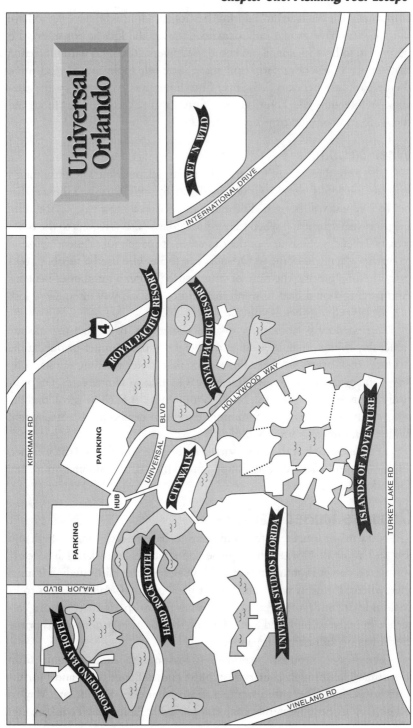

complaints that the rides are "dorky." Best of all, adults who have yet to have kids, or who have grown kids, or who have left the kids at home, or who never plan to have kids at all can come to Universal Orlando without feeling that they're in a kiddie park. And those snobbish sophisticates who think theme parks are beneath them may find themselves won over by the dazzling architecture, the luxurious accommodations, the gourmet food, and the wide array of nighttime entertainment.

When to Come

There are three major questions you must ask yourself when planning a visit to Universal Orlando: How crowded will it be? What will the weather be like? When will my schedule allow me go? For most people, the third question will determine when they go, regardless of the answers to the other two. The dictates of business or the carved-in-stone school calendar will tend to dictate when you come to Orlando. For those who can be flexible, however, carefully picking the time of your visit will offer a number of benefits. And parents should bear in mind that school officials will often allow kids out of classes for a week if you ask nicely.

During slow periods, the crowds at Orlando's major theme parks are noticeably thinner than they are at the height of the summer or during the madness of Christmas week. On top of that, hotel rates are substantially lower and airfare deals abound. Likewise, Orlando in winter can seem positively balmy to those from the North, although it's unlikely you will find the temperature conducive to swimming (except in heated pools). Spring and fall temperatures are close to ideal.

Let's take a look at these two variables: the tourist traffic and the weather. Then you can make a determination as to which dates will offer your ideal Orlando vacation.

Orlando's Tourist Traffic

Most major tourist destinations seem to have two seasons — high and low. For most of Florida, the high season stretches from late fall to early spring, the cooler months up North. Low season is the blisteringly hot summer, when Floridians who can afford it head North. Orlando, thanks to its multitude of family-oriented attractions has five or six distinct "seasons," alternating between high and low, reflecting the vacation patterns of its prime customers — kids and their parents.

The heaviest tourist "season" is Christmas vacation, roughly from Christmas Eve through January first. Next comes Easter week and Thanksgiving weekend. The entire summer, from Memorial Day in late May to Labor Day in early September, is on a par with Easter and Thanksgiving.

There are two other "spikes" in attendance: President's Week in February and College Spring Break. Various colleges have different dates for their Spring Break, which may or may not coincide with Easter; the result is that the period from mid-March through mid-April shows a larger than usual volume of tourist traffic. The slowest period is the lull between Thanksgiving and Christmas. Next slowest (excluding the holidays mentioned earlier) are the months of September, October, November, January, and February. Tourism starts to build again in March, spiking sharply upward for Easter/Spring Break, then dropping off somewhat until Memorial Day.

It would be nice to know how theme park attendance rises and falls from month to month. That information is a closely guarded trade secret, but fairly reliable *annual* estimates are available. Here are annual attendance figures for Orlando area parks for 2001 as estimated by the trade paper *Amusement Business*:

Rank*	Park	Attendance
1	The Magic Kingdom	14,700,000
3	EPCOT	9,000,000
4	Disney-MGM Studios	8,300,000
5	Disney's Animal Kingdom	7,700,000
6	Universal Studios Florida	7,200,000
7	Islands of Adventure	5,500,000
8	SeaWorld Orlando	5,100,000
11	Busch Gardens Tampa	4,600,000

Numbers represent the parks' national rankings. Disneyland, California, was number two, Universal Studios California was tied with SeaWorld Orlando for number eight.

In other words, on any given day, the largest crowds will tend to be at the Disney parks. If you've been a Disney regular, Universal Orlando will seem quite manageable by comparison. Of course, this pattern could well change. If Universal Orlando lives up to its potential, we could see the day when the crowds at Disney and the crowds at Universal are about the same.

While there is a definite advantage to timing your visit for one of Orlando's slack periods, you will probably still be amazed at how many other people are lining up to see the same things you are. What counts as a small crowd to an Orlando theme park may seem like a horde to you. The best advice is to avoid the absolutely busiest times of the year if possible. I find the slow months of fall and spring to be ideal. I even enjoy January, but I'm not the sunbathing type. If you come during the summer, as many families must, plan to deal with crowds when you arrive and console yourself with the thought that, in bypassing Disney, you've automatically avoided the worst crowds.

The Best Day of the Week to Visit

A fair bit of advice has been written about the best days of the week to visit the various Orlando area theme parks and I've written my share of it. In the fullness of time, however, I have come to believe that such guidance is of limited use, for a number of reasons. First, as I've already mentioned, if you're anywhere near normal, theme park crowds are going to seem overwhelming most of the time anyway. Second, there's a problem with averages. You could well arrive on the "slowest" day of the week only to find that there's been an atypical blip in attendance.

One reason for attendance being unpredictable is the frequent special events and corporate promotions that can flood the parks with an extra several thousand people or even close them altogether. To cite just one example, I was visiting Islands of Adventure on a day when a major car manufacturer was hosting thousands of its customers as part of a special promotion. Not only did these lucky folks get early admission to the park, so that when the rest of us mere mortals were allowed in the place was packed, but the park closed early so that the favored few could have the place to themselves until late into the night.

Note: In theory, you can get advance warning about these park-flooding events by calling Guest Services, but only 48 hours prior to the actual date of the event.

That being said, one popular view has it that Saturday and Sunday are good days to visit Universal Studios Florida on the theory that most folks start their vacations on the weekend and that most of those who come to Orlando go to Disney first. Following this theory, Monday through Wednesday become the "busy" days. However, my recent experience suggests just the opposite. I found fewer people in the parks on weekdays and bigger crowds on the weekends. Go figure.

It is also more than likely that Universal Orlando will attract still larger crowds now that it has three on-site resort hotels open. Therefore, it will be a good while before anyone will be able to hazard an educated guess as to which are the busiest days of the week at the parks. And even then, it will only be "on average."

Finally, there is no reason to cram a visit into a day or two (although many people insist on doing just that). If you decide to make Universal Orlando your primary Orlando destination, you can get a fourteen-day Orlando FlexTicket (see *The Price of Admission*, below) that offers unlimited admission to both Universal Orlando parks, as well as some others nearby. The per-day cost of these tickets is quite reasonable and they remove the insane pressure that can come with a park-a-day touring schedule.

The Best Time of Day to Visit

If it's hard to guess which day of the week is best, it is possible to give sound advice on what time of day to come to the parks, regardless of the day of the week or the time of year.

For optimum touring conditions, plan on arriving at the park early, very early. The gates open anywhere from 15 minutes to an hour prior to the official opening time. The parking lot opens even earlier. This is especially true during busy periods; if you are visiting during one of the lulls you can probably afford to sleep in a bit.

Arriving crowds peak at about 11:00 a.m. and then level off. Many families and the faint of heart start leaving about 4:00 p.m. Thus, your best shot at the more popular rides is before 11 and after 4. During the heat of the day you can catch the shows in the large theaters that offer posted starting times and shorter lines. You may also find that in the hour before closing many rides have no lines at all.

Of course, CityWalk is another matter. Things don't start hopping there until 8:00 or 9:00 p.m. and the place stays open until 2:00 a.m. Factor that in to your planning. I don't know about you, but a day that starts at seven and ends at two the next morning doesn't sound like a vacation to me.

Orlando's Weather

Orlando's average annual temperature is a lovely 72.4 degrees. But as we've already noted, averages are deceptive. Here are the generally cited "average" figures for temperature and rainfall throughout the year:

	High (°F)	Low (°F)	Rain (in.)
January	71	49	2.3
February	73	50	2.8
March	78	55	3.2
April	83	59	1.8
May	88	66	3.6
June	91	72	7.3
July	92	73	7.3
August	92	73	6.8
September	90	73	6.0
October	85	66	2.4
November	79	58	2.3
December	73	51	2.2

(Source: Orlando/Orange County Convention & Visitors Bureau)

Use these figures as general guidelines rather than guarantees. While the average monthly rainfall in January might be 2.3 inches over the course of many years, in 1994 there were 4.9 inches of rain that month and in 1996 almost 4 inches fell in the first two days alone. January of 1996 and 2001 saw lows dip into the twenties.

I find Orlando's weather most predictable in the summer when "hot, humid, in the low nineties, with a chance of afternoon thunderstorms" becomes something of a mantra for the TV weather report. Winter weather tends to be more unpredictable with "killer" freezes a possibility. As to those summer thunderstorms, they tend to be localized and mercifully brief (although occasionally quite intense) and needn't disrupt your touring schedule. I was once in Orlando for a summer week when it rained somewhere every day but never on me. On the other hand, I got nailed every day on another summer week there. Another thing to bear in mind is that June through September is hurricane season, with July and August the most likely months for severe weather.

Gathering Information

Universal Orlando maintains a number of phone lines that provide recorded information about prices, opening hours, and special events. These numbers can also be used to get in touch with Universal Orlando Vacations if you are interested in booking a package. Toll-free numbers that work in the United States and Canada are (800) 711-0080, for Universal Vacations, and (888) 322-5537, for general park information. For the hearing impaired, there is a TDD line at (800) 477-0672. If you are calling from other countries outside the U.S. or are already in Orlando, the number to call is (407) 363-8000, which is the main switchboard. This one seems to have more options for recorded information than the others. However, by pressing "zero," you can speak with an "attraction representative" at any time if you have specific questions or requests.

The Internet

There are a number of resources on the Internet you may want to check out before your trip. The main Universal Orlando site can be found at www.universalorlando.com, and while it will win no usability awards, it has perhaps the most "official" information. It has sections on both parks, City-Walk, and the resorts as well as information about upcoming special events. If you are interested in booking a package vacation that includes a hotel room and other add-ons, the web site for Universal Studios Vacations is www.universalstudiosvacations.com.

Note: Universal changes the configuration of its web sites with some regularity. If any of the links given here don't work, try logging on to www.universalstudios.com and clicking through to the section that interests you.

An excellent source of pre-trip intelligence can be found at www.disboards.com. The "dis" in disboards stands for "Disney Information Station," but the site has a discussion board devoted exclusively to Universal Orlando. On the home page, scroll down and click on the link for "Universal Studios/Islands of Adventure Forums." When the page loads, bookmark it. This is the place to come for the latest discoveries and rumors and a good place to ask those unanswered questions.

Getting There

Universal Orlando is located near the intersection of the Florida Turnpike and Interstate 4 (abbreviated I-4 and pronounced "Eye Four"). It is bounded by Kirkman Road on the east, Vineland Road on the north, Turkey Lake Road on the west, and I-4 on the south. Universal Boulevard runs through the park property from the International Drive tourist district to Vineland Road.

There are four entrances to the park complex. The main entrance is via the Universal Boulevard overpass from International Drive. There are also entrances from Kirkman, Vineland, and Turkey Lake. The Kirkman Road entrance sits on a main thoroughfare and is quite busy. The other entrances seem almost anonymous by comparison. Perhaps because of that, they tend to be the lesser used and, therefore, the quickest ways into the park. All entrances feed cars down broad, palm-lined boulevards to a toll-plaza-like entrance between the two huge, multilevel parking garages sandwiched between Universal Boulevard and Kirkman Road.

Practically speaking, the entrance you wind up using will probably depend on the direction from which you approach.

From International Drive

If you are staying in one of the many hotels in the International Drive area, your obvious approach is up Universal Boulevard, crossing I-4 to the main entrance. This approach provides a nice view of the Royal Pacific Resort and Islands of Adventure as you cross the Interstate.

From the south on I-4

Coming from the south (that is, traveling "east" on I-4), the most direct route into the park is to take Exit 75A, International Drive, and turn left at the top of the ramp. This puts you on the Universal Boulevard approach. There are two other alternatives, however. On especially busy days, when the overpass at Exit 75A can be backed up, you might save a little time by getting off at Exit 74, Sand Lake Road. Turn left off the ramp, under the Interstate and then right almost immediately onto Turkey Lake Road. You can't miss it;

just follow the "Universal Orlando" signs. Just opposite Dr. Phillips High School, you will see the Universal sign on your right. Your third choice is to drive past Exit 75A and take the left hand Exit 75B, which feeds you onto Kirkman Road; the entrance to the park will be on your left at the first light.

From the north on I-4

For visitors approaching from the north (that is, traveling "west" on I-4) your best bet is Exit 75B, but you won't be able to take the immediate left turn into the park. That's because there's not enough room to get across four or five lanes of traffic to the far left lanes to turn into the park. In fact, a wisely placed road divider prevents you from even trying. The signs direct you to proceed north to Vineland, turn left, and use the entrance on Vineland. Another alternative is to turn right onto Major Boulevard almost immediately upon exiting I-4. Major is a divided road, so it's easy to make a U-turn. Once you do so, you will be pointed straight at the Universal Orlando entrance when you return to the intersection.

Another alternative is to drive past 75B and take Exit 74B. This will take you to Hollywood Way, where you can turn right and head straight to the parking garage.

From the Florida Turnpike

Whether you are coming from the north or south, take Exit 259 and follow the signs to Tampa via I-4, then get off I-4 at either 75B or 74B.

Parking at Universal Orlando

Whichever entrance you use, you will arrive at the tollbooth entrances to the two huge "parking structures"; one is five levels high, the other six, and they hold a total of 20,000 cars. At the booth, an attendant will collect your daily parking fee of $8 ($10 for RVs, buses, and trailers). Annual Pass holders can show their pass for **free** admission to the parking lots. Parking is **free** to everyone after 6:00 p.m., which offers an extra incentive to visit CityWalk's restaurants and clubs or see a movie on a day you don't have a ticket to the parks.

Don't bother asking the booth attendants for maps to the park or parks you'll be visiting that day; they don't have them. You'll pick up these guides later.

Once you have paid the parking fee, you will be directed to your parking space. Your parking options are virtually nonexistent. You will be directed in such a way that the two parking structures are filled in the most efficient way possible. The parking structures are ingeniously designed so that as one level fills up cars are routed directly to the next level, without having to corkscrew upwards as you do in most multistory parking lots.

One of the great things about Universal Orlando's parking is that most of it is covered, thus protecting you and your car from the broiling Florida sun and those sudden afternoon downpours. During the busy summer season, however, the open roof is filled fairly early in the day to spare the lot attendants the worst of the sun and heat. Great for the employees, not so great for you. That means that if you arrive at midday you may find yourself parked on the roof. I am told that if this is not acceptable to you (and I believe it shouldn't be), you can ask the attendant to direct you to sheltered parking. It may take some polite persistence but it can be done.

The various sections in the two structures are named after movies or characters (Jaws, Jurassic Park, Cat in the Hat, and so forth); rows are indicated by numbers, with the first digit indicating the level. Thus "Jaws 305" would be on the third level. As always in these situations, it's a good idea to make a written note of your parking lot location.

Universal Orlando claims that the farthest parking space is just a nine-minute walk from CityWalk. That may be stretching (or shrinking) the point, but moving walkways speed your journey.

Handicapped Parking. Handicapped parking spaces are provided close to the main entrance on Level 3. Follow the signs for handicapped parking and you will be directed accordingly.

Preferred Parking. If you'd like to shave a few minutes off your walk, you can pay $11 for a parking space that's almost as close to the main entrance as the handicapped spaces.

Valet Parking. Get in the Hollywood spirit by having an attractive young attendant park your car for you as you pull up right at CityWalk. The fee is $8 if you stay for less than two hours and $15 for over two hours. Annual Pass holders pay a flat rate of $8 no matter how long they stay. Just follow the signs. If you are coming just for lunch Monday through Friday, between 11:00 a.m. and 2:00 p.m., you can have your parking stub validated at most full-service CityWalk restaurants (Emeril's validates at all times including dinner and on weekends). A stay of under two hours is **free** and two to four hours is $8, but a stay of over four hours will cost you the full $15, even with validation.

Passenger Drop-Off. If you're in a generous mood, you can drop your family off near CityWalk before you go off to park the car. Look for the signs directing you to the drop-off area, which is just across Universal Boulevard from the Valet Parking area.

Parking for Resort Guests. If you are staying at one of the on-property resort hotels, use any of the entrances and follow the signs to your hotel. All of the hotels have separate gates, with separate, paid parking facilities for guests. Non-guests can also use these lots but at rates higher than those charged to guests and considerably higher than the fee levied at the main theme park parking garages. In other words, the hotel parking lots do not provide an economical alternative to parking in the main parking structures.

Alternatives To Driving

If you are staying at an off-site hotel, look into the **Super Star Shuttle** bus service that ferries guests at area hotels to Universal Orlando, SeaWorld, and Wet 'n Wild. There are about eight separate routes and hotels as far afield as downtown Orlando and the Route 192 corridor in Kissimmee participate in this program. The service is typically **free** to guests, but some hotels may charge a small fee. In theory, you must be a guest of a participating hotel to use this service, but this is seldom if ever enforced. Hotels near a pickup point, cheerfully send their guests next door to catch the shuttle.

Unfortunately, information on routes, schedules, and which hotels are currently participating is hard to come by, although you might try calling (866) 482-9077. The best bet is to ask the hotel you are planning to book whether they participate in the program. Once at Universal Orlando, you can stop by the bus station between the parking garages and CityWalk to see which routes service which hotels. The service runs from the hotels to Universal Orlando all day, with fewer departures in the afternoon. Return trips don't start until about 4:00 p.m. You should be able to pick up a printed schedule for your route from your hotel or the driver.

If you are staying along the International Drive corridor, you can hop on the **I-Ride Trolley** to reach the corner of Kirkman Road and Major Boulevard (stop number five on the Main Line). From there, follow the walking directions given below. The trolley is 75 cents for adults and 25 cents for those 65 and over. Kids 12 and under ride **free**. Exact change is required. All-day and multi-day passes are available at many hotels and retail shops along I Drive. For more information, call toll-free (866) 243-7483 or view a route map at www.iridetrolley.com on the Internet.

You can also reach the parks via public transportation; Orlando's **Lynx buses** cost just $1 (25 cents for seniors 65 and older), exact change required. These fares are likely to rise to $1.25 and 50 cents, respectively, on January 1, 2003. A weekly bus pass costs $10. Route 21 links downtown Orlando with the I-Drive corridor, passes through the Major Boulevard hotel area (see *Chapter Six: Staying Near the Parks*) and stops near the Hub in Universal Orlando. Route 24 links Universal Orlando to the I-Drive hotels north of Sand Lake Road. If you're staying in the Walt Disney World area, bus routes 301 and 302 will bring you to the Kirkman Road side of Universal's property.

For more information, call (407) 841-2279 or visit www.golynx.com on the Internet. On the web site you will be able to download maps of the routes that interest you.

It is actually possible to **walk to the parks** at Universal Orlando, although very few people do it. If you are staying at one of the hotels located along Major Boulevard on the Kirkman Road side of the property (see *Chapter Six*), you can reach CityWalk in 15 to 30 minutes, moving at a purposeful pace. From Major Boulevard, follow the signs for valet parking and you will find an escalator that takes you to CityWalk. If you are staying on the other side of I-4, at one of the hotels near Universal Boulevard, you are looking at a minimum walk of 30 minutes, maybe closer to an hour. Coming from this direction, look for the bus drop off station and take the escalator leading to the Hub (see below).

Of course, if you are staying at one of Universal's on-property resort hotels (See *Chapter Five: The Resort Hotels*) you should take advantage of the free water taxis or shuttle buses to CityWalk.

Arriving at Universal Orlando

From your parking space, you will walk to the nearest of a series of escalators and moving sidewalks that will funnel you to "**the Hub**," a large circular space on the third level with access from both parking structures and from the bus station. In the Hub, you can rent a wheelchair ($7), but not strollers or electric convenience vehicles. For those, you'll have to wait until you reach the theme parks. The Hub also has restrooms and a few vending kiosks if you just can't wait to get that Universal t-shirt.

From the Hub, it's a straight shot along more moving sidewalks to City-Walk, Universal's dining, shopping, and entertainment venue. In CityWalk, you can continue straight ahead to Islands of Adventure or hang a sharp right and head for Universal Studios Florida.

Whichever park you choose to visit, you will cross a bridge over the artificial canal system that links the resort hotels to the parks and arrive at an attractive entrance plaza where you will find a row of ticket windows and, nearby, a Guest Services window, of which more later.

You should also be sure to pick up a map of the park you are visiting. The "Studio Guide" for Universal Studios Florida and the "Adventure Guide" for Islands of Adventure are large fold-out brochures with a map of the park and a listing of restaurants, shops, and helpful information. A separate insert lists show times and various seasonal attractions. On the front will be listed the park's official opening and closing times and the dates for which the information in the insert is valid, which could be for just the one day on which you receive it or for several days or weeks. If you don't receive one when you pay for your ticket, additional copies of the guides are available just inside the gates and at various shops throughout the parks.

Opening and Closing Times

Universal Orlando is open 365 days a year. In the slow seasons, the park may open at nine and close at six. During the high season, the park may open at eight and close at eleven. The gates may open a few minutes prior to the "official" time, but there is no "early entry" program allowing access to the parks an hour or more prior to the posted opening time. But if you can't enter early you can stay late. Typically, the last visitors aren't shooed out until an hour or more after closing time.

As noted previously, opening and closing times can also be affected by special events. If the park will be closing early, there should be a large sign posted near the entrance gates informing you of this sad fact. You can also double-check today or tomorrow's official hours by calling (407) 363-8000, the main information number.

Tip: Take your time leaving the parks at night unless you're absolutely exhausted (a strong possibility). Strolling slowly through these magical streets under a moonlit sky, hand in hand with that special someone, can be an unforgettable experience when you are among just a handful of people in the park.

The Price of Admission

Universal Orlando has a variety of ticket options, with a variety of bells and whistles. These choices offer great flexibility but they can get a bit confusing. First of all, when we talk about "admission" we are talking primarily about the two theme parks. There is no admission charge to visit CityWalk, although you will have to pay cover charges to enjoy the nighttime entertainment in the clubs and restaurants. There are single-day "passes" to each park, along with two- and three-day options. Then there are several Annual Pass options. On top of that, there are multi-day, multi-park tickets that let you visit some of Universal's nearby neighbors as well. Let's try to sort through all the choices.

Note: The information below may change. All prices given below include tax. They are subject to change without notice and most likely will go up slightly sometime during 2003. Whatever your choice, children under three are admitted **free**. All that being said, prices were as follows when this book went to press:

Single-Day Passes

Single-day passes are valid for only one park, not both. You can choose which park you wish to visit.

One-Day Universal Studios Florida Pass OR
One-Day Islands of Adventure Pass:

Adults:	$52.95
Children (3 to 9):	$43.41

Multi-Day Passes

Multi-day passes offer unlimited park to park access. They also include seven days of admission to CityWalk's nightclubs. If you don't use the second (or third) day of your pass, it remains valid forever, but you cannot transfer it (i.e. give it to someone else).

Two-Day Universal Orlando Pass:

Adults:	$100.65
Children (3 to 9):	$ 86.87

Three-Day Universal Orlando Pass:

Adults:	$116.55
Children (3 to 9):	$102.77

Note: Universal sometimes offers a "Third Day Free" promotion, but it requires that you use all three days within a seven-day period.

CityWalk Party Passes

CityWalk's entertainment venues levy a "cover charge" whenever there is live entertainment on offer. If you wish, you can purchase a CityWalk Party Pass for $9.49, including tax. It offers admission to all entertainment venues for the evening, so you don't have to pay a separate cover at each club or restaurant. However, if you purchase a two- or three-day theme park pass, you can use that pass for seven consecutive nights of nightclub admission in CityWalk. The clock starts ticking on the first day you use the pass. In other words, you could buy a three-day pass, spend three days exploring the two theme parks, going to bed early each night, and then spend the next four nights enjoying CityWalk. This is an excellent incentive to buy the multi-day passes. For more on the CityWalk Party Pass, see *Chapter Four: CityWalk*.

Annual Passes

At the moment, Universal Orlando offers a number of Annual Pass options. One offers admission to both parks. The other, the Celebrity Annual Pass, applies only to Universal Studios Florida. This begs the question, why not an Annual Pass just for Islands of Adventure? It is possible that, in the future, Universal may decide to offer one; if they do, it is logical to assume that the cost will be the same as for the Universal Studios Florida pass. On the other hand, they may phase out the Universal Studios Florida Celebrity Annual Pass, so your only option would be a pass that includes both parks. Time will tell.

Two-Park Annual Pass:

All ages:	$169.55

Universal Studios Florida Celebrity Annual Pass:

Adults:	$95.35
Children (3 to 9):	$79.45

In addition to the freedom to come and go as you please, Annual Passes confer a number of other benefits, including free parking and free use of the kennels for your pets. You will also receive a 20% discount on souvenir purchases in the parks and a 10% to 15% discount on food (not alcohol) at many of the park restaurants, although not at the walk-up stands. The Annual Pass will get you a 20% discount on a CityWalk Party Pass and a 10% discount on food in most of CityWalk's restaurants (15% at Latin Quarter).

There are additional discounts and privileges that change from time to time; they are outlined in the brochure you receive with your Annual Pass and changes will be announced in the annual passholders' newsletter, which is published quarterly. For the very latest information on the Annual Pass call (407) 224-7750.

If you'd like to save some money, consider the Power Pass. It gives you unlimited two-park access but there are some important restrictions. First of all, there are blackout dates: every weekend in July, the first two weekends in August, December 24 through January 1, and April 13 through 26, 2003 (Spring Break time). Also, you will receive no discounts at park restaurants and shops and you will have to pay for your parking.

Two-Park Power Pass:

All ages:	$105.95

Bear in mind that Annual Passes take the form of a photo ID card, so there's no chance of lending, passing on, or selling your Annual Pass to someone else. Every time I visit, the cheerful gate attendant checks my Annual Pass to see if that's my smiling face on my card.

Florida Resident Specials

Universal frequently makes special offers designed to encourage those who live closest to the parks to visit more often. A typical Florida Resident Special involves a reduced price for admission to both parks during slower periods of the year. To get these deals you must be able to show proof of Florida residence such as a Florida driver's license or some other document linking you to a Florida address. The best way to find out what Florida Resident Specials might be available to you is to call (407) 363-8000, press "0," and ask for information.

The Star Treatment

If an Annual Pass doesn't offer enough ego gratification, consider a **Non-Private VIP Tour**. For $127.20 you can join a group of up to 14 other VIPs for a five-hour escorted behind-the-scenes tour of the park of your choice. Not only will you see things that ordinary visitors don't, you will be whisked to the head of the line for "at least seven" attractions and be guaranteed the best seats. These tours start at 10 a.m. and noon.

If you'd like to corral up to 14 close friends, you can all take a private eight-hour **Exclusive VIP Tour** for $1,802. That gives you nearly 60 percent more time and reduces the per-person cost by about $7. What's more, this tour starts when you want it to and can be customized to your group's special interests (so it doesn't have to last eight hours if you don't want it to). The group must be preformed, that is you can't join another group. Nor does your group have to total 15. You can bring five friends or ten, or go all by yourself. The cost remains the same.

If you'd like to do a VIP Tour of both parks, that can be arranged too. These tours last two days, one day for each park. The **Two-Day, Two-Park Non-Private VIP Tour** costs $243.80, a $10 per person pre-tax discount off the cost of two one-day tours booked separately. The **Two-Day, Two-Park Exclusive VIP Tour** option costs $3,180 for a group of up to 15 (a $28 per person pre-tax discount). If you book a one-park VIP tour and then decide to use the VIP tour option for the other park within ten days, they will extend the same modest discount.

If you'd like to cram both parks into the same day, your only option is to take the **One-Day, Two-Park Exclusive VIP Tour**; there is no non-private version on this one. This one costs $2,968 for up to 15 people, lasts up to eight hours, and you can pretty much set your itinerary with your tour guide.

All VIP tours include regular admission to the park. You can get more information about both kinds of VIP tours, as well as additional options, by calling (407) 363-8295 during normal business hours, Monday through Friday. You can also request a VIP tour reservation online by logging on to www.universalorlando.com. Reservations must be made at least 72 hours in advance (two weeks prior during summer and holiday periods) and a credit card hold is required. If you must cancel your reservation, do so at least 72 hours prior to the tour; otherwise, your credit card will be charged.

If you can afford it, this is a terrific way to see the parks. I've done it and found the guides to be personable and extremely knowledgeable. Becoming a guide is a lengthy and highly competitive process and only a few who apply make the cut.

The Orlando FlexTicket

Several of the non-Disney theme parks, namely Universal Orlando, Sea-World, Wet 'n Wild, and Busch Gardens Tampa have banded together to offer multi-day, multi-park passes at an extremely attractive price. This option is called the Orlando FlexTicket and it works like this:

Four-Park, Fourteen-Day Orlando FlexTicket — Universal Studios Florida, Islands of Adventure, SeaWorld, Wet 'n Wild:

Adults	$180.15
Children (3 to 9)	$143.05

Five-Park, Fourteen-Day Orlando FlexTicket — adds Busch Gardens Tampa:

Adults	$215.46
Children (3 to 9)	$175.12

These passes are valid for fourteen consecutive days, beginning on the day you first use them. They offer unlimited visits to the parks they cover. As for parking, you pay at the first park you visit on any given day. Then show your parking ticket and Orlando FlexTicket at the other parks on the same day for complimentary parking. FlexTickets purchased at Universal Orlando also include the seven-day CityWalk Party Pass described earlier.

Unlike the Universal Orlando multi-day passes, these tickets expire. That is, if you use an Orlando FlexTicket for only five days, you can't return a month later and use the remaining nine days. These passes offer excellent value for the dollar; the four-park pass works out to under $13 a day! On top of that, they offer the come and go as you please convenience of Annual Passes, albeit for a much shorter time.

Passes may be purchased at any of the participating parks' ticket booths or through your travel agent before coming. There are a number of attractive vacation packages now being offered that include the Orlando FlexTicket plus hotel accommodations in the International Drive area and other benefits. For more information, call Universal Studios Vacations at (800) 711-0080, or contact your nearest travel agent.

Which Price Is Right?

If your schedule only allows one day at Universal Orlando, the choice is both simple and complicated. Simple because you'll only need a one-day pass, complicated because you must choose between two wonderful parks. If you've already visited Universal Studios Florida, then you will clearly want to opt for Islands of Adventure. Even if this is your first visit to Orlando, I would still recommend Islands of Adventure. It's new, it's special, and it's the one all your friends back home will want to hear about. On the other hand, if you hate roller coasters and enjoy "edutainment," you might find Universal

Studios Florida more to your liking. Read the chapters that follow and make your own decision.

Given the fact that unused days on the multi-park Universal Orlando Passes never expire, consider purchasing a three-day pass even if you have only two days. That third day will cost just $15.90 (for an adult). If you use it one year later, assuming the one-day admission remains at $52.95, you have made 333% on your money. If only my mutual funds did that well!

Annual Passes become a good investment when you know you will be returning to Orlando within the next 12 months. The cost of a regular Annual Pass is significantly less than the cost of two two-day passes. It is even less than the cost of three one-day passes, when you add the $8 daily parking fee.

Think twice before grabbing a Power Pass, however. To my mind, this option makes sense only if you have figured a way around paying for parking. The dollar difference between a regular annual pass and the Power Pass is roughly eight days of paid parking. Factor in the blackout dates and the money you lose by not getting a discount on meals and shopping and the Power Pass looks even less attractive.

The Orlando FlexTicket is also an excellent buy for people whose main interest is Universal. You can spend one day each at the other parks and the remaining eleven or twelve days coming and going as you please at the two Universal parks. The per-day cost is $13 to $15, which adds up to a lot of entertainment bang for the buck.

If you have any doubts about whether you will enjoy the theme park experience, you can hedge your bets. You can upgrade any pass to a more expensive pass while you are still at the park. The price you pay will be exactly what you would have paid if you'd purchased that pass when you first arrived.

Discounts

Getting a discount to Universal Orlando is a good bit harder than it used to be, but it is still possible to save a few bucks. Here's how.

AAA. Members of the American Automobile Association receive a $3 per ticket discount for all members of their party, up to six people, at the gate on the two-day Universal Orlando pass only. The policies on AAA discounts change frequently, so double-check by calling one of the toll-free numbers given earlier.

AAA members can also buy their tickets through a local AAA club office, in which case the discount will no doubt be better and will vary from club to club. Once inside the parks, your AAA card is good for a 10% discount at the shops and restaurants.

Coupons. The Orlando area is awash in throwaway publications aimed at the tourist trade. They all contain discount coupons for many attractions in the area, including the major theme parks. When they are available, a typical discount is $2.50 off for each of up to six people. Discount coupons must be presented at the ticket windows at the parks and do not apply to Annual Passes or VIP tours.

Discover Card. Paying for your tickets with a Discover Card gets you a $10 discount on the admissions price.

Fan Club. Members of the Universal Fan Club get an array of discounts. Membership is free but the catch is you must enroll through your employer, which must participate in the program. The Fan Club program is available to companies with more than 100 employees (more than 50 in Florida). For information on how to get your company enrolled, send an email to fanclub@universalorlando.com.

Medical Discounts. Disabled guests receive a 15% discount. If you have a medical condition that prevents you from enjoying Universal's more intense or active rides — even if you do not consider yourself "disabled" — go to the "Guest Services" window near the ticket booths to inquire about a disability discount. This is a good strategy for grandparents who know they'll be sitting out *Back To The Future, Dueling Dragons,* and some others. You will not be asked for documentation to prove you have a disability or other medical condition.

Ticket Brokers. Another major source of discounts is ticket brokers. There are dozens of them scattered around the tourist areas, many of them located in hotel lobbies. Ticket brokers concentrate on the major attractions and the dinner shows that are an Orlando staple. Discounts for the major theme parks aren't as good as they used to be. At most you will be able to shave a few bucks off the price of the popular Universal Orlando passes. At worst, you will pay full price in exchange for the convenience of not waiting in a long ticket line at the parks.

One place worth checking out is the Official Visitors Center at 8723 International Drive, which is operated by the Orlando/Orange County Convention and Visitors Bureau. There you will find plenty of discount tickets, coupon books, and the free Orlando Magicard, which offers a broad array of discounts at hotels, restaurants, and attractions.

On the Internet. Ticket brokers are cropping up on the Internet. One of them, Ticketmania, offers Universal Orlando passes for about $2 to $10 off, depending on the pass. To this they add a $4 per order shipping fee ($5 for delivery outside the United States), although from time to time they offer free shipping. The Ticketmania web site is www.ticketmania.com.

Timeshare Come-ons. Some ticket brokers advertise Universal tickets for an eye-popping $20 or even for free. The catch is you must agree to sit through a presentation on timeshare properties. There's "no obligation," of course, but you can expect to be subjected to a concentrated hard sell. Another thing to consider before going for these super-cheap tickets is that the tickets Universal sells to the timeshare tour folks are heavily restricted; for example, they do not allow park-to-park access.

Travel Agents. Travel agents with a valid IATAN or CLIA card and a printed business card receive complimentary one-day admission to the parks. Other members of their party (up to six) will each receive a $2.50 discount on a one-day pass, $5 on a multi-day pass.

Vacation Packages. If you purchase a vacation package from your travel agent, one that includes airfare, hotel, and a rental car, as well as passes to Universal Orlando, you are probably getting a very good buy on the tickets. If you are making Universal Orlando the primary focus of your trip, these package deals offer excellent value and make a lot of sense.

Buying Tickets

Your best bet is to buy tickets before you come to Orlando, since the clock doesn't start ticking on your Passes until you turn them in at the parks. If you use a travel agent, allow several weeks to receive your tickets. You can also visit your local AAA office if you are a member, or try the services of Ticketmania, described above.

If you wait until you get to Orlando, you can purchase tickets at the park when you arrive for your visit, but I recommend purchasing your tickets before then, especially if you have only one or two days to spend at Universal Orlando during high season. This will save precious time. Your best bet is to buy tickets at the park a day or so before your visit, perhaps during a visit to CityWalk. A good time to purchase tickets at the park is in the late afternoon. Tickets can also be purchased at the Universal Studios store in the Orlando International Airport, where many tourists begin their Orlando adventure.

Universal Express

Long lines are the biggest complaint people have about theme parks. Wouldn't it be great if you could just get on every ride without having to cool your heels in line for an hour or more? Well at Universal Orlando there are two closely related programs that let you do just that.

Universal Express for Everybody

Both parks are dotted with high-tech electronic kiosks that allow you to book a ride time on your favorite attractions. The kiosks look and operate a bit like ATMs and each kiosk handles bookings for one or more nearby rides.

You begin the booking process by swiping your ticket through a slot, or running your annual pass under a bar code scanner. Next you choose the ride you wish (if there is more than one offered by that kiosk) and a one-hour window in which you'd like to ride. The machine provides you with a small chit, called an Express Pass, with your reserved time printed on it.

When the time comes to ride, you return to the attraction and look for the special Universal Express entrance, which will be clearly marked, and hand your chit to an attendant. Then head to the front of the line and enjoy the ride. The system monitors bookings to assure that no one has more than a 15-minute wait.

You can hold only one Express Pass at a time. To get another, you must either use the pass you have, wait until the one-hour window in which you chose to ride has passed, or wait two hours from the time you got your pass (the time is printed on the chit).

Those who have used the FASTPASS program at Walt Disney World will find the system familiar. The main differences with the Universal system are that it works for almost all rides, not just the most popular, and it allows you to choose your own ride time instead of assigning you one.

Universal Express for Resort Guests

Guests at the on-site resort hotels (see *Chapter Five*) get the best deal of all. They can use their room keys (which look like credit cards and are personalized with the guest's name) to gain immediate access to the Universal Express queues. Simply flash your key at the attendant and you are in. Better yet, you can use this perk all day and ride each ride as many times as you wish.

At check in, you can ask for a key for every member of your party, so everyone staying in the same room can take advantage of this perk at his or her own discretion. Otherwise, up to four people — sometimes five — can be admitted with one room key.

Your room key gives you preferred Universal Express access on the day you check in and all day the day you check out. So you could check in very early and, even though your room isn't ready, get a room key to use at the parks. When you check out, simply hang on to your room key and use it at the parks for the rest of the day.

Some attendants barely look at your room key but others do. I was once asked for photo ID by someone who wasn't sure that the bearded guy in front of her was really named Kelly.

Exceptions to the Rule

Not all rides accept Universal Express. At Islands of Adventure, the privilege is not valid at *Pteranodon Flyers* or *One Fish, Two Fish*. And while you can use it at IOA's mega roller coasters, it will not get you to the front of the separate line of folks waiting for seats in the coaster's front row. At Universal Studios Florida, you cannot use Universal Express on *Woody Woodpecker's Nuthouse Coaster* or to jump the line at the water slide in *Fievel's Playland*. The rides and attractions that feature Universal Express will be indicated by the Universal Express logo on the park map you pick up when you enter the theme parks.

Notes and Comments on Universal Express

You may sometimes hear Universal Express referred to as "Front of the Line" or FOTL. Some people mistakenly take this to mean that they will quite literally be placed on the ride ahead of everybody else who is waiting. Not so. In effect, you are placed on a separate, shorter queue. You may experience a short wait, but it should be no more than 15 minutes and is usually much less.

Tip: There is actually a downside to Universal Express. Because you miss the queue line, you miss the setup for the ride's storyline. Consequently, you don't experience the ride at its fullest. So my advice is to use the Universal Express system only when absolutely necessary or after you have ridden a ride a few times.

Universal Express is not the only way to jump to the front of the line. A few rides in each park offer "single rider lines" that can cut your waiting time dramatically. I have called them out in the *Good Things to Know About...* sections of the appropriate chapters.

Of course, Universal Express rules and policies may change, so check with Guest Services or your Universal Orlando resort hotel concierge for exceptions and restrictions at the time of your visit.

Good Things to Know About . . .

Here are some general notes that apply to both of the theme parks at Universal Orlando. Notes that are specific to the individual parks will be covered in the appropriate chapter.

Access for the Disabled

Universal Orlando makes a special effort for its disabled guests. (In fact, you are likely to see disabled people among the staff at the parks.) Special viewing areas are set aside at most rides; there are even kennels for guide dogs that cannot accompany their masters on some rides.

Wheelchairs can be rented in the Hub (see above under *Parking*), as well as inside the parks, for $7 per day. Electric convenience vehicles can be rented just inside the entrances to both parks; the rate is $35 per day, with a

$50 deposit and 24–hour advance reservation.

Auditions

If you think being a performer at Universal Orlando would be a lot of fun, you are not alone. To whet your appetite, check out the Universal Audition Hotline at (407) 224-7622, where they announce upcoming tryouts and give details on exactly what they're looking for. Who knows, this could be your big break.

Babies

Little ones under three are admitted **free** and strollers are available for rent if you don't have your own. There are also diaper changing stations in all the major restrooms (men's and women's). But that's as far as it goes. Make sure you have an adequate supply of diapers, formula, and baby food before you head for the park.

Strollers can be rented just inside the entrances of both parks. Single strollers are $7 per day and doubles are $14.

Baby "Swaps"

All rides can accommodate parents whose little ones are too small to ride. One parent rides, while the other waits in a holding area with the child. Then the parents switch off and the second parent rides without a second wait in line. It's a great system.

Breakdowns

Rides break down. They are highly complex mechanical wonders and are subjected to a great deal of stress. Some mechanical failure is inevitable. If you are in line for a ride when it breaks down, you are entitled to a pass that will give you priority access to the ride once it's working again. Since most rides are repaired fairly quickly, a breakdown can be a blessing in disguise. Simply return at your convenience once the ride is back up and be escorted to the head of the line.

Car Trouble

If you return to your car and find the battery dead, Universal will give you a free jump start. Raise the hood to alert the attendants. If the problem is more serious, they will help you get help.

Drinking

Universal Orlando provides beer at outdoor stands and in all sit-down restaurants and many fast-food outlets as well. Wine is also available. Hard liquor is served at many restaurants and at walk-up windows in CityWalk. The legal drinking age in Florida is 21 and photo IDs will be requested if there is the slightest doubt. Try to feel flattered rather than annoyed. Taking alcoholic beverages through the turnstiles as you leave the parks is not allowed.

Emergencies

As a general rule, the moment something goes amiss speak with the nearest Universal employee (and one won't be far away). They will contact security or medical assistance.

First Aid. Each park has two first aid stations. See the chapters on the individual parks for information on locations.

Lost Children. It happens all the time, and there's a good chance an alert employee will have spotted your wandering child before you notice he or she is gone. Rather than frantically search on your own, contact an employee. Found kids are escorted to Guest Services and entertained until their parents can be located.

Lost Property. Go to Lost & Found on the Front Lot at Universal Studios Florida or in the Port of Entry at Islands of Adventure and report any loss as soon as you notice it. The Guest Services window in CityWalk also has a lost and found section. Be prepared to provide as accurate a description as possible. Universal has an excellent track record for recovering the seemingly unrecoverable.

Guest Services

The friendly folks at Guest Services can answer just about any question you have and help you out when things are going wrong. If you have a problem or complaint while in the parks, seek out the Guest Services office at the front of the park (in the Front Lot at USF and in Port of Entry at IOA). If you have a question you can call (407) 224-6350 and press option #5 to speak with a Guest Services representative. If you memorize just one Orlando phone number, make it this one. You might even want to program it into your cell phone.

Leaving the Parks

You can leave either park at any time and be readmitted free the same day. Just have your hand stamped with a fluorescent symbol on the way out; when you come back, look for the "same day reentry" line and pass your hand under the ultraviolet lamp. You will also have to show your ticket again, since some tickets only allow admittance to one park. Most people use this system when they visit the restaurants in CityWalk or go back to the hotel for a quick afternoon nap, but it's a good idea for Mom and Dad to have their hands stamped when leaving the park for the day. Why? Just in case you get to the car and discover that Junior has left his E.T. doll somewhere on the grounds. The hand stamp will speed up your visit to Lost & Found.

Lockers

Electronically controlled lockers are available at both parks and allow unlimited in-and-out all-day access. They cost $5 a day and accept both bills and credit cards.

Pets

If you have pets of whatever description, inform the attendant when you pay for your parking and you will be directed to the Universal Studios kennels. Pet boarding is $5 a day for each animal and the accommodations are comfortable if not precisely luxurious. You supply the food, they supply the bowl and water. However, Universal's staff will not feed or care for your pet; they won't even touch it. If your pet needs to be walked or fed at specific times, you must return to the kennel and take care of it yourself.

Shopping by Phone

Forgot to buy a souvenir for your favorite uncle? Want to get a video preview of the parks? You can take care of both through Universal's mail order department. Call (407) 224-5800 (there is no toll-free number) and they will help you shop.

Smoking

There are smoking sections in all restaurants and smoking is, of course, permitted outdoors. An exception: smoking is not permitted in lines to the rides and attractions. Many smokers ignore this rule, probably out of ignorance. Bear in mind that many foreigners visit Universal Orlando and most of them come from countries where America's fetish with secondhand smoke seems quaint if not absurd. So before you learn how to say "Put that #@*!!% cigarette out," in French, German, Spanish, Japanese, and Portuguese, signal a passing attendant and let them take the heat.

Visiting the Resort Hotels

The Portofino Bay, Hard Rock, and Royal Pacific hotels offer plenty of atmosphere along with good restaurants and bars. You don't have to be a hotel guest to enjoy them. Feel free to stroll over from CityWalk or the theme parks for a meal or drinks or just to look around. Or take the complimentary water taxi from the dock in CityWalk.

A Note on Costs

Let's face it, visiting a theme park resort destination is not precisely a budget vacation, and Universal Orlando is no exception. A three-day visit by a typical family of four will cost nearly $400 in admissions alone. Of course, compared to other forms of entertainment, Universal Orlando offers excellent value for the dollar, as most people will agree.

Nonetheless, most of us must keep an eye on how much money we are spending, so throughout the book I have tried to give you a quick idea of how much things like restaurants and hotels cost using dollar signs.

For restaurants, I have tried to estimate the cost of an average meal, without alcoholic beverages. In the case of full-service restaurants, I have based my estimate on a "full" meal consisting of an appetizer or salad, an entree, and dessert. At the end of the book, I list hotels that are off Universal's property but convenient to the parks. For hotels, I have tried to estimate the cost of one night's stay in a double room. The cost rankings are indicated as follows:

	Restaurants	**Hotels**
$	Under $10	Under $50
$$	$10 – $20	$50 – $100
$$$	$20 – $30	$100 – $150
$$$$	Over $30	Over $150

Accuracy and Other Impossible Dreams

While I have tried to be as accurate, comprehensive, and up-to-date as possible, these are all unattainable goals. Any theme park worth its salt is constantly changing and upgrading its attractions. Restaurants change their menus; shops revamp their choice of merchandise and even the theme of the shop itself. On top of that, some attractions are seasonal; that is, they operate only when the crowds come.

What are most likely to change, alas, are prices. Like any business, Universal reserves the right to change its prices at any time without notice, so it's possible that prices will be revised after the deadline for this book. If you do run into price increases, they will typically be modest.

The Intrepid Traveler, the publisher of this book, maintains an entire web site with updated information about Universal Orlando and other non-Disney attractions in the Orlando area. Log on there for the latest on prices and new rides and attractions:

http://www.TheOtherOrlando.com

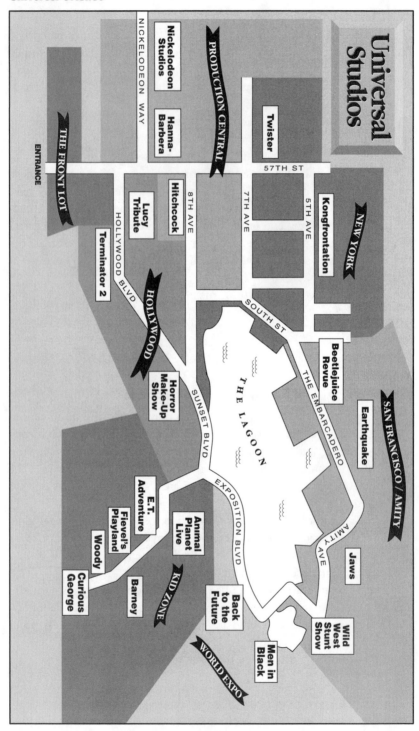

CHAPTER TWO:

Universal Studios Florida

"Ride The Movies!" the brilliant ad slogan coined by Steven Spielberg, says it all. Here is a movie-based theme park containing some of the greatest thrill rides in the world — along with a short course in the filmmaker's art (cleverly disguised as entertainment) — all sprinkled through a huge, meticulously detailed, working movie set that can make the simple act of sitting down to eat a hot dog seem like an adventure.

When Universal Studios Florida opened in 1990, it instantly became the number two draw in Orlando, right after Mickey's realm down the Interstate. With just over 100 acres and a price tag of a mere $650 million, Universal couldn't match Disney in size and scope. But that didn't mean Universal was willing to accept perennial also-ran status. There are a number of elements that set Universal Studios Florida apart from Disney and, say some, make it superior to Disney.

The word that visitors and locals most frequently use to differentiate Universal from Disney is "adult." Whereas Disney World is perceived by many as a kiddie park that adults will enjoy, they see Universal as a park conceived with grown-ups in mind. There are a number of reasons for this:

Adult Themes. Many Universal attractions are based on films and shows that appeal primarily to adults — *Jaws, Earthquake, Terminator,* and *Twister* are a far cry from *Honey, I Shrunk the Kids.*

Intensity. Whereas Disney (at least in its early days) would tend to tone down rides in the development stage lest they frighten young children, Universal Studios seems to delight in seeing just how intense they can be. *Jaws* and *Back To The Future* are prime examples.

Beer and Wine. Beer and wine are readily available at Universal. And not just in the restaurants. Don't be surprised to see a beer vendor plying those long lines on hot summer days. Some of the sit-down restaurants serve pretty decent wines by the bottle and at a few places you can get a mixed drink. In spite of the ready availability of alcohol, there is remarkably little evidence of drunkenness. Evening crowds may tend to be a bit more boisterous, but I have never seen any real unpleasantness.

There are two other elements that, while not necessarily contributing to the "adult" nature of the park, tend to set Universal apart:

Film Production. Universal Studios Florida is (as they never tire of telling you) a working studio. Virtually every corner of the park was designed in such a way that it could serve the needs of Universal's own film makers as well as those of other producers who use the facility to shoot films, TV shows, and television commercials. The New York set can be "dressed" to stand in for virtually any urban setting in the world, they claim. Don't be surprised if you see a film crew at work during your visit. You are welcome to watch if you are discreet.

Pyrotechnics. If Universal Studios Florida has a stylistic signature, something that tells you that this is a Universal attraction and not someone else's, it has to be their lavish use of fire, fireworks, and loud explosions. You can almost feel your eyebrows singe on *Earthquake, Twister,* and *Jaws.*

Dining in Universal Studios Florida

Dining at Universal is unlikely to win any kudos from die-hard gourmets. Still, Universal seems to do a pretty good job of holding prices down while serving food most people will enjoy. And if you want to have a nice meal while visiting the park, you can do pretty well. Finnegan's and Lombard's Seafood Grille, the two full-service restaurants in the park, have at least a dish or two that's better than average. Try the Catch of the Day at Lombard's or one of the Irish specialties at Finnegan's, for example, and you will feel well fed indeed.

For most families, however, the fare will be of the standard fast-food variety — most of it pretty good and not too outrageously priced considering you are a captive audience. The most conspicuous bit of price gouging is to be found in the soft drinks. Small, medium and large soft drinks are $1.79, $2.29, and $2.99 respectively, plus tax of course. You can purchase your large soft drink in a "souvenir container" and get it refilled throughout the day for $1.79 per refill, but even that option prices soft drinks at about what you'd expect to pay for a beer back home. Cost-conscious parents might want to steer thirsty little ones to the water fountains which are, mercifully, dotted throughout the park.

In addition to the standard eateries, which are described in detail later, there are innumerable street-side kiosks that appear and disappear as the crowds and weather dictate. From these vendors you can get everything from candy-coated peanuts, to soft pretzels, to fresh fruit.

Shopping in Universal Studios Florida

Without thinking too much about it, it's easy to spend more on gifts and souvenirs at Universal than you spent on admission. The standard, all-American souvenirs (t-shirts and the like) are priced only slightly higher than their off-park equivalents, and some of them are very nicely designed. Universal also offers a line of upscale clothing, with the Universal logo displayed very discreetly. You can find these items at the Universal Studios Store, as well as at a few other locations in the park. They are expensive, but worth it.

Rather than lug purchases with you, take advantage of Universal's package pickup service. Most shops will be happy to send your purchases to the Universal Studios Store, near the front entrance, where you can pick them up on the way out. Or you can simply save all your shopping for the end of your visit and stop into the Universal Studios Store while the rest of the crowd is rushing to the gate at closing time. This shop has a good, although not complete, selection of merchandise from virtually every other shop in the park. You can also shop by phone by calling (407) 224-5800.

Another option is to visit the Universal outlet store in nearby Belz's Outlet Mall on International Drive. They offer a selection of discontinued and discounted Universal merchandise, and I have heard reports that sometimes they carry items that are still currently on sale in the parks. All of Universal Studios Florida's shops will be described in some detail later.

Good Things to Know About . . .

Here are some notes that apply specifically to Universal Studios Florida. General notes that apply to both parks will be found in *Chapter One.*

First Aid

There is a first aid station on Canal Street, across from *Beetlejuice's Graveyard Revue* and just beside Louie's Italian Restaurant. You'll also find help at Family & Health Services on the Front Lot.

Getting Wet

The *Curious George* play area in Woody Woodpecker's KidZone is straight out of a water park, and kids who visit there will not be able to resist the temptation to get absolutely drenched. Parents should plan accordingly, especially on cooler days when a wet child could catch a chill. So bring a towel and a change of clothes.

Height Restrictions and Other Warnings

Due to a variety of considerations, usually revolving around sudden movements and the configuration of lap restraints, a few rides will be off-limits to shorter (typically younger) guests. The following rides have a minimum height requirement of at least 40 inches:

The FUNtastic World of Hanna Barbera (stationary seating is provided)

Back To The Future . . . The Ride

In addition, *Men In Black* has a minimum height requirement of 42 inches and *Woody Woodpecker's Nuthouse Coaster* is closed to riders under 36 inches. Any child under 48 inches must be accompanied by an adult and must be able to sit upright without help.

PG Ratings

Universal urges "parental discretion" for kids under 13 on the following rides and attractions:

The Gory, Gruesome & Grotesque Horror Make-Up Show

Terminator 2: 3-D

Alfred Hitchcock, The Art of Making Movies

Beetlejuice Graveyard Revue

In addition, *Jaws* may be too intense for very small children. Most parents seem to ignore the warnings. In this day and age (sadly, perhaps), it's hard to imagine a child being shocked by anything.

Reservations

Lombard's Seafood Grille is the only one of Universal Studios Florida's full-service restaurants to accept dining reservations. They are highly recommended at any time and especially if you are visiting during the busy season, although a reservation is not an absolute guarantee of avoiding a short wait. You can make your reservations first thing in the morning when you arrive or by phone up to 24 hours in advance. The direct line to Lombard's is (407) 224-6401.

Single-Rider Lines

To help shrink long lines, *E. T. Adventure* opens a single-rider line when things get busy. *Men In Black* has a single-rider line open all the time.

Special Diets

Lombard's Seafood Grille and Finnegan's can provide kosher meals with 48 hours advance notice. Call Food Services at 407-363-8340 to make arrangements. The Studio Guide brochure's list of dining spots calls out restaurants offering vegetarian meals and "healthy choices." In addition, Lombard's offers a nice selection of light seafood entrees and salads. If you're trying to stick to a low-fat regimen, lotsa luck. Your best bet will be the salads and fruit plates.

Special Events

The year is sprinkled with special events tied to the holiday calendar. Most of the events listed here are included in regular admission, but separate admission is sometimes charged for evening events.

Among the holiday-themed events Universal Studios puts on are:

Mardi Gras. New Orleans' pre-Lenten bacchanalia comes to Florida in the form of a nighttime parade, complete with garish and gaudy floats, lots of Dixieland jazz, and plenty of baubles and beads that are flung into the outstretched hands of the crowd.

Fourth of July. Universal Studios celebrates America's birthday with a small town celebration on steroids. It's Universal's biggest fireworks display of the year, one you will feel in the core of your being as well as see and hear. Often, fireworks displays continue nightly through the entire month of July.

Halloween. After many years at Universal Studios, the Halloween celebration moved to Islands of Adventure in 2002. It may return, but don't count on it.

Christmas. Ho, ho, ho! It's a Hollywood version of a heartwarming family holiday, complete with Franken-Santas and Christmas lights on many of the attractions.

New Year's Eve. Expect a wild street party, often with a live pop concert being taped for later television broadcast. There is an awesome fireworks display at midnight and the park stays open until 1:00 a.m.

These special events evenings can be fun if you're in the right mood. However, some people may find them an awkward and distracting overlay to the park's main business.

The Shooting Script: Your Day at Universal Studios Florida

It is perfectly possible to spend a full day at Universal Studios Florida and see everything. This is especially true if you've heeded the advice in *Chapter One* and arrived during one of the less hectic times of year. If circumstances or perversity have led you to ignore this sage advice, you will have to plan carefully and make use of the Universal Express kiosks (see *Chapter One: Planning Your Escape*) to ensure seeing as much of the park as possible in a one-day time span. At the very least, you will be able to see enough to feel satisfied. Not everyone, after all, will be equally interested in all of the attractions, and missing a few won't break anyone's heart. Even at less busy times, you might want to consider following some of the strategies set forth in this section. Lines for more popular rides can grow long enough to make the wait seem tedious even in slack periods.

A little later, I will give you a blow-by-blow description of every attraction, eatery, and shop in the park. Here, I will provide an overview, some general guidance, and a step-by-step plan for seeing the park during busier periods.

Doing Your Homework

It's perfectly possible to arrive at Universal Studios knowing nothing about any of the films or TV shows on which its attractions are based (although it's hard to imagine that being possible), and have a perfectly good time. Indeed, you don't need to understand a word of English to be entertained here, as the happy hordes of foreign tourists prove.

Nonetheless, there is one attraction which, in my humble opinion, will benefit from a bit of research prior to your visit. *E. T. Adventure* will make a lot more sense to those who have seen the film. This is especially true for younger kids who might find E.T.'s odd appearance a bit off-putting if they haven't seen the film. Fortunately, this is the kind of homework that's easy and fun to do. Any well-stocked video rental store will have all the research material you need.

As for *Jaws, Earthquake, Back To The Future*, and *Twister*, while they're all based on popular films, knowing the films adds little to the fun of the rides.

What to Expect

Universal Studios Florida uses the "back lot" as its organizing metaphor. The back lot is where a studio keeps permanent and semi-permanent outdoor sets that can be "dressed" to stand in for multiple locations. USF consists of six such sets — Hollywood, Woody Woodpecker's KidZone, World Expo, San Francisco/Amity, New York, and Production Central — in addition to the Front Lot. You will find a helpful map of the layout of the sets in the **Studio Guide brochure**, which you can pick up at the entrance gates or in many of the shops throughout the park. (Be sure to pick up the separate **Attraction & Show Times insert** too.) Each set will be discussed in detail in the sections that follow.

It will also help to have a basic understanding of the different types of rides, shows, and attractions Universal Studios Florida has to offer. Each type of attraction has its own peculiarities and dictates a different viewing pattern.

Rides. As the term indicates, these attractions involve getting into a vehicle and going somewhere. Some, like *E. T. Adventure*, are the descendants of the so-called "dark rides" of old-fashioned amusement parks; you ride through a darkened tunnel environment lined with things to look at. Others, like *Back To The Future*, use up-to-the-minute simulator technology to provide the illusion of hurtling across vast distances while your vehicle actually moves only a few feet in any direction.

Rides are the first major attractions to open in the morning and should be your first priority. Rides have a limited seating capacity, at least compared to the theater shows. They don't last long either; most at Universal are no longer than five minutes. They tend to be the most popular attractions because of the thrills they promise (and deliver). The result: Lines form early and grow longer as the day wears on and more people pack the park.

Theater Shows. Whereas the rides offer thrills, theater shows offer entertainment and, more often than not, education as well. They occur indoors, out of the heat and sun, in comfortable theaters. They last about 25 minutes on average. Most theater shows start running about an hour after opening time. The shows run continuously, that is, as soon as one group exits another is ushered in. While there is no schedule listed in the Studio Guide brochure, the starting time of the next show will be posted outside the theater.

Because they seat 250 to 500 people at a time, a long line outside a theater show may be deceptive. Many times you can get on line as the next group is entering and still make the show. This is not always true during the busier times, however. Ask an attendant if getting on line now will guarantee a seat at the next show.

Amphitheater Shows. These shows differ from theater shows in two major respects: They seat more people (up to 2,000) and take place in covered arenas that are open to the elements on the sides. Thus they can be hot during the summer and bitterly cold during the winter. Unlike theater shows, amphitheater shows perform on a set schedule, which is listed in the Attraction & Show Times insert that comes with the Studio Guide brochure. Because of their large seating capacity, even on the busiest days you can usually arrive for an amphitheater show 15 minutes before show time and get a decent seat. On slower days you can stroll in exactly on time or even a little late. Amphitheater shows generally don't have their first performance until at least two hours after opening.

Outdoor Shows. These are small-scale shows, typically involving a few entertainers. They occur on the streets at set times announced in the Attraction & Show Times insert.

Displays and Interactive Areas. These two different types of attractions are similar in that you can simply walk into them at will and stay as long as you wish. That's not to say you won't find a line, but, with the exception of *Fievel's Playland*, lines are rare at these attractions.

All the Rest. There's a great deal of enjoyment to be derived from simply walking around in Universal Studios Florida. The imaginative and beautifully executed sets make wonderful photo backdrops and, when things get too hectic, you can even find a grassy knoll on which to stretch out, rest, and survey the passing scene.

Academy Awards

If you have a limited time at Universal Studios Florida, you probably won't be able to see everything. However, it would be a shame if you missed the very best the park has to offer. Here, then, is my list of Academy Awards:

Back To The Future . . . The Ride. Still the most exciting and imaginative simulator ride ever created.

Terminator 2: 3-D Battle Across Time. With this show, the award for "best 3-D attraction in Orlando" moves from Disney to Universal.

Curious George Goes To Town. Just for kids and just wonderful.

Jaws. A wet and wild updating of those old haunted house rides on the boardwalk. Ride it at night.

Earthquake — The Big One. Special effects explained and demonstrated with wit and imagination.

Animal Planet Live! Hilarious and heartwarming antics of your favorite Hollywood stars.

Runners-Up

These aren't on my list of the best of the best but they make many other people's lists and they are very, very good.

Men In Black: Alien Attack. A ride-through video game pits you against the universe.

The FUNtastic World of Hanna-Barbera. *Back To The Future* on training wheels still packs a wallop.

The Gory, Gruesome & Grotesque Horror Make-Up Show. Fun and games with dead bodies and strange critters.

Twister. A perfect opportunity to get blown away.

E. T. Adventure. A bicycle ride to E.T.'s home planet is like *It's a Small World* on acid.

The One-Day Stay

If you are staying at an on-site hotel and thus have preferred access (see *Chapter One: Planning Your Escape*), then you can largely ignore the following advice and proceed as you wish.

1. Get up early. You want to arrive at the park before the official opening time. Allow at least half an hour to park your car and get to the main en-

trance. If you arrive extra early, don't worry, there will already be people there waiting and Universal Studios will do its best to keep you all amused, usually by having costumed characters come out to mix and mingle and pose for photos.

2. Since you were smart enough to buy your tickets the day before, you don't have to wait in line again, at least not for tickets. Position yourself for the opening of the gates and go over your plan one more time.

3. As soon as the gates open, have your pass validated and move briskly to *Back To The Future*. Many people will break into a run. A lot of them will stop first at *T2: 3-D Battle Across Time*, but resist the temptation. *Back To The Future* has a much more limited capacity and the wait gets lengthy very soon after opening.

As soon as you exit *Back To The Future*, move quickly to *Jaws* and ride. Don't be tempted as you pass *Men In Black*; you can always return later and use the single-rider line.

Option: If *E. T. Adventure* is high on your list, go there first and then head for *Jaws*; if not, save E.T. for late in the day when many of the kiddies and their exhausted parents will have left.

4. After *Jaws*, head past *Earthquake* to ride *Kongfrontation*. Due to its popularity and more limited seating capacity, the line for Kong gets longer faster, so it's wise to see it first. After Kong, see *Twister*, then backtrack and ride *Earthquake*.

Tip: If the lines are too intimidating at any of the rides, use a nearby Express kiosk to reserve a later ride time.

5. If *The FUNtastic World of Hanna-Barbera* is on your list, head there now. If the line is short, ride it. If the line looks too long, head on to *T2*. Now the time has come to start checking out the theater and amphitheater shows. Hitchcock is just across the street from *Hanna-Barbera* and well worth seeing.

6. At this point, you will have been on the most popular rides and seen a show or maybe even two. The crowds are beginning to get noticeably larger and the sun is high in the sky. Take a break, maybe eat lunch. If the park is particularly crowded and you feel you are "running late" you may want to limit your lunch to quick snacks you can carry with you as you move from line to line. There are plenty of outdoor kiosks dispensing this kind of "finger food."

7. Continue your rounds of the shows you want to see. Check in periodically at any rides you missed (or would like to try again). You may be pleasantly surprised.

8. As the crowd thins towards closing time, circle back to the rides you missed. A great time to find shorter lines to even the most popular rides is about an hour before the official closing time.

9. The park doesn't lock the gates at the scheduled closing time. Many shops will still be open, so this is a good time to buy your souvenirs; you'll have saved some prime touring time and won't have to lug them around for so long. Many of the smaller eateries will be open as well. And you'll have plenty of time to visit *Lucy: A Tribute* before heading for your car.

The One-Day Stay for Kids

For selfless parents who are willing to place their child's agenda ahead of their own, I submit an alternative one-day plan that will serve the needs of younger children — age eleven and below, maybe seven or eight and below. In my experience, many young children are preternaturally sophisticated and often better equipped to handle the more intense rides than their elders. Presumably, you know your own child and will be able to adapt the following outline as needed.

1. Get to the park bright and early. As soon as you are in, visit *E. T. Adventure.*

2. If you have very young kids, it'll be too early for *Barney* so head to *Hanna-Barbera,* if they are over 40 inches tall.

3. Depending on your kid's tolerance, check out *Jaws, Men In Black* (42-inch minimum), *Kongfrontation,* and *Earthquake,* in that order. (I am assuming your child is too short for *Back To The Future.*)

Tip: If the lines are too intimidating at any of the rides, use a nearby Express kiosk to reserve a later ride time.

4. Next, check show times for *Barney* and the *Animal Planet Live!.* See them in the appropriate order. Try to steer your little ones away from *Barney's Backyard, Fievel's Playland,* and *Curious George,* explaining that you'll return later.

5. Visit Nickelodeon and break for lunch.

6. After lunch, let the kids burn off steam at *Fievel's Playland, Barney's Backyard,* and *Curious George* while you get some much-needed rest and plot out the remainder of the day. Remember, too, that the heat of the day is the best time for your little ones to get soaked at *Curious George.*

THE FRONT LOT

In movie studio parlance, the front lot is where all the soundstages, as well as the administrative and creative offices are located — as opposed to the back lot, which contains the outdoor sets. Here at Universal Studios Florida, the Front Lot is a small antechamber of sorts to the theme park proper, which can be looked on as one huge back lot. On the Front Lot you can take care of minor pieces of business on your way into the park — like picking up more money from the ATM or renting a stroller — and here you can also return when things go wrong — to register a complaint at Guest Services, or seek nursing aid for an injured child, or check Lost & Found for that priceless pearl earring that flew off in *Back To The Future*. You will find the following services on the Front Lot:

To your left as you enter the park are ...

Lockers. There are two small bays of electronically controlled lockers. The rental fee is $5 for the day with in and out access, and the machines accept both bills and credit cards. If these are full, you can find more lockers on the other side of the plaza.

Mail. You'll find a small U.S. Postal Service drop box to the right of the lockers.

Phone Cards. Also to the right of the lockers is a phone-card vending machine.

Vacation Services. If you've come to Universal Studios Florida for the day and like what you see, you can upgrade your one-day pass to any of Universal Orlando's multi-day pass options. The price you paid for your one-day pass will be deducted from the price of the multi-day pass. There are some simple rules: Upgrades must be purchased before you leave the park. Everyone in your party who wants one must show up with their one-day pass stub in hand. Free or complimentary passes are not eligible for upgrades.

Upgrades are non-transferable and Universal enforces this feature by requiring your signature on the pass and requesting photo ID when you return, which can be the next day or five years hence. The pass stays valid until you use it. If you *really* liked your visit, you can also sign up for an Annual Pass here.

Dining reservations can also be made at Vacation Services.

Stroller & Wheelchair Rentals. Wheelchairs are $7 a day and strollers $8. Double strollers are $14. A motorized "electric convenience vehicle" (ECV) is yours for $35 for the day with either a $50 refundable deposit or the deposit of a photo ID. A 24-hour advance reservation is suggested to ensure getting an ECV.

To your right as you enter the park are ...

Guest Services. This office performs a wide variety of functions. You can pick up information and brochures about special services and special events. If you have a complaint (and, just as important, a compliment) about anything in the park, make your feelings known here. Guest Services personnel will often make good on an unfortunate experience by issuing a free pass for another day.

First Union Bank. This is a full-service branch of a local bank. This is where to head if you need to cash (or buy) traveler's checks, exchange foreign currency, or get a cash advance on your credit card. It's even open on Sundays.

ATM. Next to the bank is an outdoor ATM, where you can get a cash advance on your Visa or MasterCard credit card at any time. The machine is also hooked into the Cirrus, Honor, Plus, Star, NYCE, Mac, Maestro, and Exchange (the Armed Forces Financial Network) systems for those who would like to withdraw money from their bank account back home.

Studio Audience Center. This should be your first stop if you want to see one of the television shows being taped on the nearby soundstages during your visit to Universal Studios. A show can have an audience of 50 to 300 and tape one to six episodes on a single day. Each show will have a minimum age requirement, which can vary greatly. Tickets are free and distributed on a first-come, first-served basis. Show up early. However, there will not inevitably be something going on at the time you visit, so try not to be disappointed if you come up empty.

You can call (407) 224-6355 to see what might be available during your visit. They say they usually know about tapings only two weeks or so in advance.

Family & Health Services. Nursing aid is available here, under the Studio Audience Center marquee, should you need it. There is also a "family bathroom" if, for example, you need to assist a disabled spouse. A special room is set aside for nursing mothers. If you just need to change a diaper, you will find diaper-changing facilities in restrooms throughout the park.

Lost & Found. The Studio Audience Center window does double duty as Lost & Found. Items that if lost elsewhere would probably be gone forever have a surprising way of turning up at theme parks. The good feelings the park experience generates must make people ever so slightly less larcenous. Universal personnel always check the rides for forgotten belongings. Items are kept for 30 days. You can call (407) 224-6355.

Lockers. Here are more of those electronic lockers, with still more lockers just around the corner in a narrow passageway that leads to Hollywood Boulevard and the T2 theater. Daily rental is $5, which allows unlimited in and out access.

Shopping on the Front Lot

The Front Lot may be a prelude to the park proper, but Universal has shrewdly located a number of shops here that cater to the needs of both the arriving and departing guest.

On Location

This should be your first stop if you've left the camera at the hotel or find yourself short of film. And if you forgot sunscreen, sunglasses, or tote bag, On Location can help you out there as well. In addition you will find a constantly rotating inventory of t-shirts, baseball caps, and the like.

If you have your photo taken by a roving photographer in the park, there's no obligation to buy a print, but if you just can't resist, this is where you claim your pictures. All pictures are digital and are held for three days. They only print them out if you order. Prices range from $13 for a single 5 x 7 to $30 for more elaborate packages.

Studio Sweets

You can't miss this small shop on your left as you enter the park. Scoop-your-own bulk candy goes for $2.20 for a quarter pound, but single cookies are over $2. There is also a wide assortment of tinned cookies and candies. Chocolate-dipped apples go for $7. Chocolate and fudge, which comes in a variety of flavors, often with added nuts, is sold for about $14 a pound.

Universal Studios Store

By far the largest store in the park, the Universal Studios Store is located just next to (in fact, it surrounds) Studio Sweets. Here you will find a representative sampling of the wares to be found in the various smaller shops scattered about the park. If you want to save all your souvenir shopping until the end of your visit, you should be able to get something appropriate here. Just be aware that the selection is not exhaustive and that the special item you admired elsewhere might not be for sale here.

If the store can be said to specialize in anything, it's clothing. In the store's children's section, you will find a selection of t-shirts and other kiddie gear priced from about $14 to $40. You will find a wide variety of options for adults, starting with simple t-shirts at about $16 and going all the way to jackets for over $100. In between, you are sure to find something you'll like. Even with the inevitable Universal Studios logos, much of the clothing displayed here is very stylish and in impeccable taste.

They haven't forgotten toys and plush dolls for the kids and, of course, the Universal Studios Store has a generous selection of other souvenir merchandise, everything from refrigerator magnets to mugs, emblazoned with various film and TV series names, faces, and logos.

It's A Wrap

It's A Wrap (studio lingo for "we've finished shooting the movie") is a nifty name for this vest-pocket souvenir stand that thoughtfully straddles the exit to the park. That means, if you're on your way to the car and suddenly remember that you forgot a present for Auntie Em, you can run back and get something without reentering the park. The selection is limited, running heavily to t-shirts and gewgaws like key chains and the like, although there is a small selection of sale items offering some nice bargains.

HOLLYWOOD

Although I haven't taken out a tape measure to check, Hollywood is probably the smallest "set" at Universal Studios Florida. It is about two city blocks long, stretching from *Lucy: A Tribute* near the park entrance to The Garden of Allah motel near the lagoon. Along the way is an imaginative and loving recreation of the Hollywood of our collective subconscious. The Hollywood set was primarily a shopping and dining venue until the opening of *Terminator 2: 3-D Battle Across Time* made it a major stop on everybody's tour of Universal's Greatest Hits.

Terminator 2: 3-D Battle Across Time

Rating: ★ ★ ★ ★ ★
Type: A "3-D Virtual Adventure"
Time: About 20 minutes
Kelly says: The best 3-D attraction in Orlando

Most attractions based on movies are created and developed by specialists at the parks. This time, *Terminator 2* director, James Cameron, and Arnold (The Austrian Oak) Schwarzenegger figured they could do it better themselves. And, boy, did they ever! Reports are that $60 million was spent to create this show. You'll get their money's worth.

Given its location at the top of Hollywood Boulevard, near the Studio gates, T2 has become everyone's first stop when entering the park (though not yours, if you follow my advice), so be prepared for long lines. Even if you don't see lines outside, the huge interior queue can hold over 1,100 people, about a show and a half's worth. On the other hand, the theater holds 700 people and the line moves fairly quickly.

Once you step off the street, you are in the newly rebuilt headquarters of Cyberdyne, the not so nice corporate giant of the T2 flick, which is out to refurbish its image and show off its latest technology. The pre-show warmup, which takes place in a large anteroom to the theater itself, features a delicious parody of the "Vision of the Future" corporate videos and television commercials that are becoming increasingly common these days. The pre-show also gets the plot rolling: Sarah Connor and her son John have invaded Cyberdyne and commandeered the video screen to warn us against the new SkyNet project (which sounds remarkably like President Bush's proposed National Missile Defense system). According to these "terrorists" (as the Cyberdyne people describe them), SkyNet will enslave us all. The Cyberdyne flack who is our host glosses over this "unfortunate interruption" and ushers us into the large auditorium. There we settle into deceptively normal looking theater seats, don our "protective glasses," and the show begins.

And what a show it is. I don't want to give too much away, but suffice it to say that it involves a spectacular three-screen 3-D movie starring Ah-nold himself, along with Linda Hamilton and Eddie Furlong (the kid from *Terminator 2*). In one of the more inspired touches, the on-screen actors move from screen to stage and back again, Arnold aboard a roaring motorcycle. The film's special effects are spectacular and the slam-bang, smoke-filled finale has people screaming and shrieking in their seats.

The Gory, Gruesome & Grotesque Horror Make-Up Show

Rating: ★ ★ ★ ★
Type: Theater show
Time: 25 minutes
Kelly says: For younger teens and horror movie buffs

How to take something gory, gruesome, and downright disgusting and turn it into wholesome, funny family fare? Universal has solved the problem with this enjoyable (not to mention educational) foray into the ghastly art of make-up and special effects for the horror genre. The key is a horror make-up "expert" with a bizarre and goofy sense of humor who is interviewed in his make-up lab by an on-stage host and straight-man. During a laugh-filled 25 minutes, he leads us through a grisly show-and-tell of basic horror movie tricks and gimmicks.

Tip: The subject matter is undeniably gross and the performers are given fairly wide latitude to ad-lib. Some people may find either the subject matter or the humor (or both) beyond the bounds of good taste. The easily offended, then, should give this show a miss. Universal rates it PG-13.

Using the inevitable volunteer from the audience (to very amusing effect), we learn how harmlessly dull knifes can be made to leave bloody trails on bare human flesh and thanks to video projected onto two screens we get a brief history of extreme makeup from Lon Chaney to Eddie Murphy. Also on hand are the actual mechanical werewolf heads that were used for the still stunning transformation scene in *An American Werewolf in London*. The show ends with a preview of a new, remotely controlled monster and yet another dirty trick played on a "volunteer."

As always, the show instructs while it entertains. Everyone will have a keener understanding of basic horror effects, and young children will be sternly warned about the importance of safety at all times. ("Don't do this at home . . . Do it at a friend's house!")

The waiting area for this show is the lobby of the Pantages Theater, where you can peruse a multimedia display about the making of *The Mummy Returns* while waiting for the show to begin.

The best seats in the house. If all you want to do is enjoy the show, the oft-repeated Universal refrain is absolutely true — every seat's a good seat. Exhibitionists hoping to be selected as a volunteer should be aware that the performers have a predilection for young women seated in the first row.

Lucy: A Tribute

Rating:　　★ ★
Type:　　Museum-style display, with video
Time:　　Continuous viewing
Kelly says:　　Best for adults with a sense of history

Lucy: A Tribute is a walk-in display honoring the immortal Lucille Darlene Ball. It's hard to miss, since you bump into it almost as soon as you enter the park. There's hardly ever a crowd, so feel free to breeze on by and take it in later. If you run out of time … well, truth to tell, you haven't missed much. Still, fans of the great redhead (and who isn't?) will find at least something of interest here, even if it's just a reminder to pull down those Lucy videos at home and take a four hundredth look.

The "tribute" is simply a large open room ringed with glassed-in display cases, like shop windows, crammed with Lucy memorabilia — photos, letters, scripts, costumes, and Lucy's six Emmys — including the posthumous Governor's Award presented on September 17, 1989. One of the more interesting windows contains a model of the studio in which the ground-breaking *I Love Lucy* show was shot. It was the first show shot with the three-camera method still used today. A fascinating footnote: The sets in those days of black-and-white TV were actually painted in shades of gray (furniture, too) to provide optimum contrast on the home screen. Continuously running videos feature Bob Hope and Gale Gordon reminiscing about Lucy, while brief clips remind us of just how much we really did love Lucy. You'll hear the people next to you saying, "Oh, I remember that one," or "I lo-o-o-ved that one." There's some interesting material here about Lucy's career before she became a television icon. In one corner, an interactive video system offers an *I Love Lucy* trivia quiz. The idea is to get the Ricardos and Mertzes cross-country to Hollywood by answering five multiple-choice questions. But, careful! You lose gas by guessing wrong. Real Lucy and Ricky fanatics should have no problem, but for most people the quiz will be no pushover.

Selected Short Subjects

Hollywood Street Entertainment

Hollywood Boulevard keeps hoppin' with a regular menu of bouncy, rhythmic musical entertainment, most of it with a Latin beat. The headline attraction is **Sarita**, a sort of Carmen Miranda clone, who sings, dances, works the crowd, and organizes a zany conga line right down the middle of the street. **Lucy and Ricky**, as in Ricardo, also show up. Sometimes Ricky does a double act with Sarita and sometimes he gives the Great Redhead the chance at show biz stardom that always seemed to elude her on the classic sitcom. Live music is provided by a hard-working combo that regularly changes costume but never the personnel.

Farther down the road, at Mel's Diner, an attractive young boy-girl a capella group called **Double Date** performs amid the 50s-vintage hot rods. Their doo-wop renditions of songs you might remember from *American Graffiti* are sure to please, although those with keen ears and a few years on them might notice that some of the lingo isn't much older than the performers. Show times for these acts are listed in the Attraction & Show Times insert that comes with the Studio Guide brochure.

Shrek also puts in an appearance from time to time, sometimes near the Garden of Allah, where you can line up to have your photo taken with the amiably antisocial ogre. This is not a guy in a furry costume but an elaborately made-up actor who does an exemplary job of bringing the animated character to three-dimensional life.

Universal Studios Radio Broadcast Center

Right next to the Brown Derby (see below) is a fairly inconspicuous radio studio. From here popular disk jockeys from around the U.S. and Canada, and from as far away as London and Belo Horizonte, Brazil, broadcast live shows to the folks back home.

If something's going on during your visit, you'll be able to watch through the picture windows. The audio feed will be piped to the outside. Even if there's no show on the air, peek in and check out the clever ceiling treatment inside.

Trick Photography Photo Spot

This is one of several spots in the park where you can take your own souvenir photo using the "hanging miniature" technique pioneered in the early days of filmmaking. You get a stand on which to position your camera and step-by-step instructions to make double sure you get it right. There are even footprints telling you where to place your subjects. Then you can photograph your family in front of the (real) Pantages Theater, with the (painted) Hollywood hills and the rest of the Los Angeles skyline stretching into the distance. Even if you don't have a camera, you should take a peek through the lens provided for the camera-less just to see how the trick works. It's nifty.

Eating in Hollywood

Beverly Hills Boulangerie

What:	Sandwiches, sweets, and coffee
Where:	At the corner of Hollywood Boulevard and Plaza of the Stars
Price Range:	$ - $$

This charming little bistro blends the current craze for coffee bars with a tasty array of breakfast and dessert baked goods. It's an unbeatable combination. If you're visiting during one of the less crowded times of year (so you don't have to dash right off to *Back To The Future*), you might want to pause here for a fortifying, if calorie-laden breakfast. Sit outside on sunny days to entertain yourself with the passing parade.

There are gigantic blueberry, banana-nut, and bran muffins and roly-poly chocolate croissants. If you subscribe to the when-on-vacation-start-with-dessert philosophy, why not start the day off right with an eclair, or a slice of raspberry cheesecake? Most pastries and muffins are in the $2 to $4 range. Coffees range from the plain (for about $1.50) to fancy cappuccinos for a little over $2.

Later in the day, you can stop in for a smoked turkey or ham and Swiss sandwich on your choice of baguette or croissant. Or soothe your conscience with a Health Sandwich of Swiss cheese, sprouts, cucumbers, and avocados. Sandwiches are in the $6 to $7 range and come with a tasty side of potato salad. You can also get salads here if you purchase them with soup ($5) or a sandwich ($8). Domestic and imported beer is available for around $4.

Mel's Drive-In

What:	Fast-food burger joint
Where:	At the end of Hollywood Boulevard, across from the lagoon
Price Range:	$ - $$

Remember the nostalgia drenched drive-in restaurant from *American Graffiti*? Well here it is in some of its splendor. No curvy car hops, alas, but you will see a mouth-watering array of customized vintage cars parked outside.

Inside, you will find a fairly typical fast-food emporium with fifties decor. Place and pay for your burger or hot dog and fries order at the cashier, then step forward to pick it up, wrapped in paper. If the food and non-service won't bring back memories of those great cheeseburgers and real-milk shakes you had way back when, at least there are jukeboxes to flip through at the tables. There is also an outdoor seating area that looks out to the park's central lagoon.

The menu is limited and prices low to moderate. The typical burger and fries meal will set you back about $9. Soft drinks are your only beverage choice here. Mel's is a good spot for a quick bite with kids who like no surprises with their meals, but I can't help but think that Universal is missing a bet here. I for one would be willing to pay a higher price for a dining experience that would more closely evoke the ambiance of the diner in the movie, complete with gum-chewing waitresses on rollerskates.

Schwab's Pharmacy

What: Ice-cream parlor
Where: In the middle of Hollywood Boulevard
Price Range: $

Schwab's is famous in Hollywood lore as the place where a sharp-eyed talent scout discovered a sweater-clad, teenaged Lana Turner sipping soda at the counter. At Universal Studios, Schwab's lends its name to a small, black-and-white tiled, vaguely forties-ish ice-cream parlor featuring Häagen-Dazs products. Milk shakes and ice cream floats run about $3; sundaes are $4, and apple pie a la mode just a bit less. Or you can order a turkey breast, chicken salad, or ham and cheese sandwich (about $7). Although there are a few tables, Schwab's is primarily aimed at those looking for a quick — and portable — snack.

In keeping with its namesake's primary business, Schwab's also stocks a small supply of over-the-counter headache and heartburn remedies. For those intent on spending the whole day riding *Back To The Future*, Schwab's very thoughtfully provides Pepto Bismol.

Cafe La Bamba

What: Cafeteria-style barbecue restaurant
Where: Across from Mel's and the lagoon in the
                    Hollywood Hotel
Price Range: $ - $$

Cafe La Bamba serves up ample portions of rotisserie chicken and barbecued ribs at moderate prices. On top of that, the ambiance is a cut above your average fast-food restaurant. Evoking a Spanish mission courtyard with adobe walls and tiled floors, it offers some charming corners just a few steps away from the cafeteria lines plus a delightful outdoor seating area that looks across to Mel's and the lagoon.

Most chicken entrees are in the $7 to $9 range. The barbecued baby back ribs are $11 and a cheeseburger platter is $8. Desserts are about $3. At the Cantina Bar, you can get a frozen alcoholic drink, beer, or cocktail.

Shopping in Hollywood

Hollywood Boulevard funnels visitors from the studio entrance to the central lagoon and serves as a primary route for visitors on their way out. Much of it has been given over to a variety of shopping experiences. The Boulevard itself is an imaginative recreation of major Hollywood facades, some of which still exist and others of which have vanished into the realm of cherished memories. It makes for a pleasant stroll and a fitting introduction to the movie-themed fun that awaits you in the rest of the park.

The following description begins at the end of the Boulevard closest to the entrance and proceeds towards the lagoon.

Silver Screen Collectibles

Silver Screen Collectibles opens onto the Plaza of the Stars, just across the street from the Universal Studios Store. At the other end, it merges with *Lucy: A Tribute*.

Expect to find t-shirts and other merchandise featuring cartoon characters. On a recent visit, Betty Boop was featured. Farther along is a hodgepodge of blown up publicity photos of stars past and present and large movie posters. The too-small book selection revolves around a few major stars of yesteryear.

The real star of Silver Screen Collectibles is the special Lucy section, strategically located at the entrance/exit to *Lucy: A Tribute*. Here you will find the Lucy Collection, a series of videos and DVDs ($15 to $20). In addition, you'll find a generous selection of books, which the true Lucy fan will find to be invaluable references, and a series of t-shirts in homage to the great redhead. (My favorite is the Vitameatavegemin shirt at $18.)

The Brown Derby

The original Brown Derby was a hat-shaped eatery that opened in Hollywood in 1929 and has long since been demolished. Universal Studios has copied the shape (in smaller scale) and devoted the tiny space to — what else? — hats! Inside you will find a cozy circular space, topped with a photographic frieze of famous stars of the past in a variety of headgear and filled to the brim with hats of all descriptions. Casual, stylish, or downright wacky, they're all here at prices ranging from $15 to $50.

Photo Op: There are lots of wonderfully way-out creations on display here. Although they have price tags, my guess is that they are seldom purchased but tried on hundreds of times a day. It's a great chance for some fun family portraits.

Studio Styles

The studio the name refers to must specialize in music videos for teeny-bopper pop stars because the clothes and accessories offered here seem aimed squarely at 16 year old girls or at least women with the figure of a 16 year old. Some of it is fun, most of it is slinky and/or brief. Prices range from about $7 for accessories to $98 for a jeans jacket with a nighttime scene of Hollywood airbrushed on the back.

Cyber Image

If you see *Terminator 2: 3-D Battle Across Time* (and you should), you can't miss this T2 memorabilia shop; you walk right through it when you leave the theater. Here's your chance to dress just like Arnold in black leather jacket ($150), muscles not included. For the less well heeled there are T2 and "No Fate" t-shirts for $18 to $25. Videos of the Terminator films are $15.

Williams of Hollywood Photo Studio

Back across Hollywood Boulevard, you'll find Universal's somewhat wan version of what has become a fairly familiar tourist town come-on. Here you can take advantage of a small costume and prop collection to dress up and have a solo or group photo taken in your choice of themes — wild West, Civil War, or prohibition gangster ($25 to $80 depending on the number of people in the shot and the size and number of prints).

WOODY WOODPECKER'S KIDZONE

Although its intense thrill rides and movie-themed edutainment have brought Universal Studios Florida a reputation as an "adult" theme park, it hasn't forgotten the kiddies. Woody Woodpecker's KidZone, located along a winding avenue off the central lagoon, is a perfect case in point. If you have children under ten, you could very easily spend an entire day here, with only an occasional foray to sample other kid-friendly attractions in the park. There's a nice balance here, too, from stage shows to play areas to kiddie-scale "thrill" rides. I describe them in roughly the order you encounter them as you wend your way deeper into Woody's KidZone.

Tip: At the end of the Hollywood set, past Cafe La Bamba, look for the Gardens of Allah Villas on your right. Cut through here for a shortcut to Woody's KidZone and the *E. T. Adventure.*

Animal Planet Live!

Rating: ★ ★ ★ ★ +
Type: Amphitheater show

Time:	About 25 minutes
Kelly says:	Fun for just about everybody

This vastly entertaining spectacle is a blatant, extended, and altogether delightful commercial for a cable TV network that shall remain nameless. It also shows off the handiwork of Universal's animal trainers and their furry and feathery charges. It's all done with the droll good humor and audience participation that characterize all of Universal's shows. Kids and adults are pulled from the audience to serve as foils for several amusing routines.

The show alternates between live action on stage and video footage on a large overhead screen showing what's going on backstage at a television studio staffed entirely by animals. In one amusing bit, a pig (the "Ham Cam") goes on location to capture live action footage of the audience. In a more enlightening segment, we learn how birds can be filmed in flight using a large fan and some trick camera work.

Just which animals you see will depend to some extent on what's hot and recent in Universal's film lineup. Most entertaining on a recent visit was Bailey, an orangutan whose comic timing would be the envy of most human professionals. Intellectually, you know that the animal is merely running through a series of learned responses. You can even spot the trainer giving the signals. But the interplay between them is so sharp and the ape's broad takes to the audience so casually hilarious that you'll really believe this is comic acting at its best.

In between the fun and games, the show sneaks in a few points about the serious business of producing "behaviors" that can be put to use in films. Most interestingly, when an animal balks at performing a trick, the trainer doesn't merely gloss over the rough spot and get on with the show. Instead, he works patiently with the animal until the behavior is performed correctly. We learn that what for us is light entertainment is serious business for the folks (both two- and four-legged) on the stage.

The best seats in the house. There really are no bad seats for this one. However, if you'd like a shot at serving as a landing strip for a very mercenary bird, try sitting in the middle section about four or five rows from the back of the auditorium.

E.T. Adventure

Rating:	★ ★ ★ ★
Type:	Gondola ride
Time:	5 minutes
Kelly says:	Kids love this one (some adults do, too)

E.T. is one of Universal's most popular rides for people of all ages, with the result that the lines can become dauntingly long. While signs announcing wait times can generally be trusted, the sign here is misleading. It only tells you how long it will take to get inside. On busy days, there can be another wait of 15 to 20 minutes inside the building before you reach the ride itself. Plan accordingly.

Based on the blockbuster movie that crossed sci-fi with cuddly toys, the *E. T. Adventure* takes us where the movie didn't — back to E.T.'s home planet. In a filmed introduction to the ride, Steven Spielberg, who directed the film, sets up the premise: E.T.'s home, the Green Planet, is in some unspecified trouble, although it looks like an advanced case of ozone hole, which is turning the place a none-too-healthy looking orange. You have to return with E.T. to help save the old folks at home. How to get there? Aboard the flying bicycles from the film's final sequence, of course. The fact that Spielberg doesn't bother to explain how we'll survive the rigors of interstellar travel aboard mountain bikes tells us that this ride is aimed at the very young. How to save the planet? That's not explained either although it seems that E.T.'s "healing touch" and our mere presence will be enough to revive the place.

Tip: Moving to the far right (as you face the screen), will put you closer to the doors to the next chamber, thus first in line for the next phase of the adventure.

After this brief setup, the doors to the right open and we line up to tell a staffer our first names and get the "passports" we will need for the journey. These are thin pieces of plastic with a mysterious bar code on one side.

Passports firmly in hand, we walk through a cave-like tunnel into the misty, nighttime redwood forests of the Northwest. This set is a minor masterpiece of scenic design and some people think it's the best part of the adventure. As we wend our way along a winding "nature trail" amidst the towering trees, we make out the animated figure of Botanicus, a wise elder from E.T.'s planet, urging us to hurry back. Here, too, we glimpse the jury-rigged contraption E.T. used to communicate in the film.

As we get ready to collect our "bikes" (look for E.T. to pop his head out of the basket on the front), we turn in our plastic "passports" to another attendant and are directed to the staging area. The bikes are actually 12-passenger, open-sided gondolas hanging from a ceiling track. They have bicycle-like seats, each with its own set of handlebars. The lap bars slide into place and we "take off" on our adventure.

This ride might be likened to a bike with training wheels. It has many of the aspects of more thrilling rides — sudden acceleration, swoops, and turns — but toned down so as not to be truly frightening. In the first phase of the ride, we are zipping through the redwoods, dodging the unenlightened grown-ups who want to capture E.T. for study and analysis. Police cars and jeeps roar out of the darkness on seeming collision courses with our frail vehicle. This section can be a little scary for small kids and a little loud for older adults. Soon, however, we are soaring high above the city in the ride's most enchanting interlude. We rise higher until we are in the stars themselves and are then shot down a hyperspace tunnel before we decelerate abruptly and find ourselves in the steamy world of E.T.'s home planet.

It's an odd cave-like environment but soon, apparently buoyed by our arrival, the place perks up and we are flying through a psychedelic world of huge multicolored flowers in wondrous shapes, past talking mushrooms and plants (or are they creatures?) with dozens of eyes. All around are little E.T.s, peeping from under plants, climbing over them, and playing them like percussion instruments. It's all rather like Disney's *It's A Small World* on acid. Those who were in San Francisco during the sixties have seen this all before, but youngsters will doubtless find it enchanting.

All too soon, E.T. is sending us back to our home but not before a final farewell. Here is where we get the payoff for giving the attendant our name at the beginning of the ride. E.T. thanks each of us personally in his croaking computer-generated voice.

I am not as captivated by this ride as some. Apparently, Spielberg created a whole new cast of characters for this ride, but, other than Botanicus, they are hard to identify, much less get to know. And the humans in the woods look too much like department store mannequins for my taste. Still, these are minor carps. Much of the ride is fun indeed and it will appeal to younger children and their timid elders, who can get a taste of a "thrill" ride without putting the contents of their stomachs at risk.

This is also one of the few rides at Universal where seeing the film on which it is based will definitely add to the appreciation of the experience. Without this background, much of the ride may seem merely odd. This will be especially true for younger children who will be better able to empathize with E.T. and his plight if they've seen the movie.

The best seats in the house. On the whole, the left side of the gondola provides better views than the right, especially of the city. Best of all is the far left seat in the first of the three rows.

Tip: When the *Animal Planet* show lets out (about 25 minutes after the posted show time), the crowds stream over to get on line for E.T. Time your visit accordingly.

Note: There are two Universal Express entrances in this ride, one outside and a second shortly after you enter the forest inside the building.

Fievel's Playland

Rating: ★ ★ ★
Type: Hands-on activity

Time: As long as you want

Kelly says: For young and very active kids

Based on Steven Spielberg's charming animated film, *An American Tail*, about a shtetl mouse making his way in the New World, Fievel's Playland is a convoluted maze of climb-up, run-through, slide-down activities that will keep kids amused while their exhausted parents take a well-deserved break.

Don't forget to bring your camera for great photo ops of the kids amidst the larger-than-life cowboy hats, victrolas, water barrels, playing cards, and cattle skeletons that make up this maze of exploration.

The highlight is a Mouse Climb — a rope tunnel that spirals upwards. At the top, kids can climb into two-man (well, two-kid) rubber rafts to slide down through yet another tunnel to arrive at ground level with enormous grins and wet bottoms. Don't worry, there's also a set of stairs to the top of this water slide.

Photo op: A shot of your kid hitting the bottom of the slide makes a great souvenir and a ground-level video monitor of the top of the slide lets you know when your little darling is about to descend.

This is a place you can safely let the kids explore on their own. The ground is padded. However, kids less than 40 inches high will have to drag a grown-up (or maybe a bigger sibling) along to ride the water slide. There's seldom a wait to get in to *Fievel's Playland* but long lines do form for the water slide. If time is a factor and if you will be visiting one of the water-themed parks on another day, you can tell the kids that there are bigger, better water slides awaiting them tomorrow.

Note: Even though this attraction is aimed squarely at the kiddie set, don't be surprised if your young teens get in the spirit and momentarily forget that romping through a kid's playground is not the "cool" thing to do.

A Day in the Park with Barney

Rating: ★ ★ ★

Type: Theater show with singing

Time: About 20 minutes

Kelly says: For toddlers and their long-suffering parents

According to the publicity, Universal's Barney attraction is the only place in the United States where you can see Barney "live." For some people, that may be one place too many. But for his legions of adoring wee fans and the parents who love them, this show will prove an irresistible draw. Even old curmudgeons will grudgingly have to admit that the show's pretty sweet.

The first tipoff that this is a kiddie show is the fact that it's the only attraction at Universal with its own stroller parking lot. And it's usually full. After the young guests have availed themselves of Mom and Dad's valet parking service, they enter through a gate into Barney's park, complete with a bronze Barney cavorting in an Italianate fountain.

When the show begins, we are all ushered into a stand-up pre-show area where Mr. Peekaboo and his gaudy bird friend Bartholomew put on a singing, dancing warm-up act that wouldn't be complete unless the audience got splashed. Then, using our imaginations, we pass through a misty cave entrance sprinkled with star dust to enter the main theater.

Inside is a completely circular space cheerfully decorated as a forest park at dusk. Low benches surround the raised central stage, but old fogies may want to make for the more comfortable park benches against the walls. The sightlines are excellent no matter where you sit, although Mr. Peekaboo reminds us that once we've chosen a seat we must stay there for the entire show.

The show is brief and cheery and almost entirely given over to singalongs that are already familiar to Barney's little fans. Barney is soon joined by Baby Bop and B.J. and the merriment proceeds apace, complete with falling autumn leaves, a brief snowfall, and shooting streamers. By the end, the air is filled with love — literally.

True star that he is, Barney stays behind after the show to greet his young admirers, a few of whom seem overawed to be so close to this giant vision in purple. One point I found particularly amusing was that the stage crew has very little to clean up after the show. The kids are remarkably efficient in policing up the fallen leaves and streamers. Now if only we could get them to do that back home!

The theater audience empties out into **Barney's Backyard**, which is the day-care center of your dreams. Here, beautifully executed by Universal scenic artists, is a collection of imaginative and involving activities for the very young, from making music to splashing in water, to drawing on the walls. For parents who are a bit on the slow side, there are signs to explain the significance of what their kids are up to. A sample: "Young children have a natural inclination towards music [which] encourages the release of stress through listening and dancing." Duh!

Barney's Backyard is where little kids get their revenge. Whereas many rides in the park bar younger children on the basis of height, here there are activities that are off limits to those over 48 inches or even 36 inches. Kids will love it. Grown-ups will wish there were more of it.

Tip: This wonderful space has a separate entrance and you don't have to sit through the show to get in here. Keep this in mind if the family's youngest member needs some special attention or a chance to unwind from the frustrations of being a little person in a big persons' amusement park.

Woody Woodpecker's Nuthouse Coaster

Rating:	★ ★ ★
Type:	A kiddie roller coaster
Time:	About 1 minute
Kelly says:	A thrill ride for the younger set

Woody Woodpecker's Nuthouse Coaster is described as a "gentle" children's roller coaster, knocked together by Woody from bits of this and that, running through a nut factory. The eight cars on the "Knothead Express" are modeled after nut crates; they run along 800 feet of red tubular steel track supported by bright blue steel poles, which are in turn held together with knotty boards and rope. The ride features some mild drops and tilted turns but it shouldn't prove frightening to any child who meets the 36-inch minimum height requirement.

Curious George Goes To Town

Rating:	★ ★ ★ ★ ★
Type:	A water-filled play area
Time:	Unlimited
Kelly says:	It will be hard to drag kids away

Woody's KidZone turns into a water park in this elaborate play area themed after the illustrated books about George, the playful monkey, and his friend The Man in the Yellow Hat. Expect your kids to get sopping wet here and enjoy every minute of it.

The fun begins innocently enough with a small tent housing a play area for very young children. Nearby is one of those padded play areas with jets of water shooting up from the ground in random patterns. Little ones still in diapers love it. But the main attraction lies a few steps farther along, in the town square. On opposite sides stand the Fire Department and the City Waterworks, dubbed "City H2O." On the second floor balcony, five water cannons let kids squirt those below mercilessly. On the roof of each building is a huge water bucket which fills inexorably with water and, with the clanging of a warning bell, tips over, sending a cascade of water into the square below as kids scramble to position themselves under it for a thorough soaking.

Behind the facades of this cartoonish town square lies a two-level, kid-powered, waterlogged obstacle course. All sorts of cranks, levers and other ingenious devices give kids a great deal of control over who gets how wet. Most kids take to it with fiendish glee. The concept isn't unique to USF, but the version here is one of the best I've ever seen.

When your kids are ready for a change of pace, they can repair to the **Ball Factory**, behind the town square. This cheerfully noisy two-level metal structure is filled with thousands of colored soft foam balls. The noise comes from the industrial strength vacuum machines that suck balls fromthe floor and send them to aimable ball cannons mounted on tall poles or to large bins high overhead. Some vacuums send balls to stations where kids can fill up mesh bags with balls they then take to the second level balcony to feed into the ten "Auto Blasters" that let them shoot balls at the kids down below. It's a scene of merry anarchy and many adults quickly get in touch with their inner child and become active participants in the chaotic battle raging all about. Those ball bins, like the water buckets outside, tip over periodically pummeling eager victims below and replenishing the supply of balls.

This is one attraction that can keep kids happily occupied for hours on end. It will also appeal to the older kids in your family who might find some of the other offerings in Woody Woodpecker's KidZone too "babyish." It's not unusual to see ever-so-hip young teens thoroughly enjoying themselves as they splash about with their younger siblings.

Tip: Bring a towel and a change of clothes for the kids if the weather's cool. This is also a good activity to schedule just before you leave the park, either for the day or for a nap-time break.

Selected Short Subjects

Character Meet and Greet

Here's your chance to meet and mingle with some of Hollywood's heavyweights. That's right, George Jetson, Fred Flintstone, Woody Woodpecker, Yogi Bear, and the rest of the gang. They show up periodically in the circular plaza at the entrance to KidZone to meet their adoring public and, yes, sign autographs. Don't expect much in the way of scintillating conversation, however; they're the strong silent type. Appearances take place on a fairly continuous basis from about 11:45 a.m. to 3:45 p.m. with the stars spelling each other off.

Eating in KidZone

Animal Crackers

What: Hot dog stand with outdoor seating

Where: On Exposition Plaza, next to Universal's Cartoon Store

Price Range: $

This walk-up fast-food counter serves up a restricted menu of quick snacks. Hot dogs and fries are about $5. Chicken fingers (about $8) is the most expensive item on the menu. Ice cream bars can be had for a little over $3. If you're looking for something a bit more substantial, or a place to eat in air-conditioned comfort, take the short stroll to the International Food and Film Festival in World Expo (see below).

Shopping in KidZone

E.T.'s Toy Closet

This vest-pocket shop is devoted to everybody's favorite alien, surely the homeliest homunculus ever to worm his way into a child's heart. Soft E.T.s are $10 to $35. Children's and adults' t-shirts are around $16 to $19. Perhaps your best bet is a souvenir photo of your child on a bike with E.T. in the basket and a huge silver moon as backdrop ($11 to $16).

Universal's Cartoon Store

Cuddly plush toys and gaily decorated children's wear is the stock-in-trade here. What will be on display when you visit is anyone's guess, as the stock here changes rapidly — although with *Animal Planet Live!* just across the way, expect a lot of animal plush toys and Animal Planet video tapes.

The Barney Shop

Here's where your little one will plead with you for a Barney doll. Reflecting the powers of persuasion wee ones have over parents and grandparents, they range in price from $10 for smallish Barneys to $41 for the largest. For children who balk at taking naps, there are pillows ($20) in the shape of the heads of various characters from the show. Videos are about $15 and Barney books are $3 and up. There is also a small selection of kiddie toys.

WORLD EXPO

The theme of World Expo is a typical World's Fair Exposition park. The result is a display of contemporary architecture and design that manages to be at once very attractive and rather characterless, although the *Men In Black* building looks quite zippy at night. Fortunately, people don't come here to muse on aesthetics. As home to two of the park's most exciting rides (*Back To The Future . . . The Ride* and *Men In Black*), World Expo's broad open spaces are filled with happy people, making a visit here highly enjoyable.

Back To The Future . . . The Ride

Rating:	★ ★ ★ ★ ★
Type:	Slam-bang simulator thrill ride
Time:	4.5 minutes
Kelly says:	The best theme park ride in Orlando

For many people, this is the ride that made Universal Studios Florida famous. And with good reason. *Back To The Future . . . The Ride* is a bone-jarring, stomach-churning (the official disclaimer posted outside describes it as "dynamically aggressive") thrill-a-second rocket ride through time and space. For once the warnings directed towards expectant mothers and those with heart problems, bad backs, and a tendency to motion sickness don't seem like lawyers' overkill. It's easy to see how this ride could trigger a premature birth or otherwise encourage what's inside to come outside in dramatic fashion.

Tip: Those in wheelchairs can still take this ride if they are able to transfer themselves from their wheelchair to the ride vehicle. Ask the attendant if you're not sure.

That mammoth building at the back of World Expo is the Institute of Future Technology where that wild and wacky Doc Brown (played on video monitors with gleeful aplomb by Christopher Lloyd) is conducting yet another series of time travel experiments. Those of us who willingly get on the invariably long lines to this attraction are "volunteers" who have agreed to test out Doc's new eight-seater convertible DeLorean — all in the interests of science. Trouble is, that not-too-bright but very resourceful Biff Tannen has stowed away in 1955 and is loose on the premises — a key bit of intelligence which we discover (via those video monitors) before Doc does. Biff has tied up some attendants and stolen the keys to one of the experimental DeLoreans. When he learns the truth, Doc goes, well, ballistic. "This could end the universe as we know it," he screams with characteristic understatement.

Suddenly, our mission has changed. Far from being mere passengers, we are now charged with giving chase to the evil Biff and engineering a time/space collision that will send Biff and his vehicle reeling back to the present.

That's the set-up. What follows is harder to describe. Suffice it to say that you're off on a four and a half minute, high-speed odyssey that will seem like eternity to some and all too brief to others. Along the way, you will zoom through the streets of Hill Valley's future, into the ice caves of its distant past, and smack into the slavering maw of a tyrannosaurus rex, always just a few tantalizing feet behind the errant Biff.

This ride raised the bar on thrill rides when it first opened. It has yet to be matched. It is, quite simply, the best simulator-based ride in Orlando, period, end of discussion.

Back To The Future . . . The Ride is actually two identical rides, located side by side in the same building. Each ride contains twelve identical eight-seater DeLoreans, each in its own "garage." The cars are arranged on three levels: four on the bottom, five in the middle, and three on the top. As you proceed into the maze of ramps that lead into the Institute, you will be guided to one of these levels. Once inside, you will wait first in a staging area and then in a cramped anteroom to your vehicle's garage. All along, the imaginative video introduction keeps you posted on Biff's caper while preparing you for the rigors of time travel. When you are in the final anteroom, an amusing safety warning featuring a family of hapless crash dummies explains the dangers of the DeLorean you're about to squeeze into.

At last the door opens and you see your DeLorean (and the wobbly group who just rode in it groping for the exit). If you look up you can see a gray void looming overhead. Once everyone is seated, the padded lap bars lock into place and the sides of the car fold down. It's a tight fit.

Tip: Try for the front seats. The view is better and rear seat passengers can expect to get their heads banged against the (padded) rear wall of the car. And heed the warnings about securing your personal belongings. Cameras, wallets, glasses, and the like have been known to disappear into the time-space continuum.

Suddenly you're airborne in a cloud of liquid nitrogen smoke and a flash of strobe lights that mask the DeLorean's rise up and out of the garage below. Your vehicle is actually an open-air cousin to the high-tech simulators used to train airline pilots. Like a box on stilts it hovers a few feet off the ground, but for all you know or care you might as well be in the depths of interstellar space.

You are now facing a mammoth, curved movie screen that completely fills your line of vision and represents the true genius of this ride. Other simulator-based rides use a movie screen that serves as a window to the outside of your spaceship or other vehicle. With *Back To The Future*, you are outside and the environment wraps around you. The illusion is startling, not to mention sometimes terrifying.

The movement of the simulator's stilts is surprisingly modest. You never actually move more than two feet in any direction. But try telling that to your brain. The kinetic signals sent by your body combine with the visual signals received from the screen to convince you that you are zooming along at supersonic speeds, making white-knuckle turns at dizzying angles. Matching the technological wonder of the concept is the care that went into making the multi-million dollar 70mm Omnimax film in which you become a key participant. Its budget reportedly rivaled that of most major feature-length films. It was directed by that living legend of special effects, Douglas Trumbull, and as they say in the movie biz, every penny they spent is on the screen.

The best seats in the house. The best way to experience this mind-boggling attraction is from the front row of the middle car of the middle row of

DeLoreans. Regardless of which of the two "theaters" you enter, this car is designated as "Car Six." This position points you directly at the center of the domed screen. You'll experience less distortion of the image (and, not incidentally, reduce any tendency towards motion sickness) and you'll be less likely to be distracted by glimpsing other cars out of your peripheral vision. (By the way, in the unlikely event you find yourself bored during your umpty-umpth ride, especially if you're off to the side of the bottom row, looking around at the other cars will give you a deeper appreciation of just how clever this ride is.)

Unfortunately, there's no easy way to position yourself to get the optimum seat. It's pretty much luck of the draw. If the lines are short or nonexistent, you might ask an attendant to point you to car number six (they'll know what you're talking about). That might at least get you to the right level. Otherwise, you'll just have to keep trying until your lucky number comes up. For die-hard fans that'll be something they can live with.

Tip: If you're prone to motion sickness but still want to savor the special thrills of this ride, take a Dramamine or a similar over-the-counter anti-motion sickness pill, before you leave for the park. Popping one just before entering will not protect you. During the ride, keep your eyes focused on Biff's car dead ahead to avoid too much conflict with your inner ear's balancing mechanism. If you find yourself getting uncomfortably nauseated, shut your eyes and tell yourself to relax. Remember, the ride lasts less than five minutes. Some queasy riders report getting relief by turning their gaze away from the screen and focusing on an adjacent car.

Men In Black: Alien Attack

Rating: ★ ★ ★ ★
Type: Interactive ride with laser weapons
Time: 4 minutes
Kelly says: This one gets addictive

Men In Black, the ride, is a bit like stepping inside one of those video arcade games, with the element of competition thrown in just to make things interesting. The experience begins when you visit "The Universe and You" a science exhibit left over from the New York World's Fair of 1964. Soon you discover that it's just a cover to enable you to apply for admission to the elite corps of MIB. You are not alone and the wait can get lengthy. Fortunately, snaking your way through the MIB building is an entertaining experience and devotees of the film will find much familiar here. A lengthy and amusing orientation film featuring Rip Torn and Will Smith is worth watching in full even when there's no line. Farther along, a training film starring two amusingly retro cartoon characters, Doofus and Do-Right, provides safety instructions for the testing vehicles that await you.

Tip: If you are by yourself or don't mind having your party split up, look for the single-rider line. It is invariably much shorter than the main line and a real time saver. Or use the kiosk outside to reserve a ride time.

Eventually, you are assigned to a vehicle with five other recruits. At each seat is a laser gun and a personal scoreboard that keeps track of hits. You are cruising through a target range, testing your marksmanship, when an urgent bulletin announces that a Prison Transport full of nasty space bugs has crashed landed in the middle of Manhattan. At once, you are reassigned to a dangerous but exciting mission. You and another team are dispatched, side by side, to do battle with the aliens through the dark and gritty streets of New York.

What follows is a few minutes of chaotic fun. Aliens in every imaginable buggy shape pop up from garbage cans and taxi hoods, from around corners and in shop windows. It's a super-sized sci-fi version of those old shooting galleries down at the boardwalk. Your job is to zap them before they zap you. When the bugs score a hit, your vehicle is sent into a tailspin. At one point, you discover that aliens have infiltrated the vehicle of the other team and you must fire at your own comrades. (*Tip:* Aim for the Fusion Exhaust Port, which is at the back of the vehicle, *above* the head of the rider in the middle seat.)

Then your MIB trainer (Will Smith from the movie) appears on a giant screen to warn you that a particularly nasty bug is bearing down on you. I don't want to give too much away but suffice it to say that it's big enough to swallow two MIB training vehicles. Gulp!

The vehicles are not simulators but they do allow for sudden swoops and 360-degree spins, which are both thrilling and discombobulating. And while the two vehicles depart at the same time and cruise along side by side for most of the ride, their progress can be affected by the direct hits scored by the aliens. As the battle progresses, every rider builds an individual score based on their success in targeting the enemy (you will see the tiny red dots of the laser guns dancing on the alien targets); the individual scores contribute to the overall team score. There is a sneaky way to significantly increase your score that I'll let you discover on your own.

Tip: The maximum possible score is 999,999 and it can be done. I know because I've seen it done (not by me, alas).

At ride's end, both vehicles are once again cruising side by side as Will Smith appears on another screen to announce which team came out ahead. The combined scores of each vehicle are posted for all to see. Then, Smith breaks the news on how your team did: Galaxy Defender, Cosmically Average, or Bug Bait.

In a final clever touch Smith uses his neuralizer to erase your memory of the whole experience and you emerge to discover that you have just completed your visit to "The Universe and You," which turns out to be about the possibility of life in outer space. "Are we alone?" the sign asks. "Of course we are," is the reassuring answer.

MIB is a lot of fun and it's hard to imagine anyone having serious complaints. Kids who are video game addicts will probably want to ride again and again to improve their scores. Obviously there is at least some skill involved in wielding the laser guns because individual scores in a vehicle can vary by as much as several hundred thousand points. On the other hand, the experience is so chaotic that it is hard to know how well you are doing or get the kind of visual feedback that would help you fine tune your aim.

The best seats in the house. Riders on the outside of the vehicles (i.e., in the seats that are the farthest from the loading platform) tend to score higher than those in other seats. My guess is that this is because they are closer to the targets and get to see them first. The hyper-competitive among you may want to take note of this.

On the way out, you can pause to purchase a photo of your laser-gun wielding team in the training vehicle. The cost is $12, $16, or $26 depending on the size. Even if you don't want to buy, you may want to check the photos (displayed on TV monitors) because they show the individual score of each rider — a great way to claim bragging rights.

Selected Short Subjects

MIB Agents

A pair of gung-ho but not too bright MIB agents appears from time to time in front of the attraction of the same name in search of an alien on the loose. Somewhere amongst you lurks a Rigillian and the agents select the most likely suspects from the crowd and do some surefire tests to detect the odd alien out. Did you know, for example, that aliens can't dance? It's great fun and the outcome is not always the foregone conclusion it might seem at first glance.

RobOasis

In the *Men In Black* plaza, on the way to *Back To The Future*, is this clever advertisement for Coca Cola. Here a tiny alien, who is something of a Coke fiend ("Take me to your liter!") sits in a tiny space ship and prattles on about his Earth mission. To either side are niches in the shape of old-fashioned glass Coke bottles. Step in and have your entire body suffused with a fine misting spray of cool water. A great refresher on a hot day.

Eating in World Expo

There's only one real restaurant in World Expo, but that doesn't mean there aren't a lot of places to get something to eat. Kiosks pop up seasonally as the weather and the crowds dictate and there are some permanent outdoor refreshment stands in the broad plaza outside the *Men In Black* building.

International Food and Film Festival

What: A multicultural cafeteria

Where: On Exposition Boulevard, next to *Back To The Future*

Price Range: $ - $$

This is as fancy as it gets in World Expo. This large, loud cafeteria-style food emporium is divided into sections by cuisine. You can choose among Italian, American, Asian, or Ice Cream (my nationality). Entrees range from $5 to about $8, and the food is a notch or two above typical fast-food quality. Salads and desserts are listed separately and are available at any of the counters. At the walk-up ice cream counter, which is located outside near the entrance to the restaurant, prices start at $2.50 and go up to about $5 for a brownie sundae. Be aware that some sections may be closed when you visit. Only soft drinks are served here.

Video monitors scattered around the large seating area play familiar films dubbed in what may be unfamiliar languages. On the walls are posters advertising movies, some of them in their overseas, retitled versions.

Tip: The rear wall is all glass and looks out on *Animal Planet Live!* — a great opportunity to take a second (if somewhat obstructed) look at one of Universal's most enjoyable attractions.

Shopping in World Expo

Back To The Future — The Store

There's a DeLorean smashing through the walls of this compact circular shop, and the walls themselves are plastered with newspaper headlines of the past and future. There are the expected *Back To The Future* souvenirs to be found here, including mugs and the like featuring the OUTATIME license plate logo. A DeLorean model kit goes for $25 and *Back To The Future* clothing, from t-shirts to denim jackets, costs $13 to $70. Picking up on the time theme, the store also features a small selection of watches and clocks.

MIB Gear Shop

This spacious, high-ceilinged shop sells clothes for MIB agents. Everything from t-shirts ($14 to $24) to windbreakers ($30) is in the black, white, and orange color scheme MIB agents seem to prefer. You will also find some sleek MIB glassware, mugs, and cups ($5 to $15) along with a wide variety of action figures and toys tied into the movie. There are even a few books on UFOs.

Expo Art

On Exposition Boulevard, outside the International Food and Film Festival, you will find several tent-like structures housing some of Universal Studios' most attractive souvenirs. Under one tent, as many as four caricaturists hold forth, turning out devastatingly accurate portraits for remarkably reasonable prices. Black and white sketches are just $14, or $20 for a couple. With color added, the prices go to $20 and $35 respectively. For an extra $12, you get a frame with glass. (You'll find more caricaturists in San Francisco/Amity.)

Other tents appear from time to time offering touristy crafts such as your name painted in fanciful letters or intricate hair wraps for women.

SAN FRANCISCO / AMITY

Juxtaposing California's San Francisco and New England's Amity might seem jarring at first, but in the movies anything is possible. In fact, the two areas are quite separate; the double-barreled name for this "set" is more a matter of convenience than anything else.

San Francisco/Amity is distinguished by the presence of *Jaws*, the wonderfully scary boat ride. The San Francisco part is also packed with eating places, some of them quite nice indeed.

Jaws

Rating: ★ ★ ★ ★ +
Type: Water ride
Time: 5 minutes
Kelly says: A scare-fest for kids of all ages

Welcome aboard, as Captain Jake takes you on a sightseeing tour of peaceful Amity harbor. As the waiting line snakes toward the dock, you get your first inkling that something might be amiss. Television monitors broadcast an appropriately hokey local news show about the strange doings in Amity, complete with interviews with the real Sheriff Brody (who complains that Arnold Schwarzenegger would have been a much better choice than Roy Scheider to play him in the movie).

The conceit, of course, is that you are in the real town of Amity and that the blockbuster film *Jaws* was not fiction but fact-based. One not unwelcome by-product of the film is that the sleepy town is now a major tourist draw, allowing Captain Jake to make a good living as the best — make that the only — sightseeing company offering visitors tours of the island.

As your tour boat is about to leave the dock, your friendly but cocky guide shows off a grenade launcher for effect. He tells us that since the great white was killed way back in '74, Amity's been pretty peaceful. He points out Sheriff Brody's house on the left and then heads out of the harbor.

This being a Universal ride, it doesn't take long for things to go ominously amiss. A crackling, fragmented radio transmission from Amity 3, a returning tour boat, is a clear signal that danger lies ahead, but the guide assures us nothing's wrong. A turn around a rocky promontory reveals the other tour boat shattered and sinking on our left. A huge dorsal fin breaks the surface, we feel a slight bump as Jaws passes beneath us, and the thrills begin.

Jaws (for that is the shark's universally agreed-upon name) breaks water on our left, showing off his gaping maw and savage teeth. Our now panicked tour guide fires off a few grenades but they go wide of the mark, sending up harmless geysers of water around his target.

A quick turn into a dark boathouse promises safety, but we know better. The edgy nerves of fellow passengers provide much of the fun here until Jaws himself crashes through the wooden boathouse on the right.

Back out in open water, we're in for another close call as Bridle's shoreside gasoline depot erupts in flames. The heat on the left side of the boat is intense and a wall of flame blocks our way. Our intrepid guide steers straight for the conflagration as our only route to safety and, mercifully, the flames die down to let us pass. Relief is only momentary, however, as Jaws lunges at the boat from the left, lifting his head high out of the water. The guide nudges the boat into a gap in a floating dock where an electrical cable has fallen into the water. Jaws lunges from our left again but this time he gets the cable before he gets us. He dies in a spectacular shower of electrified water and sparks. A little farther along, what appears to be his charred corpse bobs to the surface. But there's life in the old boy yet and he makes another attempt on the hors d'oeuvres floating by. A final volley from the grenade launcher and we are at last out of danger and glide back to the dock without further incident, barely five minutes after we left.

This is a water ride and, as you are informed several times before embarking, you will get wet. Some people just don't seem to believe it. One of the extra added amusements of this ride is watching fastidious tourists take out a tissue and carefully wipe off the damp seats before sitting down. Don't bother. There's a lot more where that came from. If you come to the park in the winter, when temperatures can be on the cool side, you might want to consider protecting yourself with a cheap plastic poncho.

The best seats in the house. Where you sit can make a difference on this ride. Inveterate thrill seekers will not be satisfied with anything but the outside seat, whichever side it's on. On balance, the left side offers the most thrills, especially the furnace blast of the gas depot explosion. The right side has the best view of Jaws' entrance into the boathouse. My favorite seat is the far left of row five. Since Jaws rises from the water, those on one side of the boat will have a slightly obstructed view of his appearances on the other side. The obvious solution is to take this ride more than once. Early risers, who get to the park before the gates open, can usually cycle through the ride several times before the lines become too daunting. I highly recommend riding *Jaws* at dusk when the special effects are particularly spectacular.

While there is a certain shock value to be derived from the element of surprise, this ride is not truly scary. At least for most grown-ups. Little ones may disagree. The shark, while a masterpiece of clever engineering, always betrays its latex and aluminum origins, at least close-up. Still, this doesn't detract from the fun, especially the first few times. As you take your third, fourth, and fifth turns around the harbor, you'll probably find yourself deriving equal enjoyment by looking behind you to see the gasoline depot automatically reconstructing itself in preparation for the next boatload of happily terrified tourists.

Earthquake — The Big One

Rating: ★ ★ ★ ★ +
Type: Show and ride
Time: 20 minutes, ride portion is 3 minutes
Kelly says: A treat for special effects buffs

If you've come to *Earthquake — The Big One* for yet another shake and bake thrill ride, be patient. You'll get your chills and thrills in due time, but first Universal Studios wants to teach you a thing or two about the painstaking behind-the-scenes ingenuity and craftsmanship that make film effects so special.

Earthquake — The Big One is actually three somewhat different attractions rolled into one — all inspired by the spectacular disaster movie that became the first film in history to win an Oscar for special effects. The experience begins in a theater lobby displaying a fascinating collection of sepia-toned photographs taken shortly after the great San Francisco quake of 1906. Also displayed here are the matte paintings used in the making of *Earthquake*. Matte paintings are painstakingly realistic paintings on glass, with a key area blacked out.

A Universal aide mounts a podium and does a brief show and tell about how weather is simulated in films. The next order of business is to choose some in the crowd for special business. The selection process involves asking for volunteers, cajoling and, if necessary, dragooning people into service. If you're interested in becoming part of the show, standing near the podium may help. The roles available are a stunt double, two U-boat officers and a "weather grip" — usually a small kid.

When the three doors at the back of the lobby open, the crowd files into a long narrow room, which serves as a stand-up movie theater. There, a short film featuring Charlton Heston, star of the original *Earthquake*, describes some of the techniques used to conjure up the total destruction of Hollywood for the film as well as other disaster effects. It's a fascinating mini-documentary that will have you shaking your head in admiration for the cleverness of those movie wizards. Most fascinating is the way high-speed photography lets the filmmaker slow down the snapping of a building and produce a startlingly realistic sequence.

When the film ends, a curtain rises on a portion of the actual model city used in the filming. The chest-high buildings are in their shattered, postquake condition. It's worth lingering a moment to get a closer look. It took model makers six months to build and it was destroyed in six seconds. The cost: $2.4 million — and those are 1974 dollars!

As you file into the next room, you enter a larger theater, and this time you get to sit on benches. Here is where the casting session you saw in the staging area pays off. Before you is a set depicting two sets. To the left, in front of an electric blue background, is a mock-up of the conning tower of a submarine. To the right is a three-story high set representing the demolished stairwell of a high-rise building.

The "stunt double" is issued blue coveralls and a safety harness and informed that he or she will be recreating the scene of an earthquake victim being lowered down the stairwell shaft. The others take their positions as submariners on watch, while the "weather grip" gets ready to pull a large rope that will dump hundreds of gallons of water on the storm-tossed U-boat.

I don't want to give away what happens next, but suffice it to say the results are surprising, informative, and funny in approximately equal measure. When the demonstration is over, the audience is ushered in to the final phase of the *Earthquake* experience.

This is the part most people come for, a simulated ride aboard San Francisco's BART (Bay Area Rapid Transit). The train (with open sides and clear plastic roof) pulls out of the Oakland station, enters the tunnel under the Bay, and soon emerges in the Embarcadero station. There is an ominous rumble and the train's P.A. system announces, with the false optimism that is something of a running theme in these rides, that this is just a minor tremor and there's nothing to worry about. Hah!

Soon the earthquake reaches eight on the Richter scale and the Embarcadero station begins to artfully fall apart. Floors buckle and ceilings shatter. The car you're in jerks upward, while the car in front of you drops and tilts perilously. Then the entire roof caves in on one side, exposing the street above. A propane tanker truck, caught in the quake, slides into the hole directly towards us. The only thing that prevents it from slamming into the train is a steel beam, which impales the truck and causes it to burst into flame. Next, what looks like the entire contents of San Francisco Bay comes pouring down the stairs on the other side. And it's still not over. An oncoming train barrels into the station directly at us, but the buckled track sets it on a trajectory that narrowly misses us.

All too soon, the terror is over and the train backs out of the station, returning us to "Oakland." As it backs out, you can see the Embarcadero station methodically reconstruct itself in preparation for the next "take."

The best seats in the house. For the first two parts of the Earthquake experience, it really doesn't matter where you are, although if you'd like to get a better look at the destroyed Hollywood model, you should try to get to the front. That means entering through the far left door and staying toward the back of the line.

You enter the train station through doors on the rear wall of the second theater. Those seated in the back of the theater will tend to wind up on the right hand side of the train; those seated toward the front on the left. Those seated on the right of the theater will tend to wind up toward the front of the train and those on the left toward the back. There is some room to maneuver for position left or right once on the BART platform, especially if the crowds are smaller. There is less opportunity to move from the front of the train to the back or vice versa.

The train holds about 200 people and is divided into three sections. The first section (that is, the car to the far left as you enter the BART station), has its seats facing backwards. The other two sections have seats facing forward. This arrangement assures that people in the first section won't have to turn around to see most of the special effects the ride holds in store. The front of each section has a clear plastic panel but the view is somewhat obstructed. Avoid the first two rows of a section, if possible. I have found that the best view is to be had in the middle of the second car. The major attraction for those sitting on the right (as the train enters the tunnel) is the flood, which can get a few people wet. The more spectacular explosion of the propane tanker and the wreck of the oncoming train are best viewed from the left. As always, the outside seats are the primo location.

Earthquake — The Big One is unique among the thrill rides at Universal

Studios in that it combines an instructional component along with the fun and games. You will emerge from the experience with a much deeper appreciation for the unseen geniuses who make the incredible seem so real on the silver screen.

Beetlejuice's Graveyard Revue

Rating: ★ ★ ★
Type: Amphitheater show
Time: 20 minutes
Kelly says: Best for young and pre-teens

Beetlejuice started out as a streetside performer on the New York set and proved so popular that he was "discovered" by Universal Studios and given his own amphitheater show. The addition of a set, pyrotechnics, and what sounds like several million dollars worth of sound equipment hasn't changed the show's basic appeal, just made it louder.

The set is a jumble of crumbling castle walls, complete with a mummy's sarcophagus and a more modern coffin. The "plot" is nonexistent. Beetlejuice, your host with the most, emerges from the mummy's tomb in a burst of fireworks that is literally blinding. He immediately gets to the business at hand, summoning the Wolfman, Dracula, Frankenstein, and the ever lovely Bride of Frankenstein from their ghostly lairs for your listening pleasure. It looks at first like it will be a real horror show — an Andrew Lloyd Webber opera! Fortunately, Beetlejuice steps in and before your very eyes — well, behind a wall of smoke actually — the cast changes into suitably hip attire. Then they begin, appropriately enough, to wail.

The premise is wafer thin and the classic Universal monsters theme goes completely out the window when, presumably to even out the gender distribution, two girls named Hip and Hop are added to the lineup. But what the show lacks in sophistication and coherence, it more than makes up for in energy and good-natured fun. And noise. The sound volume is guaranteed to wake the dead. The tender-eared and the old at heart should consider themselves suitably forewarned.

Some of the songs seem oddly matched to the performer. Dracula, for example, gives a stirring but puzzling rendition of "La Vida Loca," but the Bride of Frankenstein (in a sexy little outfit that should remind the men in the audience that they're not dead yet) sings the more appropriate "I Will Survive." And conceiving Frankenstein as a heavy metal guitarist is inspired.

The choreography is straightforward and energetic, and those who have yet to see their first Vegas extravaganza or Broadway musical will find it a lot of fun. Add some mildly raunchy Beetlejuice-ian humor, a brief romp through the first few rows of the audience, regular appeals for audience participation in the form of wolf wails and hand clapping, and you have a recipe for cheerfully mindless entertainment.

There are really no bad seats for this one. An interesting seating choice would be next to the pit in the center of the house, where the sound and light techies run the show. If your kid has dragged you to the show for the fifth time, you can amuse yourself watching these wizards ply their high-tech trade. Seating is pretty much first-come, first-served, although at peak periods attendants may direct you to a seat to speed the flow.

Wild, Wild, Wild West Stunt Show

Rating: ★ ★ ★ +
Type: Amphitheater show
Time: 15 minutes
Kelly says: A bang-up stunt-fest

What's a Wild West show doing cheek by jowl with the *Jaws* ride in Amity? Don't ask, just sit back and enjoy yourself.

This slam-bang bit of foolishness features a handsome cowboy stunt man, his goofy sidekick, a noble steed, and a trio of villains — Ma Hopper and her "twin" boys who are evil, ornery, and stupid in approximately equal measure. Along the way, the gang gets to show off all the standard western movie stunts like falling off buildings and horses, breaking bottles and chairs over each others' heads, and generally wreaking havoc. There is also a liberal dose of pyrotechnics, with a bang-up finale that owes a debt to Buster Keaton's silent classic, *Steamboat Bill Jr.* In fact, ear-splitting explosions seem to be to Universal shows what Green Slime is to Nickelodeon — something of a corporate logo.

Despite the violence, it's hard to imagine this show offending or scaring anybody. The performances are so broad that the show reads more like a cartoon than the westerns on which the action is based. True, some of the explosions and gun shots are loud and startling, but that's all part of the fun. Another part of the fun for some people will be sitting in the splash zone. It's near the well, but just in case you forget, there are several announcements that point out its precise location, and like they say, you will get wet.

Tip: There are some 2,000 seats in this arena so, on all but the most crowded days, you need not arrive much before the posted show times. There are typically four shows a day. They are listed in the Attraction & Show Times insert to the Studio Guide brochure you received when you entered the park.

Selected Short Subjects

The Amity Boardwalk

Between *Earthquake — The Big One* and *Jaws* is a winding stretch of road that offers up a typical New England boardwalk as a child might see it — bright and shining. Of course, the originals are a lot shabbier and far more weather-beaten, the games a bit more threadbare, but never mind. This is the movies, after all, and with the genius of the best set designers Universal has to offer, everything should be perfect.

Here you can try your skill at knocking over plastic glasses with a whiffle ball, tossing a softball into a farmer's milk can, or playing skee-ball. If you fancy yourself a superhuman, try ringing the bell with a mighty blow of your sledgehammer. You can also test the skill of the Amazing Alonzo who bets you $3 or $5 that he can guess your weight or age. Most games cost $2 and, as with the seaside attractions they mimic, the odds are heavily weighted towards the house. Universal, however, makes it easier to win at least something and the prizes, while modest (or ugly, depending on your mood), are a cut above those you'll find along, say, the Jersey shore.

Although the Boardwalk is several cuts above the Arcade in New York (see below), I react in much the same way: Why bother? If you've seen all this before, you may react the same way. If, however, you hail from a part of the world where this kind of folksy seaside recreation is not part of your collective subconscious, you may want to pause and give it a whirl. Many people do. All things being equal, I'd recommend saving yourself for the more authentic (if more downscale) versions you'll encounter on your next visit to the New England seashore.

Trick Photography Photo Spot

Just before you cross the bridge across the lagoon to Expo Center, you encounter one of those clever spots where you can use the "hanging miniature" technique to snap a unique souvenir photo. Here, you can pose your family in front of the Space Shuttle, ingeniously plunked down on top of the Institute of Future Technology in the background.

Eating in San Francisco/Amity

The San Francisco/Amity area enjoys the distinction of having the most eateries of any of USF's six sections, thanks largely to the leisurely way it snakes along the lagoon. Here, roughly in the order you encounter them as you proceed from World Expo around the lagoon to New York, are your choices:

Brody's Ice Cream Shoppe

What:	Quick-service ice-cream parlor
Where:	Near the entrance to *Jaws*
Price Range:	$

Need a quick fortifier? A sugar jolt is close at hand at this ice cream stand. Cones and sundaes are the order of the day at prices ranging from about $3 to $5.

Captain Quint's Seafood and Chowder House

What:	Fried seafood at picnic tables
Where:	Along the Amity boardwalk
Price Range:	$ - $$

Stop here for a quick al fresco seafood like fish & chips or fried scallops ($8) or a shrimp and scallop combo with fries ($10). Clam chowder and lobster bisque is $5. There is some very good beer served here ($4) along with the usual array of soft drinks. All seating is outdoors at weathered picnic tables. Venture around behind the snack stand and sit by the lagoon for one of the nicest views in the park.

McCann's Fruit & Beverage Co.

What:	Sidewalk stand
Where:	Along the Amity boardwalk, amid the pitch and skill games
Price Range:	$

For a change of pace, look for this quaint little stand selling fresh apples, oranges, and seasonal fruits along with an array of refreshing drinks alluringly displayed in buckets of ice.

Midway Grill

What:	Outdoor snacking at picnic tables
Where:	Along the Amity boardwalk, amid the pitch and skill games
Price Range:	$

The sign says "Hot dogs ★ Sausage ★ Fries" and the menu is scarcely more elaborate than that. Grilled Italian sausages and Philly cheese steaks are about $6, hot dogs are $4, and beer is about $5. Walk up to the window and take your snack along as you stroll the Midway, or sit at a nearby picnic table.

Boardwalk Funnel Cake Co.

What:	Walk up stand
Where:	Along the Amity boardwalk

Price Range: $

This stand sells, what else?, funnel cakes ($4) with a variety of toppings (79 cents each) that include apple, strawberries, and chocolate. Soft serve ice cream is also available ($2.50 to $3.50).

San Francisco Pastry Company

What: Small pastry and coffee shop
Where: Across from *Earthquake — The Big One*
Price Range: $

Right at the entrance to Lombard's stands this tempting alternative. It features most of the pastries you found at the Beverly Hills Boulangerie in Hollywood ($3 to $4) as well as coffee, cappuccino, and soft drinks. Sandwiches are about $7 as is a fruit plate. There are no tables inside and a small outside seating area, so many customers will have to take their snacks to one of the scenic spots along the nearby waterfront.

Lombard's Seafood Grille

What: Elegant restaurant evoking Fisherman's Wharf
Where: On the lagoon, across from *Earthquake —*
              The Big One
Price Range: $$ – $$$$

Lombard's is a full-service restaurant boasting the most elegant decor at Universal and the best food. The main dining room exudes an industrial-Victorian aura, with brick walls, filigreed iron arches and tapestry-covered dining chairs. The room is dominated by a huge, square, centrally located saltwater fish tank like something Captain Nemo might have imagined. Windows on three sides look out over the lagoon. All in all, the atmosphere is charming.

The food here, which is strong on seafood, is excellent and my favorite at USF. Appetizers cost $5 to $8 and range from simple bisques and chowders to a sumptuous shrimp cocktail. For the main course, I would suggest splurging on the grilled, blackened, or herb-crusted fish. The Catch of the Day menu insert lets you know what's available and gives the current market price. Expect to pay $18 or so for your fish entree, but don't expect to be disappointed. Other entrees ($14 to $20) reflect the diverse cuisine of San Francisco and include Cioppino, a Ginger Stir Fry, Shrimp Alfredo, and a Nob Hill Sirloin Steak.

Special mention should be made of the salads ($11 to $16), which are not merely healthy but delicious as well. Try the Seafood Lover's Cobb Salad, a medley of cold shellfish and veggies, or get blackened seafood of your choice served warm over a bed of field greens with raspberry balsamic vinegar.

There is an exceptional dessert here, the San Francisco Foggie, which is served in an enormous martini glass. On a bedrock of chocolate brownie rises a Nob Hill of ice cream, as a fog bank of whipped cream rolls in off the Bay. A drizzle of caramel sauce and a sprinkling of almond slivers complete this delicious creation (about $5).

Reservations can be made by calling (407) 224-6401.

Chez Alcatraz

What: Outdoor stand

Where: On the lagoon, between Richter's and Lombard's Seafood Grille

Price Range: $

Right at the water's edge, next to Shaiken's Souvenirs, Chez Alcatraz offers quick snacks at moderate prices. Seafood chowder or chili is $5; a blackfin crabmeat cocktail and a smoked turkey croissant are $7. Seating is outdoors and unshaded.

Richter's Burger Co.

What: Fast-food burger joint

Where: On the lagoon, across from *Earthquake —
The Big One*

Price Range: $$

That's Richter as in scale, and just in case you didn't get it the first time, one glance at the damaged interior of this warehouse-like structure will let you know that the theme here is pure *Earthquake*. It's a fun environment in which to chow down on standard burger fare.

The Big One ($7) is a burger or cheeseburger served with "a landslide of fries," while the San Andreas (about $7) is a chicken sandwich. Frisco shakes, chocolate and vanilla, are about $3.

The decor is fun and imaginative, and worth more than a passing glance. At the back, you'll find tables with a lagoon view and a balcony offering a great bird's-eye view of the New York end of the lagoon.

Shopping in San Francisco/Amity

Shaiken's Novelties & Souvenirs

This is a souvenir shop in search of a theme. Despite the earthquake-related name and its location next to Richter's, Shaiken's offers up a fairly standard selection of Universal t-shirts and other wearables, at the usual prices ($16 and up). You can, however, pick up a DVD of *Earthquake*, the film that inspired the ride.

Salty's Sketches

Stop under the awning by the San Francisco Pastry Company to have one of Universal's expert caricaturists immortalize your goofy grin for posterity. These artists must all have studied under the same master because their styles are almost identical and the quality of the renderings excellent.

The cost is also surprisingly moderate given the high quality of the finished product. Black and white sketches are just $14, or $20 for a couple. With color added, the prices go to $20 and $35 respectively. For an extra $12, you get a frame with glass.

Quint's Surf Shack

Tucked into an old wooden lighthouse (look up as you enter), this shop celebrates the surfer lifestyle in clothes. For women, there is brightly colored and quite attractive beach and resort wear at prices ranging from $20 to $50. For men, there are Hawaiian style shirts (about $50) and gaudy, baggy swim trunks ($44). For both, there are t-shirts and shorts that let you play lifeguard.

NEW YORK

Compared to some others on the lot, the New York set seems downright underpopulated — with attractions, eateries, and shops, that is. Whole streets in New York are given over entirely to film backdrops. Gramercy Park, Park Avenue, the dead end Fifty-Seventh Street that incongruously ends at the New York Public Library, and the narrow alleys behind Delancey Street contain nary a ride or shop. These sets, however, provide some wonderfully evocative backgrounds for family portraits, especially the library facade, with a collection of familiar skyscrapers looming behind it. They also include some clever inside jokes for those familiar with the movie industry. Check out the names painted on the windows of upper story offices along Fifth Avenue and see if you can spot them. Of course, New York does have attractions. In fact, it has two of Universal Studios' most popular draws, one of them a guaranteed blockbuster. It also serves up some of the nicest dining experiences to be had in the park.

Twister ... Ride It Out

Rating: ★ ★ ★ ★
Type: Stand-up theater show
Time: 15 minutes
Kelly says: Amazing in-your-face special effects

Here is an attraction that will almost literally blow you away. Based on the hit film of the same name, *Twister* is a theater show without seats that leads you through three sets for a payoff that lasts all of two minutes. But what a two minutes it is!

The journey begins as you snake though a waiting line in Wakita, Oklahoma, around large props from the film. You are entertained by two disk jockeys ("the storm chasers of rock and roll") from WNDY ("windy") who spin peppy rock songs with appropriately stormy titles. You will be kept cool by large fans that blow a fine water mist over the crowds. As you draw closer to the Soundstage on which the real adventure unfolds, the entertainment gives way to videos of actual tornadoes, some of which are really scary.

The line may seem formidable but don't despair. This show can handle 2,400 people each hour, so the line moves fairly quickly. Once inside, the show follows a familiar three-part format. In the first chamber, themed as the prop room for the film, you watch a video in which the vivacious Helen Hunt and an oddly wooden Bill Paxton set the scene. If you missed the movie, this segment gives you the information you need to understand what the film and this attraction are all about.

The second chamber is themed as the ruined interior of Aunt Meg's house from the movie. Trees and the front end of an automobile protrude through the ceiling, where a string of video monitors continue the introduction process. There is not a great deal of "edutainment" in this attraction, especially as compared to, say, *Earthquake*, but what little there is happens here. We get a brief explanation of how high-end computer software was used to re-create tornado physics and see some production shots that illustrate how some of the niftier scenes in the film were created.

Then it's on to the final chamber where the "real" show happens — live, in-person, and right before your eyes. You enter a set where you stand on a three-level viewing area under the deceptive protection of a tin roof. In front of you is the Wakita street that runs past the Galaxy outdoor movie theater where a "Horror Night" double feature of *The Shining* and *Psycho* is being shown. The street is deserted, but no sooner is everyone in place than all heck breaks loose and the inanimate objects before you take on a scary life of their own.

The best seats in the house. You will have a great experience here no matter where you stand. However, die-hard thrill seekers will want to be as close to the action as possible. Stay to the right as you are ushered into this final chamber if you want to stand in the front row. Most people hug the railing, but you can form a second row and make your way to dead center if you wish.

I don't want to give too much away about what happens next but you've probably already figured out that you'll be living through the vortex of a twister. Some of the effects are versions of what you may already have seen while riding *Earthquake*. But when the twister arrives stage center, just feet away, you will gape in awe and wonder, "How'd they do that?"

Tip: This is a wet, if not precisely soaking, experience. A poncho might be in order if you're really fussy. Otherwise, you probably will find the sprinkling fun, even refreshing. Interestingly enough, I have gotten wetter in the back row than I have in the front.

Kongfrontation

Rating: ★ ★ ★ +
Type: Aerial tram ride
Time: 4.5 minutes
Kelly says: More handsome than scary

Pass through the huge columns of Pennsylvania Station along New York's Fifth Avenue and you will soon find yourself in a gritty re-creation of a New York subway station, specifically the Roosevelt Island aerial tram station by the Fifty-Ninth Street Bridge. As you snake your way to the tram platform, past graffiti-dense concrete walls and posters advertising forthcoming Universal films, television monitors keep you posted.

Since-departed newspeople from New York station WWOR tell us of sightings of King Kong on a rampage. When you finally board the 40-person aerial tram, the tram conductor assures you there's no danger. Somehow the padded lap bar that lowers into place suggests otherwise.

Very shortly after the tram leaves the station, the truth becomes clear. Kong is not headed for the city limits but is dead ahead and in no mood to be trifled with. What's worse, the tram cannot stop. On the left you see a subway car toppled from its elevated track, burning brightly; a police car is wrecked on a fire hydrant which sends a geyser skyward.

Turn a corner and there is Kong himself, on the left, hanging from the Fifty-Ninth Street Bridge. A police helicopter hovers nearby ready to pump him full of lead and it looks like we're going to be caught in the crossfire. An enraged Kong lunges for the tram, which takes a glancing blow and almost plummets into the river. It looks like we're in the clear as we glide into Roosevelt Island, but there is Kong again, this time rising threateningly out of the shattered roof of an industrial building. He's close — very close — and he grabs the tram car and gives it a thorough, bone-jarring shaking. Only a huge fiery explosion behind Kong saves you, because Kong drops the tram. Then, less than five minutes after departure, you glide to safety in the Roosevelt Island station. Video monitors lower from the ceiling with a Channel 9 news update. There you are, high above the East River, reacting in terrified delight to the gigantic Kong.

This ride has been significantly intensified since its debut. If you rode it several years ago, you may be surprised by the new bumps and drops. Still, *Kongfrontation* is far from the scariest ride at Universal. The sudden dropping of the tram and the shaking may give you a momentary start, but the real fascination in this ride is the craftsmanship behind the mammoth figures of Kong himself. They are beautifully done and far too attractive to be frightening. Best of all is the full-figure of Kong hanging from the bridge. A second or third look reveals that the figure has been artfully foreshortened to make it look bigger and taller than it actually is. What's more, these huge animated figures are close enough to offer excellent photo ops. Flash photography is forbidden (although I've never seen anyone disciplined for ignoring the rule), but there's enough ambient light to pose a reasonably accomplished photographer no problem at all, especially if you use fast film or a digital camera.

The best seats in the house. If it is at all possible, you should ride *Kongfrontation* more than once, hoping for end row seats on both the right and the left of the car. Those on the left have a terrific view of Kong on the bridge; those on the right get to stare the magnificent beast straight in the mouth. Those on the left will also be prominent in the video news report that ends the ride.

As you exit this ride, you will have a chance to be photographed in the grip of a life-sized Kong (actually just the head and hand). It's a clever shot, the giant prop is another masterpiece of the set maker's art, and you just might find the result worth the $11 to $16 charge.

Selected Short Subjects

Arcades

Why anyone would pay good money to get into Universal Studios Florida and then waste their time in a video arcade is beyond me. On the other hand, the two Arcades in New York never seem to lack for customers, so what do I know? Perhaps the answer lies in the fact that most patrons are teenagers who probably didn't pay for their own admission.

The Blues Brothers

The Dan Ackroyd-John Belushi routine that made a better *Saturday Night Live* sketch than it ever did a movie is immortalized in this peppy street show, which currently holds forth from a makeshift stage on Delancey Street. The warm-up comes courtesy of a belting blues singer whose gospel-tinged renditions of blues standards are a show in and of themselves. Then, backed by a live sax player and a recorded sound track, Jake and Elwood goof and strut their way through a selection of rock and blues standards, winding up with a rousing, extremely high-decibel version of "Soul Man."

The genial performers, who are look-alikes only to the extent that one is tall and lanky and the other short and stout, do the material justice, and Jake's hyperkinetic dance steps are a highlight of the show. If you like your rock straight and unadulterated, you should enjoy it. Performances are listed in the Attraction & Show Times insert to the Studio Guide brochure you were handed as you entered the park, but Jake and Elwood take no chances; they cruise the lot in their funky revamped cop car promoting the show.

Extreme Ghostbusters

Subtitled "The Great Fright Way," this brief (15-minute) street show takes place against the New York Public Library facade at the back of the New York set. The show gets off to a promising start with Beetlejuice singing "Start spreading the ooze" to the tune of "New York, New York." When the Ghostbusters arrive, the ghost with the most turns the tables on them, casting a wicked spell that forces them, quite against their wills, to perform in a gender-bending medley of some of the sillier pop genres of the past forty years. From the girl groups of the sixties, to rap, to the boy bands that are a current obsession, the guys get to do a bit of everything. There's even a Madonna number. It's all great fun and the Ghostbusters dance and lip sync (as Beetlejuice cattily points out) with gusto.

Historical note: This location is where Beetlejuice got his start as a street performer before hitting the big time with his *Graveyard Revue* and the Ghostbusters used to have their very own show not far away, in the building *Twister* now occupies.

Street Breaks

Break dancing has become a staple of New York street entertainment and the troupe of dancers here is a cut or two above what you're likely to see in Times Square. If hip hop is your beat and acrobatic dancing is to your taste, then this show won't disappoint.

Eating in New York

Finnegan's

What:	Irish pub and sit-down restaurant
Where:	On Fifth Avenue across from *Kongfrontation*
Price Range:	$$ - $$$

Finnegan's has two parts and two personalities. The first is a full-fledged Irish pub complete with live entertainment and walls crowded with beer and liquor ads and offbeat memorabilia. Cozy up to the antique bar and order a yard of ale if that's your pleasure, or choose from a classy selection of domestic and imported beers. Guinness stout, Harp lager, and Bass ale are available on draught and the menu thoughtfully describes the differences among these three types of brew. Hard cider and wine are also available.

The other half of Finnegan's is a full-service restaurant hidden behind the false facades of the New York lot. The decor here is pared down and perfunctory, reflecting the room's other identity as a movie set. Fortunately, the food is anything but pared down or perfunctory. The theme is Irish and British Isles, with generously sized entrees to match. Appetizers (in the $6 to $7 range) include "Irish Chicken Stingers," Cornish pasties, and Scotch eggs.

Among the entrees ($11 to $22), London Times fish and chips is traditional, right down to the newspaper it's served in. The shepherd's pie is a juicy souvenir from the Emerald Isle, topped with perfectly browned mashed potatoes. There's also bangers and mash (sausage and mashed potatoes), Irish stew, and (of course) corned beef and cabbage. All entrees are accompanied by hearty steamed vegetables in a light nutmeg-tinged sauce.

For lighter appetites, there is a suitably authentic potato and leek soup (about $4), and sandwiches in the $10 to $12 range. Best bet for dessert is the warm bread pudding with a dollop of vanilla ice cream ($5).

Louie's Italian Restaurant

What: Cafeteria-style Italian restaurant
Where: At the corner of Fifth and Canal, near the lagoon
Price Range: $ - $$

Louie's is a remarkably successful re-creation of the ambiance of New York's Little Italy section — tiled floors, marble-topped tables, and cafe chairs. The only hint you're at Universal Studios is the cafeteria style serving area and the odd ceiling with its jagged edges and movie lights that remind you that the restaurant can do double duty as a film set.

The fare is standard Italian and just the basics. Pizza slices are in the $4 range or $17 to $19 for whole pies. Entrees include lasagna, spaghetti, and fettucini alfredo. They range from $6 to just over $7. Subs and panini are also on offer for about $6 or $7. Caesar salad is $4 or $5 depending on size, and a bowl of minestrone costs a bit under $3. There is imported Italian beer (about $4) as well as Bud, Bud Lite, and wine. In one corner of the restaurant, there is a counter selling coffee, cappuccino, and pastries ($3 to $4).

The quality is above average, as well, making Louie's my favorite USF cafeteria. Louie's is quite large and makes a good place to duck in out of the sun or rain for a rest.

Shopping in New York

Aftermath

This is the cleverly named shop that you can't avoid after *Twister*. There are plenty of *Twister* souvenirs here, from the very inexpensive to t-shirts for $18 to $25. There are more mugs here than in most shops ($5 to $15). If you have a thing for plush cows (please, I don't want to know about it), then you will enjoy the large selection offered here ($13 to $40). There are a few books about tornadoes aimed at inquisitive youngsters.

Safari Outfitters

You will find Safari Outfitters just to the right of the entrance to *Kong-frontation*. Those exiting from that ride are funneled right through this shop, so it can get crowded. There are King Kong dolls with black leather faces and hands ($15 and $30) and a nifty line of King Kong t-shirts for $14 to $26 and, of course, you can also get videos of the original *King Kong* and the re-make. At the back of the shop is the giant Kong head, where you can have your picture taken in the monster's grasp ($11 to $16). If you skipped this earlier, you can come back at your leisure to fill this gap in your photo-graphic record.

New York Candy Co.

Second Hand Rose, the name on the sign over the door of this candy store, made sense when it served as an outlet for discontinued and dis-counted merchandise. That function has apparently been taken over by a Universal outlet store in the nearby Belz Outlet Mall on International Drive. What you will find here now is a by-the-pound candy store much like Stu-dio Sweets on the Front Lot. This shop, however, does have an extensive se-lection of Pez dispensers. Collectors take note.

PRODUCTION CENTRAL

Production Central is modeled on a typical film studio back lot. Essen-tially, it is a collection of soundstages and has a resolutely industrial feel to it. But what it lacks in architectural pizzazz, it more than makes up for in enter-tainment value.

The FUNtastic World of Hanna-Barbera

Rating: ★ ★ ★ ★
Type: Simulator ride
Time: 5 minutes

Kelly says: For younger thrill seekers

Note: This ride is scheduled to close to make way for an attraction based on Jimmy Neutron. It may have already closed by the time you visit. For more information on the new ride, see *Previews of Coming Attractions*, below.

If you've logged any time at all in front of the television screen on Saturday morning, you are familiar with the handiwork of Bill Hanna and Joe Barbera. They were perhaps the most successful animation team outside the Disney empire and the creators of Yogi Bear, the Flintstones, the Jetsons, and Scooby-Doo and the gang. Their pared-down animation style spearheaded the explosion of mass-produced cartoons for TV.

Despite the kiddie-orientation of *The FUNtastic World of Hanna-Barbera*, this ride is not kid's stuff — at least in terms of the wallop it packs. It is second only to *Back To The Future* in its bone-jarring, inner-ear-discombobulating effects. If you were shaken up or made queasy by *Back To The Future*, approach this one with care. On the other hand, if you are uncertain about your susceptibility to motion sickness, you may want to try this one before hazarding the more violent lurches of *Back To The Future*. (There is a row of stationary benches in the front for little ones and those who wish to forego the thrill ride aspect of the show.)

As you are ushered into the antechamber to this ride, Yogi Bear and Boo Boo appear on overhead screens. Before long they are joined by Hanna and Barbera themselves — the real guys, not cartoon versions. As the two animators explain some of the basics of their art, the plot thickens. The evil Dick Dastardly, accompanied by his cohort, Muttly the dog, becomes incensed when he learns that Hanna-Barbera's next feature will not be built around him. Seeking revenge, he kidnaps Elroy, the Jetson's child, and takes off into hyperspace. Now the game is afoot. We will have to take chase in our own spaceship, with Yogi himself at the controls. Ominously, we are informed that Yogi is not the best of pilots.

The interior of the spaceship is actually a movie theater divided into twelve eight-seat sections. Each section is a simulator car, very much like those in *Back To The Future*. When the show begins, the screen in front of us becomes the windshield of Yogi's spaceship and we are off on a light-speed chase after Dastardly. Using his hyperdrive capabilities, he leads us on a merry chase through both time and space. Along the way, we roar through the streets of Bedrock, nearly collide with Shaggy and Scooby-Doo inside a haunted castle, and end up, happily but bumpily, in the future where Elroy is reunited with his grateful parents.

The best seats in the house. As the line approaches the entrance to the antechamber, it divides in two. By choosing the left lane, you will wind up towards the back or middle of the theater. If you position yourself in the middle of the group in the antechamber, you stand a good chance of ending up in the middle of the theater. In my opinion, the best seats are in the middle of the house in the last, or next-to-last row. From there, you get the best, least distorted view of the screen.

After the show, the audience files out through an "interactive area," a large open space with imaginative cartoon-like stage settings evoking Bedrock, Jellystone Park, and the Jetson's space city. The theme is the animation process and those who pay attention can learn something about how their Saturday morning cartoon shows are created.

Photo Op: There are several spots for a souvenir photo here. The best is a kid-sized version of the Flintstone's car, set against a colorful prehistoric cartoon vista. There's also a pint-sized version of a Bedrock living room where you can pose your loved ones lounging on a rock sofa.

Scattered about the room, in no apparent order, are illuminated signs on which Scooby-Doo outlines the process whereby an idea becomes a finished cartoon. Most people ignore these. Too bad. They are fun and informative. A fun game for older kids would be to decipher the order of the process. Try this one during an afternoon downpour and offer a prize.

Most of the kids are immediately drawn to the consoles that give the interactive area its name. In Bedrock, kids can dance along a piano keyboard painted on the floor and make a choir of prehistoric birds squawk out a tune. In Jellystone Park, they can try their hands at adding appropriate sound effects to a Yogi Bear cartoon. And in Space City, they can put outline figures of George Jetson, Rosie the robot, and Astro the dog through their animated paces.

Tip: The interactive area can be entered at any time through the Hanna-Barbera Store. So, if you are on a tight schedule, you might want to skip this feature. You can always come back later in the day after you have visited your must-see attractions.

Alfred Hitchcock: The Art of Making Movies

Rating:	★ ★ ★ ★ +
Type:	Theater show
Time:	40 minutes
Kelly says:	A special treat for Hitchcock buffs

Note: This show is scheduled to close to make way for an attraction based on the Shrek animated films. It may have already closed by the time you visit. For more information on the new attraction, see *Previews of Coming Attractions*, below.

This earnest homage to one of the cinema's true geniuses will be a must-see for Hitch's fans. Younger visitors may find themselves wondering what all the fuss is about. One reason is that, in the limited amount of time available in the theme park format and the need to keep up the pace, much of Hitchcock's artistry is left on the cutting room floor. The shocking images and the plot twists are here, but the clever set-ups (Hitchcock's famous "MacGuffins") and the maddeningly leisurely pace with which he built unbearable suspense are missing. Even so, there's a lot of entertainment value here. Hopefully, those unfamiliar with Hitchcock's work will be spurred to visit the video store back home and check it out.

If you have to wait, you will be entertained by interviews with Hitchcock explaining the basics of his screen philosophy. If you are fortunate enough to be able to walk right in at showtime, you may want to come back later, just to catch the pre-show video.

About 250 people are cycled through the attraction at each show. You pick up a pair of 3-D glasses at the entrance and form up in an anteroom decorated with a three-dimensional collage of artifacts and stills from the master's oeuvre. A simulated celluloid strip winds around the room near the ceiling bearing the titles and dates of all of Hitchcock's 53 films, from *Pleasure Garden* in 1925 to *Family Plot* in 1976. If you have the time, try to count how many of them you've seen and make a list of the ones you've always been meaning to rent one of these days.

The first stop in this multi-phase show is the Tribute Theater where you see a large-screen compilation of clips from Hitchcock's films narrated by Hitch himself, thanks to the clever use of scenes from his 1950s television show and other archival sources. Those familiar with the vast scope of Hitchcock's filmography will have fun trying to identify the stars and films as they whiz by at MTV-like warp speed. Others will get some small sense of the antic humor that was always just below the surface in many Hitchcock films.

The real attraction, of course, has to do with those glasses you've been holding on to. Hitchcock's *Dial M for Murder* (1954) was originally designed to use the then popular 3-D process. However, by the time the film was ready for release, the studio decided that the craze had passed and *Dial M* was released "flat" — that is, in two dimensions.

The strangulation scene and the famous stabbing with the scissors is shown and suddenly it looks as though something has gone terribly wrong in the projection booth. But it's just part of the show, as a flock of crazed birds slashes through the screen and a newly shot sequence shows off the shock and fright possibilities of the 3-D process.

Next, you file to your left into a second theater — the *Psycho* sound stage. To the left, high on a hill, is the ghostly Bates house that has become an American icon. To the right is the Bates Motel office, its "No Vacancy" sign blinking ominously in the rain. Here, you get an all too brief lesson in how genius can transform simple elements into spine-chilling terror. Your on-screen host, Tony Perkins, who played Norman Bates in the horror classic, notes that *Psycho* was based on a true incident, one that also inspired the later *Texas Chain Saw Massacre*. How times change! Hitchcock's famous "shower scene," which is painstakingly analyzed in film schools around the world, is widely recognized as one of the scariest sequences ever put on film, yet he never shows the knife cutting skin and never shows a bloody wound.

The best seats in the house. Your guides are always assuring you that every seat is a great seat. In this case, it's true. Other than trying to avoid the very first row in the Tribute Theater, don't bother jockeying for position. Dual screens on the *Psycho* sound stage make sure everyone sees the action.

For my money, the best part of *Alfred Hitchcock: The Art of Making Movies* happens after the show proper. The final component is a two-story "interactive" area with a variety of devices that are used to illustrate various aspects of Hitchcock's craft. Two involve audience participation.

One demonstration re-creates the final sequence of *Saboteur*. This 1942 film was one of the first Hitchcock made in the United States, and what a calling card it was. Norman Lloyd, who played the villain of the piece and who later went on to direct and produce for Hitchcock's TV show, narrates a video explanation of how Hitchcock created the illusion of the bad guy falling from the torch of the Statue of Liberty. Volunteers from the crowd play the bad guy at two different points in the sequence — when he's hanging on for dear life and when he slips from the hero's grasp and falls to a grisly death. The results are combined with bits of the original on the video monitor. The cleverest part is the way the "falling" villain stays in one place, while the camera pulls away from him on a vertical track.

Photo Op: After the demonstration, have a friend take a picture of you standing on Lady Liberty's torch!

The other live demo involves the sequence on the carousel from *Strangers on a Train*. John Forsythe, another Hitchcock star, narrates the explanation of this one and an audience volunteer is the victim. Upstairs, Jimmy Stewart is your on-screen host for a discussion of two Hitchcock films in which he starred — *Rear Window* and *Vertigo*. Try your hand at peering through the binoculars as you attempt to spot the murderer in one of the windows of the apartment buildings across the way! Take it from me, it ain't easy.

Note: When crowds are thin, there may only be one live demonstration, usually the *Saboteur* sequence.

One of Hitchcock's most beloved trademarks was his penchant for making a brief, silent walk-on appearance in each of his films. It was the filmmaking equivalent of the artist's signature on a canvas. A very entertaining video narrated by Shirley MacLaine, reprises many of these appearances, including the way he managed the seemingly impossible challenge of appearing in *Lifeboat*, a movie that takes place entirely on a small boat cast adrift in the Atlantic.

Tip: The interactive area is relatively small but seldom gets as crowded as it should because many people choose to skip it in their rush to get to the next attraction. Big mistake. This section will reward those who savor it at their leisure. However, if you skip the interactive displays in the interests of saving time, you can walk back into this area later by entering the Bates Motel Store from the Eighth Avenue side. The live demonstrations are geared to the exit of the crowds from the main show (about every 20 minutes), but the rest of the section can be enjoyed at any time you have a few spare moments to kill — perhaps during one of those Florida afternoon showers!

My guess is that a lot of people who have never seen a Hitchcock film go through this attraction and have a wonderful time. However, there's no escaping the fact that the more you know about the master's work, the more fun you will have. On the other hand, if your curiosity is piqued by what you see, you can buy videos of Hitch's greatest hits in the Bates Motel Store.

Nickelodeon Studios Game Lab

Rating: ★ ★ ★
Type: Interactive theater show
Time: 25 minutes
Kelly says: For kids 10 and under

Nickelodeon Studios Florida is a studio within a studio. Nick (as it likes to be called) is a 24-hour cable TV network that bills itself as "the first network for kids." It maintains a presence on the Universal lot, but it is otherwise a separate entity. Even its location, at the end of Nickelodeon Way, sets it apart from the rest of the park.

Get in line and watch from a comfortable distance as the 17-foot-tall Green Slime Geyser in the plaza outside the studio rumbles to life. According to well-informed sources, this green Rube Goldberg-esque oddity is the world's only source of the green goo that features so prominently in Nickelodeon lore. (If you don't know what slime is, ask your kid.) Every ten minutes or so, it erupts with a roar, spewing gallons of bubbling lime-green goop.

Photo Op: The Green Slime Geyser in full roar makes a fabulous backdrop for yet another photo of the kids. The Nickelodeon folks have also thoughtfully provided a number of other photo backdrops in the plaza.

Your wait will be a happy one, what with the constant barrage of clips from Nickelodeon shows. When the queue moves inside it takes you past picture windows allowing you to peer into the makeup department, the gak kitchen (your kids will know what that's all about) and wardrobe. From there the line snakes through a studio piled high with props. Video monitors along the route provide a brief description of what you're seeing. Once inside the Game Lab, adults and kids are separated and herded into separate bleachers for the show Ostensibly, Nickelodeon tries out new stunt ideas for its game shows here. This is audience participation that pits the red bleachers against the blue bleachers to often amusing effect. There's a host (or hostess) and a staff of young and cheery assistants. Volunteers are picked out of the peanut gallery to play silly games that sometimes involve adults dragooned from the safety of their seating sections. One kid is pre-selected to be "slimed" with the green goo that has become something of a corporate logo for Nickelodeon. The hosts of Game Lab will sometimes conduct brief candid interviews with their pint-sized guests and occasionally turn up the kind of gems that Art Linkletter made a career of in another television age. A sample from a recent visit:

Hostess: What's your name?

Kid: Brandon.

Hostess: How old are you?

Kid: Five.

Hostess: What do you do for a living?

Kid: (After a long pause) I build houses with my blocks.

You'd have to score pretty high on the curmudgeon scale not to find that adorable.

Tip: Near Nickelodeon Studios, just past the Slime Geyser, is a little known park exit that takes you directly to the Hard Rock Cafe. You can also use this exit as an entrance.

Seeing Nickelodeon Programs

Nickelodeon, as they never tire of telling you, is a working television studio. Production goes on year round, some of it in Orlando. Does that mean you can see a show while you're in Orlando? The answer is a resounding "maybe," since most production has moved to Los Angeles.

There are two numbers to call for information on Nick shows, (407) 224-6355, which is Universal's Studio Audience Center, and (407) 363-8500, which is Nickelodeon itself. The shorter the time between your call and the date of your projected visit, the more accurate the information you will receive. If *Slime Time Live* is in production, you should be able to get tickets (first-come, first-served) near the Slime Geyser on the day of shooting at about 1:00 p.m. Kids must be six or over. Queue up early and call to check first. Another Nick-related number that sometimes features recorded information is (407) 224-NICK (6425).

It's important to remember that all the shows on Nickelodeon are videotaped for showing at a later date. That means that none of the shows they produce absolutely has to be shot on a specific date at a specific time. The studio will usually have a pretty good idea of what it will be shooting three to four months in advance, but the schedule will not be specific as to times. In addition, production is scheduled to suit the studio's needs, not yours. If a big prop breaks just before they're ready to start taping, they'll simply stop and wait until the prop is fixed. That means you won't be able to find out that a particular show tapes every day at two o'clock and show up then.

Your chances of being in the audience of a show will also be affected by when you visit. Nick likes to schedule the taping of game shows, especially the more popular ones, during peak tourist seasons — summertime and around Christmas — because they know that people come during those times hoping to be in the audience. This means that the huge audience for these shows will have a good shot at seeing them in person if they want to. Another factor that will affect your chances of seeing a particular show are the number of episodes that will be taped. Some shows are seen only on weekends. They will shoot perhaps 25 episodes during the course of the year. Other shows are "stripped." That is they are shown every day, Monday through Friday. These shows may shoot up to 40 episodes during a "season" and there may be more than one season during the course of a year. Unfortunately, it's impossible to predict when these seasons occur. Any given show will probably tape on a different schedule this year than it did last year. Again, the scheduling is determined solely by what proves to be most convenient for the studio.

You won't be able to get tickets in advance, or make reservations, or have your name put on a list. There are two reasons for this. First, the studio wants to protect itself against no-shows. The last thing Nickelodeon wants is a full house that's only two-thirds full — it looks bad on TV — and in a theme park that's mobbed with kids, it's not too hard to fill every seat the day of the show — especially when you're giving the tickets away. The other reason goes back to Nick's steadfast rule against making promises to its young fans that it might not be able to keep. It's perfectly possible that the show scheduled for that certain Wednesday two months down the road may have to be postponed at the last minute. As it is, everyone who walks through the front gate of Universal has an equal chance of getting into the audience of a show being taped that day.

Once you get to Orlando, call Nick again and double-check the production schedule. It may be more specific now. For example, three months ago, they might have been able to tell you that the show you wanted to see would be in production this week. Now they may be able to tell you it will be taping only on Wednesday, Thursday, and Friday. But just because you've called 363-8500, don't think you're the only one with this "inside" information. Nick puts out the word in a variety of ways when shows are in production. There may even be huge billboards along I-4 announcing current tapings! So even though you have the information, you'll still have to step lively to maximize your chances of getting a seat.

When you get to the park itself on the day of your visit, be alert for Nick staffers passing out tickets to arriving guests. If that's not happening, go immediately to Nickelodeon Studios, where people queue up for Game Lab. Just tell the Nickelodeon staffers there that you want to see a show that day and ask them how to go about it. They'll give you the straight poop.

You will increase your chances by getting to the park as early as possible, but don't expect a ticket just because you're first on line. Nick only begins to dispense tickets an hour or two before taping begins. Apparently, they found that when they handed out tickets too early, people wound up waiting around in the hot Orlando sun and getting irritated. Still, arriving early has its strategic advantages. Some shows will tape as many as six episodes a day; if you don't get into the first taping, you'll have a shot at the others. Another strategy that might work is going to the Studio Audience Center as soon as you arrive. It's next to Lost & Found, to your right as you enter the park. I'm told they will sometimes have tickets for that day's Nickelodeon tapings. There are anywhere from 50 to 300 tickets for each show and they go quickly once distribution begins.

A word about dress codes: If you're wearing a Shamu t-shirt and a Goofy hat, you'll still be admitted to the audience of a Nickelodeon show. You can probably expect some good-natured ribbing from the person who does the audience warm-up before all Nickelodeon shows. Just don't expect to see yourself on TV when the show airs. The camerapeople know not to give the competition free advertising in the "pick-up shots" of the audience. On the other hand, outfitting yourself as a walking billboard for Nickelodeon or Universal won't garner you any special privileges.

However, if you'd like to see your kid become a contestant on one of the shows, it will help if you pay at least some attention to junior's appearance. Nickelodeon makes a genuine effort to get a cross-section of America on its shows, but they draw the line at extreme hairstyles and odd or sloppy clothing (although they don't like to tell you as much). A few hours watching the shows themselves will give you a good set of guidelines on what Nick considers appropriate attire and grooming. My suggestion would be to avoid clothing, such as t-shirts, which openly advertises anything.

Once you've made it to the studio for the taping, the Nickelodeon staff is very good about letting you know when the episode you are watching will be aired. That way, you'll be able to tune in back home and, maybe, see yourself on the boob tube.

Selected Short Subjects

Stage 54

This small display area is used for a constantly changing series of walk-through "behind the scenes" exhibits based on recent Universal theatrical films. Typically, the exhibits showcase the artistry of the special effects wizards who create the illusion of reality in action and fantasy films. Among the films that have been showcased here are *Jurassic Park, The Mummy,* and *How The Grinch Stole Christmas.* The exhibits feature sketches, models, photos, and mock-ups along with actual costumes and props used in the films. Often the props spill out into the street in front of Stage 54. Perhaps the most interesting parts of these exhibits are the video interviews with the unsung geniuses behind the films' amazing effects. Watch and you'll get answers to the burning question, "How'd they do that?"

Trick Photography Photo Spot

This is another of those spots in the park where you can take your own souvenir photo using the "hanging miniature" technique pioneered in the early days of filmmaking. Here, you can photograph your family against a fanciful New York skyline that floats above the roofs of the adjacent New York set. This one has a brief, but fascinating, explanation of how various types of special photographic effects in film are created.

Jurassic Park Photo Op

The opening of Islands of Adventure, with a whole island devoted to *Jurassic Park,* did not mean the demise of this vest-pocket attraction carved out of a corner of the Boneyard. No ride, alas, but you can have a friend take your photo in a re-creation of the scene from the film in which T-Rex attacks the tour jeep. Depending on your acting skills, the result will look eerily realistic or merely silly — and either result is fine.

Eating in Production Central

Classic Monsters Cafe

What:	Buffet restaurant
Where:	Across from *Twister*
Price Range:	$$

Those glamorous ghouls of our collective black-and white subconscious take center stage in an eatery filled with souvenirs from zany sci-fi movies like *Abbott and Costello Go To Mars* and chillers like *Frankenstein, The Mummy,* and *Dracula.* The Creature from the Black Lagoon even floats in a big tank in the "Swamp Dining" room.

Amazingly enough, they have resisted the seemingly irresistible temptation to use terms like Monster Meals, and FrankenFries, and Mummy's Pasta on the menu, although they do serve Devil's Food Cake for dessert.

Salads are $4 to $9 depending on how fancy you like them. Pastas are about $7 to $8 and wood-fired pizzas (cheese and pepperoni) are $7 to $8. Roasted chicken dishes are $7 to $9, with roasted potatoes, onions, and fresh corn. Draft beer is available in addition to the usual assortment of soft drinks.

The food is served "buffeteria" style in Frankenstein's laboratory, which makes you wonder if eye of newt is among the condiments. You can take your pick of several dining areas — Space, Crypt, Swamp, and Mansion Dining — each with a different theme and all packed with life-sized statues, props, and photographs.

Universal Studios' early success was fueled by its inventive horror movies, and this gleefully ghastly gastronomic goulash is a fitting celebration of that bygone era.

Shopping in Production Central

Bates Motel Store

Named after the fatal motel from Hitchcock's classic *Psycho*, this small shop offers the kind of souvenirs — Bates Motel towels, soap, even shower curtains — that will make sense only to die-hard *Psycho* fans. If you are one of them, you're sure to find something to send chills down your spine every time you enter your bathroom.

Of more general interest are books about Hitchcock and videos (including some boxed sets) of his films. If the show has whetted your appetite to know more about his work, by all means browse here. If you see the Hitchcock show, you can't miss the Bates Motel Store; it's the exit.

Otherwise, you'll find its discreet entrance on Eighth Avenue right around the corner from the entrance to the main show. The cashier's counter evokes the hotel desk from the *Psycho* movies. Check out the tacky painting to the left of the cashier's desk, near Door #1. Peek behind it for a typical Hitchcockian surprise.

Surf Hut

Under an overstuffed thatch-roof palapa next to the T-Rex Photo Op you will find a colorful selection of tropical shirts, dresses, and straw hats, along with sandals, leis, towels, and other beach accessories.

The Hanna-Barbera Store

The Hanna-Barbera ride empties out into this brightly decorated toy and souvenir shop, where Scooby Doo outshines Yogi and his pals. Wearables include t-shirts and sweats at prices ranging from $12 to $25. Small plush dolls are $9 here, with larger ones available for up to $25. In addition, there is the usual selection of mugs, key rings, and the like.

Nickelodeon Kiosk

If you just can't wait, an open-air shop sells Nickelodeon merchandise as you leave the Nick Studio area. Items include story and activity books, t-shirts, and plush toys. A larger selection (and more pleasant shopping conditions) can be found just a few steps away in the Universal Studios Store on the Front Lot.

Previews of Coming Attractions

The summer of 2003 will see the opening of two, perhaps three new attractions at Universal Studios Florida, both of them based on popular animated characters with recent hit films to their credit.

Jimmy Neutron: Boy Genius, based on the film of the same name, will invite us to a demonstration of Jimmy's latest invention, a sort of super-spy intelligence-gathering gizmo that alerts us to the evil plans of the alien Yokians. In true theme park fashion, we are immediately recruited to help Jimmy save the planet. Delighted to be of service, we climb aboard the Rocket Pod (another of Jimmy's inventions) and speed off to glory. Along the way we encounter Carl and Sheen, Goddard, and Cindy Vortex, characters from the film. To quote another famous movie star, "Fasten your seat belts. It's going to be a bumpy ride."

This ride will replace the *Hanna Barbera* attraction and the official word from Universal is that guests will "ride specially designed motion-based vehicles that move in sync with a dynamic film, projected on a giant screen." Whether this means a retrofitting of the existing *Hanna Barbera* ride or something more along the lines of *Spider-Man* over at Islands of Adventure remains to be seen.

The second attraction, *Shrek 4-D*, is a "prequel" of sorts to the forthcoming sequel to the vastly popular original film. This film short, titled "Shrek and Donkey's Scary-Tale Adventure," takes us along on the honeymoon of Shrek and Princess Fiona. No ordinary film, this one is shot in glorious Ogre-Vision, described as a "sensory immersion process." If I'm read-ing correctly between the lines of the official Universal description of the new attraction, the show will share some of the 3-D film and booby-trapped seat technology of *Terminator*, with the fourth "D" being smell.

Another change may be in the works but information on this one is harder to come by. The scuttlebutt is that *Kongfrontation* will close — indeed it may be closed by the time you visit — and be replaced by an indoor coaster. The building that houses Kong is reportedly the second largest building in the world without interior structural supports (number one is the Vehicle Assembly Building over at Kennedy Space Center), so there's plenty of room. What's a mystery is the theme-ing of the new ride. *The Mummy, The Scorpion King* and *Apollo XIII* have all been mentioned as pos-sible sources of inspiration.

For more information, as it becomes available, visit:

http://www.TheOtherOrlando.com

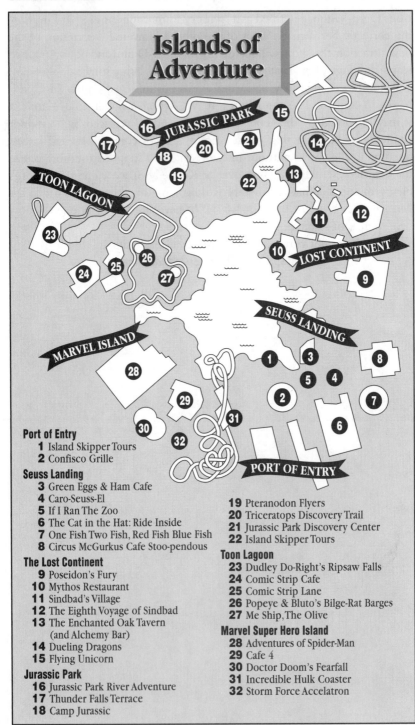

Islands of Adventure

JURASSIC PARK

TOON LAGOON

LOST CONTINENT

SEUSS LANDING

MARVEL ISLAND

PORT OF ENTRY

Port of Entry
1 Island Skipper Tours
2 Confisco Grille

Seuss Landing
3 Green Eggs & Ham Cafe
4 Caro-Seuss-El
5 If I Ran The Zoo
6 The Cat in the Hat: Ride Inside
7 One Fish Two Fish, Red Fish Blue Fish
8 Circus McGurkus Cafe Stoo-pendous

The Lost Continent
9 Poseidon's Fury
10 Mythos Restaurant
11 Sindbad's Village
12 The Eighth Voyage of Sindbad
13 The Enchanted Oak Tavern
   (and Alchemy Bar)
14 Dueling Dragons
15 Flying Unicorn

Jurassic Park
16 Jurassic Park River Adventure
17 Thunder Falls Terrace
18 Camp Jurassic
19 Pteranodon Flyers
20 Triceratops Discovery Trail
21 Jurassic Park Discovery Center
22 Island Skipper Tours

Toon Lagoon
23 Dudley Do-Right's Ripsaw Falls
24 Comic Strip Cafe
25 Comic Strip Lane
26 Popeye & Bluto's Bilge-Rat Barges
27 Me Ship, The Olive

Marvel Super Hero Island
28 Adventures of Spider-Man
29 Cafe 4
30 Doctor Doom's Fearfall
31 Incredible Hulk Coaster
32 Storm Force Accelatron

CHAPTER THREE:

Islands of Adventure

Billed as "Orlando's next generation theme park," Islands of Adventure has certainly raised the competitive bar with its assortment of cutting edge attractions, thrill rides, and illusions.

Islands of Adventure is located right next door to Universal Studios Florida, just a five- or ten-minute stroll away. Despite the proximity, Islands of Adventure is not just more of Universal Studios. It has a separate identity and, with the notable exception of Jurassic Park, its attractions draw their inspiration from very different sources from those in its sister park.

Guests reach Islands of Adventure through the Port of Entry, a separate themed area that serves much the same function as The Front Lot at Universal Studios Florida. Through the Port of Entry lies a spacious lake, dubbed the Great Inland Sea. Artfully arranged around it are five decidedly different "themed areas" — Seuss Landing, The Lost Continent, Jurassic Park, Toon Lagoon, and Marvel Super Hero Island. The "islands" of Islands of Adventure are not true islands of course; but the Great Inland Sea's fingerlike bays set off one area from the next and the bridges you cross to move from one to another do a remarkably good job of creating the island illusion. The flow of visitors is strictly controlled by the circular layout. If you follow the line of least resistance, you will move through the park in a circle, visiting every island in turn.

There are a number of themes, if you will, that differentiate Islands of Adventure from Universal Studios Florida (and from other Central Florida theme parks, too, for that matter):

Roller coasters. Islands of Adventure introduces to Orlando some heavy hitters in the increasingly cut-throat competition for bragging rights in the world of high-end steel coasters. *Dueling Dragons* in The Lost Continent features twin coaster tracks that intertwine and come within inches of collision, while the *Incredible Hulk Coaster* on Marvel Super Hero Island zaps you to the top of the first drop with what they say is the same thrust as an F-16 jet.

Pushing the envelope. Universal's designers take obvious pride in "next generation" rides and attractions that will be like nothing you have experienced before. As just one example, the *Spider-Man* ride takes the motion simulator from Universal Studios Florida's *Back To The Future. . .The Ride*, drops it into a simulated 3-D world right out of *T-2*, puts it on a moving track, and spins it through 360 degrees along the way.

More for the kids. While Islands of Adventure provides plenty of the kind of intense, adult-oriented thrill rides for which Universal Studios became famous, it makes a special effort to reach out to kids. Seuss Landing is almost exclusively for the entertainment and enjoyment of younger children. Toon Lagoon will appeal to slightly older kids, and Marvel Super Hero Island is the perfect place for adolescents to scare themselves to death.

Less "edutainment." Whereas Universal Studios Florida finds ways to teach you about making movies, Islands of Adventure seems remarkably free of ulterior motives. This place is all about good, clean, mindless fun!

More theme-ing. Although it hardly seems possible, Islands of Adventure is even more heavily "themed" than its sister park and many other parks. What that means is that the park designers have made a concerted effort to stretch the theme of each island into every restaurant, every shop, indeed into as many nooks and crannies as possible.

Better food. A major investment has been made in upgrading the image of theme park food in the newer park. See "Dining in Islands of Adventure," below.

Music. Islands of Adventure is the first theme park to feature originally composed soundtracks — one for each island — just like a movie. Of course, music is nothing new in theme parks but what is both new and exceptional at Islands of Adventure is the way the music is integrated into the park experience. It swells as you enter each island, changes gradually as you move from one part of the island to another, and as you cross from one island to another, blends seamlessly into the next island's theme. The effect is pervasive yet unobtrusive, so much so that many people may not even be aware of what a special achievement it is.

Dining in Islands of Adventure

Islands of Adventure's best-kept secret is the food. Those who truly care about the taste and quality of what they put in their stomachs and who despair of eating well in a theme park will find much to celebrate here.

Mythos, the full-service restaurant in The Lost Continent, is a gourmet dining experience that would be a credit to any cosmopolitan city. Its presence in a theme park is cause for wonderment. I suspect that annual passholders will come to the park just to have dinner. The food at Islands of Adventure's other full-service restaurant, Confisco Grille, while not up to the level of Mythos, is also very good.

The fast food in the park is a cut above the norm, too. The menu at Thunder Falls Terrace in Jurassic Park is inventive in its details and exceptional in its execution, even if the service is cafeteria style. The Green Eggs and Hamwich served in Seuss Landing is not only amusing but tasty as well. Even the lesser establishments, where the cuisine is more hot than haute, have their interesting flourishes. The Cafe 4 in Marvel Super Hero Island, for example, serves a chicken and Boursin pizza.

Best of all, given the obvious quality of the food, the prices are no more than you would expect to pay for far less adventuresome cooking at other theme parks. All of the restaurants mentioned here are reviewed in depth later in this chapter.

Shopping in Islands of Adventure

Much of what can be said about the shopping in Universal Studios Florida can be repeated for the shopping experiences offered in Islands of Adventure. However, a number of things are worth noting.

The Middle Eastern bazaar section of The Lost Continent offers a number of shops run by some very talented artisans. Look here for the kind of gifts that won't scream "bought in a theme park!" Look, too, in Port of Entry for unusual folk sculptures and decorative items.

As a writer, I take a certain pleasure in seeing so many books for sale in Seuss Landing, even if they are children's books. And speaking of the child in us all, the treasure trove of comic books to be found in Marvel Super Hero Island is nothing to look down your nose at.

If you love your stay at Islands of Adventure, consider buying the soundtrack. A CD with the music from all the islands is available at many of the shops. When you return home, it will offer you a subliminal reminder of all the fun you had at the park.

Again, let me counsel you on the wisdom of saving your shopping for the end of the day. The Islands of Adventure Trading Company in Port of Entry has a good selection of souvenirs representing all of the park's islands. There's even a Universal Store in CityWalk, which means you can shop for souvenirs days after your tickets to the parks have expired. You can also shop by phone by calling (407) 224-5800.

Universal Orlando

Good Things to Know About . . .

Here are some notes that apply specifically to Islands of Adventure. General notes that apply to both parks will be found in *Chapter One: Planning Your Escape.*

Dining Passes

It is actually possible to eat at Mythos, IOA's gourmet restaurant, without paying admission to the park. Here's how it works: Make a reservation at Mythos (see "Reservations," below) and then stop at the "Will Call" window, to the right of the ticket booths at the front entrance to the park. Tell them you have a reservation at Mythos and want an "Adventure Dining Pass." They will provisionally charge your credit card for one-day passes for everyone in your party. You then have two hours from the time of your reservation to eat and return to Guest Services. In addition, they require that you return within 30 minutes of the time you pay your check at Mythos (the time will be stamped on your credit card receipt). When you return and show your receipt, they will tear up the credit card slip; overstay your welcome and you will be charged for a one-day pass. If you find yourself running late at Mythos, alert your server to the situation and the restaurant will run interference for you with Guest Services.

If you have a pass to the park, you can use this system to invite guests to lunch. If you've been freeloading with family or friends during your Orlando vacation, this is a great way to say "thank you." It's also a good way to dazzle business associates. Although the Dining Pass program was designed with Mythos in mind, you can probably use it to visit Confisco Grille as well, if you ask.

First Aid

There is a first aid station in Port of Entry, just past the turnstiles, in the Open Arms Hotel building. A second first aid station will be found tucked away in the bazaar area near the Sinbad theater in The Lost Continent (number 12 on the map above).

Getting Away From It All

Each of the islands has a park-like, attraction-free section tucked away near the shores of the Great Inland Sea. I suspect these were designed as venues for private parties and corporate events. They are little visited by most guests and offer a terrific opportunity to escape the madding crowd. They also boast excellent views across the Sea to other islands. On days when the park is open past sunset, they are surprisingly private and quite romantic places to snuggle up with that special someone.

Getting Wet

Islands of Adventure has some great water-themed rides. They offer plenty of thrills but they pose some problems for the unprepared. Kids probably won't care, but adults can get positively cranky when wandering around sopping wet.

The three water rides, in increasing order of wetness, are *Jurassic Park River Adventure, Dudley Do-Right's Ripsaw Falls*, and the absolutely soaking *Popeye & Bluto's Bilge-Rat Barges*. Fortunately, these three are within a short distance of each other, allowing you to implement the following strategy:

First, dress appropriately. Wear a bathing suit and t-shirt under a dressier outer layer. Wear shoes you don't mind getting wet; sports sandals are ideal. Bring a tote bag in which you can put things, like cameras, that shouldn't get wet. You can also pack a towel, and it might be a good idea to bring the plastic laundry bag from your hotel room.

Plan to do the rides in sequence. When you're ready to start, peel off the outer layer, put it in the tote bag along with your other belongings, and stash everything in a convenient locker. You can use the all-day lockers in Port of Entry, but a more convenient choice is the bank of small lockers at the entrance to the *Jurassic Park River Adventure*. These lockers cost $1 an hour. The all-day lockers are more spacious but will cost you $5. You decide.

Once you've completed the circuit of rides, you will be very, very wet, especially if you have gone on some of the rides more than once. You now have a choice: If it's a hot summer day, you may want to let your clothes dry as you see the rest of the park. Don't worry about feeling foolish; you'll see plenty of other folks in the same boat, and your damp clothes will feel just great in the Florida heat. In cooler weather, it's a good idea to return to the locker, grab your stuff, head to a nearby restroom, and change into dry clothes. Use the plastic laundry bag for the wet stuff.

The alternative is to buy an Islands of Adventure rain poncho (they make nice souvenirs and are usually available at most shops) and hope for the best. This is far less fun and you'll probably get pretty wet anyway.

Height Restrictions and Other Warnings

Due to a variety of considerations, usually revolving around sudden movements and the configuration of lap restraints, a few rides will be off-limits to shorter (typically younger) guests. Here is a list of rides that have minimum height requirements, which are given in inches ("):

Pteranodon Flyers	36" min, 56" max
Spider-Man	40"
Jurassic Park River Adventure	42"
Popeye & Bluto's Bilge-Rat Barges	42"

Dudley Do-Right's Ripsaw Falls	44"
Doctor Doom's Fearfall	52"
Incredible Hulk and *Dueling Dragons*	54"

The rides in Seuss Landing require that children under 48 inches tall be accompanied by an adult.

Another problem may be encountered by taller and heavier guests. The roller coasters and *Doctor Doom's Fear Fall* employ state of the art harness-like contraptions to make sure that you don't go flying off into space. Unfortunately, not everyone fits into them.

Anyone with a chest measurement over 50 inches may have difficulty fitting into the harness and at 54 inches you can pretty much forget about it. Height is less of a problem (I am told basketball players have ridden) but some extremely tall individuals may also be out of luck. The rides in question provide a sample seat outside so you can check to see if you'll fit. These, by the way, also offer great **photo ops**.

Reservations

Mythos and Confisco Grille both accept reservations, with Confisco serving as a sort of reservation center for both restaurants. If you're really planning ahead, the central reservations number is (407) 224-9255. They will take reservations up to 30 days in advance.

Single-Rider Lines

To help shrink long lines, some rides open single-rider lines when things get busy. You will find single-rider lines at *Incredible Hulk, Doctor Doom's Fearfall, Spider-Man, Dudley Do-Right's, Bilge Rat Barges,* and the *Jurassic Park River Adventure.* There is a double-riders line at *Ripsaw Falls,* because riders must sit between each other's legs. Operation of single-rider lines is solely at the discretion of the lead ride attendant, so don't count on this time-saving ploy.

Special Diets

The map in the Adventure Guide has a special symbol for restaurants serving vegetarian meals. Confisco's and Mythos can provide kosher meals with 48 hours advance notice. Call Food Services at 407-363-8340 to make arrangements. These restaurants may also be able to accommodate other special dietary needs. Call the reservations number above a few days ahead to discuss your needs.

Special Events

The year is sprinkled with special events tied to the holiday calendar. For

Halloween, that means two admissions to the park, one for a regular daytime visit and another for the evening's special event. Daytime visitors can get a discounted admission for the evening's festivities, but this will still boost the cost of a full day by up to $25. The other events are included in the regular admission price.

Fourth of July. Islands of Adventure celebrates America's birthday with a burst of patriotic fervor. Often, fireworks displays continue nightly through the entire month of July and sometimes into August.

Halloween. From fairly modest beginnings, Universal Orlando's night-time Halloween celebration has grown into the most elaborate and hyped special event of the year. This is not to everyone's taste but the spooky-funny atmosphere in the park is infectious, with goblins and ghouls leaping out at visitors. Special walk-through attractions are created just for this event, featuring haunted mazes — dark narrow passages with "scary" surprises around every corner — and tableaux vivants based on horror movie themes. This has become an extremely popular event and each year Universal tries to top last year's show. The show now occupies much of the month of October with the price of admission rising like the undead as Halloween approaches. The separate evening admission for this one can be quite pricey.

Grinchmas. December sees Seuss Landing transformed into a winter wonderland, complete with a mini ice slide and an up close and personal encounter with the Grinch himself, who proves to be a delightful (if parentally incorrect) host.

Treasure Hunt: Your Day at Islands of Adventure

You should be able to see all of Islands of Adventure in a day, if only because the definition of "all" will be different for everyone and most people will exclude at least some of the attractions from their list of must-sees. For example, many people will have no interest in subjecting themselves to the intense thrills of the roller coasters or *Doctor Doom's Fear Fall.* Teenagers and young singles will have little or no interest in Seuss Landing, and those without children can probably skip the interactive play areas (although they're pretty nifty and worth a peek).

Those who are perverse or persistent enough to want to see literally everything Islands of Adventure has to offer can probably come pretty close in a single day, especially if they are willing to arrive early, step lively, and use the Universal Express kiosks.

Doing Your Homework

This assignment is not mandatory, but I would urge those who have not seen the original *Jurassic Park* to rent the video before visiting Islands of Adventure. This easy-to-handle research project will add to your enjoyment of what the designers have achieved in IOA's Jurassic Park.

If you have not yet introduced your small children to the magical world of Dr. Seuss, this is an excellent excuse to do so. A knowledge of "Cat in the Hat," "If I Ran the Zoo," and other Seuss books will make their visit to Seuss Landing a whole lot richer, and reading from the books is a great way to pass the time on those long car trips to Florida.

What To Expect

Islands of Adventure has many of the same kinds of attractions as Universal Studios Florida, with some notable exceptions. I refer you to the "What To Expect" section in the previous chapter for a refresher. Here I will make some additional brief comments.

Rides. The rides here vary widely in terms of "throughput" — the number of people they can accommodate per hour. *Pteranodon Flyers*, for example, has a minimal throughput, while *Cat in the Hat* processes a surprising number of riders each hour.

Roller Coasters. Coasters spawn long lines, although the ones at Islands of Adventure are so intense that sometimes the wait to ride is surprisingly brief. Both coasters have separate lines for the daring few who want to ride in the front row; for these folks the wait is often lengthy.

Amphitheater Shows. These operate on a fixed schedule listed in the park guide. Generally seating is not a problem.

Theater Shows. Only *Poseidon's Fury* falls into this category.

Displays and Interactive Areas. There are three separate interactive play areas for children; all of them can captivate your kids for hours on end. Keep that in mind when planning your touring schedule. The displays in the *Discovery Center* in Jurassic Park, while also enthralling for many children, are less likely to eat up considerable chunks of time.

All the Rest. Islands of Adventure has many more places to get away from the crowds than does its sister park. In fact, if you have a multi-day pass, you might want to bring a good book one day and just chill out along the shore of the Great Inland Sea.

Not-So-Buried Treasure

If you have limited time to spend in Islands of Adventure, or if you simply choose not to run yourself ragged attempting to see it all, here are my selections for the best the park has to offer:

Spider-Man. Quite simply the best ride in the park and the current state-of-the-art in thrill ride technology. Don't miss it.

The Roller Coasters. Those who can tolerate the cutting edge coaster experience (and you know who you are) will want to ride both *The Hulk* and *Dueling Dragons* — several times. Absolutely awesome.

Triceratops Discovery Trail. Not everyone agrees with me, but I think this is the very best animatronic attraction anywhere — when it's working.

Cat in the Hat. This kiddie ride manages to be both traditional and cutting edge.

Seuss Landing. Even if you don't go on any of the rides, you should at least take a slow stroll through this over-the-top wonderland to marvel at the design.

Popeye & Bluto's Bilge Rat Barges. A soaked-to-the-skin (but very clean) raft ride.

Mythos. This is a restaurant not a ride, but that doesn't mean the experience is any the less thrilling. The best food you've ever had in a theme park served in a very special setting.

Runners-Up

Here are a few more suggestions that aren't at the very top of my list but are well worth considering:

Jurassic Park River Adventure. River boats, raptors, and a hair raising splashdown.

Poseidon's Fury. Again, not everyone agrees with me but this special effects extravaganza is lots of fun.

The Eighth Voyage of Sinbad. Stunts that are dynamite (almost literally) with a great warm-up act.

The One-Day Stay

Let me emphasize that I do not recommend trying to cram this wonderful park into a single day; the multi-day passes and the Orlando Flex-Ticket offer excellent value and the luxury of a more leisurely pace. Realistically, however, one day is all many visitors have. In this case, if you are staying at one of the resort hotels, the preferred access your room key affords will save you enough time that you won't have to plan your visit to the park like a military campaign. The Universal Express kiosks can also save you lots of time. Nonetheless, I offer the following advice:

1. As soon as the gates open, proceed to the *Spider-Man* ride. Go straight to the end of Port of Entry and turn left. Hard-core thrill seekers should then ride *Hulk* and *Doctor Doom*, preferably in that order. If lines are short, you may want to take the opportunity to ride *Hulk* twice.

2. Now head through Toon Lagoon and Jurassic Park to Lost Continent to ride *Dueling Dragons*. If the lines to *Dudley Do-Right's Ripsaw Falls* and the *Jurassic Park River Adventure* seem short — and you don't care about getting

wet — you may want to catch them along the way.

3. At this point, it may be close to noon and time to take stock. *Poseidon's Fury* is a good choice for midday since the queue is indoors and mercifully air-conditioned. Also, check the schedule for the *Sinbad* show; you shouldn't miss this one.

4. I like to ride *Popeye & Bluto's Bilge-Rat Barges* (along with *Ripsaw Falls* and *River Adventure*) late in the day, when getting wet starts looking like a great idea (see "Getting Wet," above).

Again, those who are temperamentally averse to the giant coasters and intense thrills like *Doctor Doom*, will find it much easier to take in all of Islands of Adventure in a day. But as I've said, coaster lovers may be pleasantly surprised at how short the lines are, especially at slower times of the year, because these giants scare off a lot of people. Again, the exception is the line for the first row, which is often lengthy.

The One-Day Stay With Kids

Many kids, especially those who are tall enough to avoid the height restrictions listed earlier, will be perfectly happy going on all the rides, in which case the strategy outlined above will work just fine. However, if you have children who are too short or too timid to tackle the thrill rides, you can adopt a much different strategy.

If you fall into this category, you should make *Pteranodon Flyers* your first priority — assuming, of course, you feel your child will enjoy it. This ride takes only two people at a time per vehicle and the line gets very long very quickly.

Otherwise (and if your child is over 40 inches tall), do *Spider-Man* first. Most kids will have no problem with this one, although some of their adult guardians may. After that, you can relax and take your time.

Next, I would recommend *Triceratops Discovery Trail* for all ages followed by a trip to Seuss Landing for those who won't find it too "babyish." However, even kids who consider themselves too "sophisticated" for most of Seuss will get a kick out of *The Cat in the Hat* ride.

After that, you can pretty much pick and choose, using the height restrictions listed earlier and your child's preferences to guide you. Despite the cartoon violence, *Sinbad* is a fun show for kids; don't miss it.

When you need a break, steer your kids to an age-appropriate play area: *If I Ran the Zoo* and *Me Ship, the Olive* for younger children, *Camp Jurassic* for older ones.

Note: Whichever pan you follow, be sure to pick up an Adventure Guide and the Attraction & Show Times insert as you enter the park.

PORT OF ENTRY

The towering lighthouse with the blazing fire at the top, modeled after the ancient lighthouse of Pharos in Alexandria, Egypt, marks the gates to Islands of Adventure and the beginning of your adventure. This striking structure is only the most obvious of the metaphors used in an eclectic blend of architecture and decor that evokes the spirit of wanderlust and exploration. At the base of the lighthouse a series of sails, like those on ancient Chinese junks, shade the ticket booths for the park. Here, "customs agents" will stamp your "passport" and send you on your way.

Through these gates lies Port of Entry, a sort of storytelling experience that combines evocative architectural motifs and haunting music to build your anticipation as you enter more fully into the spirit of discovery. Universal's scenic designers have outdone themselves on this one. To centuries old Venice, they've added images of Istanbul, a soupçon of Samarkand, a touch of Timbuktu, and a dash of Denpassar to create one of the most ravishingly beautiful examples of fantasy architecture I have ever seen. Hurry through in the morning if you must, but if you are among the last to leave the park, I urge you to linger in Port of Entry and drink in the atmosphere.

As you marvel at the architectural details and the exquisite care with which the designers have "dressed" this sensuous streetscape, pay attention to the sounds that swirl around you. In addition to the chatter of your fellow adventurers, you will experience one of IOA's "next level" touches. Like all the other islands in the park, Port of Entry has its own specially composed soundtrack that unfolds as you walk along, drawing ever closer to the Great Inland Sea. But there are other inspired aural touches as well, like the muffled conversations from dimly lit upper-story windows hinting at intrigue and adventures unknown. It's a very special place.

Port of Entry serves some more mundane purposes as well. Before you pass through the gates you will find, on your left, a pale green building that houses Group Sales. If you are the leader of a group of 20 or more, this is the place to come. To the right of the ticket booths, you will find a Guest Services walk-up window marked "Will Call." Stop here if you have arranged to have tickets waiting for you. Nearby is the only **ATM** in Port of Entry, so if you are in need of ready cash, make sure to stop here before you enter the park. Once inside, you won't find another ATM until you reach the Enchanted Oak Tavern, all the way back in The Lost Continent.

Once past the ticket booths and the entrance turnstiles, you will find a spacious semicircular plaza. Directly ahead of you is a large stone archway. Behind the fantastic facades of the buildings to either side are a variety of Guest Services functions. To the left of the archway, you will find (starting from the far left)...

Universal Vacation Services. Located in the Daughters of Adventure building (established 1402, motto: "Women hold up half the sky"), this is the place to come to get your Annual Pass.

Restrooms. Because there are some things you don't need to carry on your adventures.

Lockers. There are four bays of electronically controlled lockers here. The rental fee is $5 for the day, with in and out access, and the machines accept both bills and credit cards.

Stroller & Wheelchair Rentals. "Reliable Rentals" has a large sign outside informing you that all the jinrickshaws, gliders, submersibles, and tuk tuks are either out of service, decommissioned, hired, or, in the case of the time machine, "stuck in the 6th century." Fortunately they still have strollers ($8 for singles, $14 for doubles), wheelchairs ($7), and electric convenience vehicles ($35) for rent. All prices include tax. A $50 refundable deposit and 24-hour advance reservation are required for electric vehicle rentals.

To the right of the archway, in the Open Arms Hotel building, you will find...

Guest Services. Questions or complaints? The cheerful folks here can help you out.

Lost & Found. Don't give up on that lost item. There's a very good chance a fellow tourist or a park staffer will find it and turn it in. Check back the next day, too, just in case.

First Aid. This is one of two first aid stations in the park. The other is in The Lost Continent, near the Sinbad Theater.

Now that you have replenished your wallet, stowed your excess gear, and rented your strollers, you step through that crumbling stone archway incised with the thrilling words "The Adventure Begins" and start your journey toward the Great Inland Sea and the magical islands that ring it.

Port of Entry's main (and only) street is given over to a variety of shopping and eating establishments. As you stroll along, don't be surprised if someone tries to talk you into a photographic souvenir of your visit; this is, after all, an exotic marketplace bustling with hawkers. There's no charge to have your photo snapped; at the end of the day, you can stop into De Foto's (see below), survey the results, and make your decision.

At the far end of this market street, under another crumbling archway that's being propped up by a jury-rigged contraption of giant planks and chains, the street opens out into another broad plaza on the shore of the Great Inland Sea. Amid the souvenir kiosks that dot the plaza, look for a large signboard that can help you plan your itinerary. Here a staffer stays in constant touch with the attractions throughout the park and updates the signboard with the current waiting times for the all the rides. If no wait time is posted, that means that the ride is temporarily out of commission.

Roughly opposite the Backwater Bar (see *Dining in Port of Entry*, below), on the shore of the Great Inland Sea, you might notice a dock once used by **Island Skipper Tours**, a now defunct ride that ferried passengers to a secluded dock in Jurassic Park on the other side of the park. This ride shut down some years ago but it has been periodically resurrected during especially busy times.

Tip: Nestled between *Island Skipper Tours* and the *Incredible Hulk Coaster* is a secluded park-like snarl of rock-shielded walkways along the edge of the Inland Sea. At the end, on a point of land jutting into the water, you will find some wooden benches and a little-visited hideaway that is wonderfully romantic at night.

Eating in Port of Entry

Whether you're on the way in, on the way out, or just breaking for lunch, there's both good food and fast food to be had in Port of Entry. At Confisco Grille you can make reservations for both Confisco and Mythos in The Lost Continent.

Croissant Moon Bakery

What: Sandwiches, pastries, and coffee
Where: On your right as you enter, under the second archway
Price Range: $ - $$

Every theme park needs a place, strategically located near the entrance, to serve those who thought they'd save some time by skipping breakfast only to arrive at the park starving to death. Croissant Moon Bakery opens when the park does and its popularity tends to overwhelm its minuscule indoor seating area and the small number of outdoor tables. There are two separate lines here, starting from opposite ends of the deli-like counter and both serve exactly the same fare.

For breakfast, there are muffins and such along with the house's own branded coffee. Better yet, treat yourself to one of the pastries, pies or cakes that are served here ($2 to $4). Many of them are exceptional.

Later in the day, try the Port of Call meat and cheese sandwich platters. Peppered roast beef and smoked Gouda, smoked turkey and brie, and honey-glazed ham and Swiss are $6 to $7.

Confisco Grille

What: Full-service restaurant with flair
Where: On the waterfront plaza

Price Range: $$ – $$$

The simple wooden chairs are painted green and blue and there are no tablecloths. But don't let the casual atmosphere fool you. Confisco Grille is a full-service sit-down restaurant that serves up a limited but imaginative menu that draws on far-flung culinary influences.

Part of the fun here is the decor, vaguely Mediterranean with Turkish accents, that asks you to imagine you are in the Port of Entry Customs House. The place is lit by hanging lamps in a variety of styles and decorated with bizarre items, like a stegosaurus skull, confiscated from would-be smugglers.

But the real fun is the food. The Plate Trader appetizers ($5 to $8) are described on the menu as "a perfect way to start your adventure." Take the hint and treat the table to nachos or Confisco Fries, which are served with a variety of dipping sauces. Also worth noting in this section of the menu is the Explorer's Vegetable Pizza, which crowns the Italian favorite with a medley of healthy toppings.

Burgers are done well here, too, with the mushroom and Swiss cheese version a standout. Other sandwich choices include a grilled chicken sandwich, a Tex-Mex wrap, and a club sandwich. Entrees are a mixed bag, with the House Specialty Pad Thai noodles a bit on the bland side, but the Shrimp Pasta, with roasted garlic and charred onions, is worth trying. Entree-sized salads (about $10) get high marks, too. Wines are served by the glass ($5 to $7) and the bottle (up to about $32).

Don't forget to leave room for one of the desserts, because they are terrific. The thoughtful servers escort every diner past a display of these goodies at a counter where you might be able to watch the dessert chef putting the finishing touches on one of the house specialties. Recent offerings included strawberry flan, tiramisu, and a yummy chocolate banana bread pudding, served with vanilla ice cream.

Perfect for lunch, Confisco's might make a good choice for a light dinner on days when the park is open late. (Check Confisco's closing time on your way in. It's been known to close earlier than the park itself.)

The adjacent **Backwater Bar** is too upscale to be a perfect replica of the kind of tropical dive where lonely adventurers come to drink away their memories of that low-down cheap saloon singer they loved and lost in Rangoon, but it will do in a pinch. It also makes a convenient staging area for those waiting for a table in Confisco, not to mention those who see no reason to interrupt their drinking with food. While the bar itself is small, there's a large outdoor seating area which makes for a great place to survey the passing scene while getting a buzz on.

Cinnabon

What:	Gooey pastries
Where:	Across from Confisco, on the waterfront
Price Range:	$

Another outpost of the well-known national chain (the other is in City-Walk), this walk-up stand sells classic Cinnabon pastries for about $3, with Caramel Pecanbons going for about $4. Boxes of Minibons go for a variety of prices, up to $13. Drinks range from $1 (milk) to over $3 (mochalatte chill).

Arctic Express

What:	Ice cream, funnel cakes, and waffle cone sundaes
Where:	Right next to Cinnabon
Price Range:	$

The Arctic theme seems a bit out of place here, but the "Fabulous Funnel Cakes" and "Waffle Cone Adventures" it serves will take your mind off any seeming contradictions. A variety of toppings and accompaniments are offered, including strawberries, and each category has its own version of "the works" for about $5. You can also get soft serve ice cream in sugar or waffle cones. Service is from walk-up windows and all seating is outdoors.

Shopping in Port of Entry

As you would expect of any great city along the ancient Silk Road, the main street of Port of Entry is lined with shops and bazaars filled with traders offering trinkets and treasures from near and far. Most of these emporia have one or more entrances opening onto the street but be aware that they form one continuous space inside, so they offer a cool and convenient refuge from the broiling sun or driving rain to those entering or leaving the park.

Islands of Adventure Trading Company

This is the largest of the shops in Port of Entry and it occupies most of the left-hand side of the street as you walk towards the Great Inland Sea. As the name suggests, you will find here a broad selection of souvenirs representing all the islands in the park. It's the usual array of logo-ed t-shirts and trinkets, everything from key chains, to mugs, to slick $300 black leather jackets with the IOA logo emblazoned on the back.

This is the perfect place to pick up that CD of the Islands of Adventure soundtrack. If you need a souvenir of your visit and you can't find it here, you probably aren't looking hard enough.

Ocean Trader Market

Beyond the Islands of Adventure Trading Company, stands this bazaar.

Reminiscent of a Middle Eastern souk, its sides are open to the street and shaded with tent-like canopies. Inside is a selection of offbeat handicrafts from around the globe. There is some attractive wooden folk sculpture as well, much of it very nice and some of it taller than you are. The larger pieces run up to $500 or so, but there are plenty of fetching pieces for well under $50.

In addition to the sculpture, look for the kind of unusual decorative objects that make a nice addition to your living room or a gift for a friend back home. Also on offer here are various items of lightweight, brightly colored summer clothing for the ladies and a few shirts for the guys.

De Foto's Expedition Photography

This is the place to stop for film supplies or a variety of disposable cameras. You can even replace the camera you brought with you if the spirit moves you and pick up some nice photo albums and frames while you're at it. De Foto's also offers sunscreen and suntan lotion, just in case you forgot to bring some along.

Island Market and Export

This shop is a lot of fun. It offers the kind of gifts that are not only tasteful but tasty. Much of the merchandise is food of one sort or another, from chocolates, to nuts, to cookies and sweets sold by the pound.

Port of Entry Christmas Shoppe

It's Christmas in July, or any other month for that matter, at this small shop selling tasteful ornaments for the tree and the yuletide hearth.

Port Provisions

This tiny open-air shop straddles the exit and provides a last chance to pick up something small. It also offers a limited selection of sale merchandise that's worth checking out by those in search of a bargain.

SEUSS LANDING

Probably best described as a 12-acre, walk-through sculpture, Seuss Landing adds a third dimension and giddy Technicolor to the wonderfully wacky world of Theodor Geisel, a.k.a. Dr. Seuss, whose dozens of illustrated books of inspired poetry have enchanted millions of children.

Universal designers have gone to great lengths to evoke the out-of-kilter world of the Seuss books, avoiding straight lines and square corners wherever possible. Buildings curve and swoop and sometimes seem to be on the verge of toppling over. Much of the architectural detail looks as though it was sculpted out of some especially thick cake icing and is now gently melting in the Florida sun. Even the foliage is goofy. Many of the wacky, twisted palm trees that dot the landscape were created by the fierce winds of Hurricane Andrew and loving transplanted here by Universal's grounds staff. The rest had to be painstakingly trained to create that Seussian look.

In its own cheerful, candy-colored way, the fantasy architecture here is just as successful and just as impressive as that in Port of Entry. Even if you have no interest in sampling the kiddie rides on offer here, you will have a great deal of fun just passing through.

The Cat In The Hat: Ride Inside

Rating:	★ ★ ★ ★
Type:	"Dark ride"
Time:	3.5 minutes
Kelly says:	Kiddie ride with zip

Dr. Seuss's most popular book tells the tale of what happens when two kids, home alone, allow the cat of the title to come in for a visit. Step through the doors beneath that giant red and white striped top hat, you will get your chance to relive the adventure.

This is a "dark" ride but perhaps one of the brightest and most colorful you'll ever encounter. You and your kids climb into cars that are designed like miniature six-passenger sofas and set off through a series of 18 show scenes that re-create the story line of the book. Just don't expect the static tableaux of the older generation dark rides. One of the nicer touches on this one is something that Universal describes as "a revolving, wallpaper-peeling, perception-altering 24-foot tunnel." The ride mechanism, too, is a step or two beyond the older generation of dark rides. Brace yourself for quick swoops, sudden turns, and a few 360-degree spins.

Tip: If you feel the spinning will be too much for your tot (or for you!) you can ask a ride attendant to have the spin mechanism in your car turned off.

Along the way, the ride does a remarkably good job of telling the story of the book. The fantastic animated sculptures of the cat and his playmates, Thing 1 and Thing 2, spin and twirl while furniture teeters and topples. The wise fish, who is the tale's voice of reason, cries out warnings and ignored advice until, miraculously, all is set to rights before Mom gets home. Kids familiar with the book will be delighted and those who aren't will doubtless want to learn more. This is a must-do for little ones, although a few more timid tykes may find the swoops and spins of the ride vehicles a bit startling.

While you probably won't care, this ride employs never-before-available computer systems to control the flow of 1,800 guests per hour and activate the innumerable special effects along the way.

One Fish, Two Fish, Red Fish, Blue Fish

Rating: ★ ★ ★
Type: Flying, steerable fish
Time: 2 minutes
Kelly says: Good, wet fun

Here's an interesting twist on an old carnival ride. You know, the one where you sit in a little airplane (or flying Dumbo) and spin round in a circle while your plane goes up and down. On this ride, based on the Seuss book of the same name, you pilot a little fishy. While you can't escape the circular route of the ride, you can steer your fish up or down.

Supposedly, if you follow the directions encoded in the little song that plays during the ride ("red fish, red fish up, up, up; blue fish, blue fish down, down, down"), you can avoid being doused by the water coming from a series of "squirt posts" that ring the perimeter. There are three verses to the song and, as far as I could tell, it actually is possible to stay dry for the first two by following directions. The third verse, however, tells you that all bets are off and that your guess is as good as the next fellow's. It is the rare rider who gets through the ride without getting spritzed. Not that most people care. In fact, it looks like some kids do just the opposite of what the song counsels in the hope of getting Mom and Dad soaked.

Note: On cold days, and sometimes in the cooler morning hours, the ride does not spray water on the riders, which will probably come as a relief to parents and a disappointment to little ones.

This ride is very nicely designed, with perfectly adorable little fish cars and an array of Seussian characters serving as the squirt posts. Presiding over the center of the circle is an 18-foot-tall sculpture of the Star Belly Fish from the book.

Caro-Seuss-El

Rating: ★ ★ ★ ★
Type: Old-fashioned carousel with Seuss figures
Time: About 1.5 minutes
Kelly says: For carousel lovers and little kids

This ride marks yet another design triumph. The old-fashioned carousel has been put through the Seuss looking glass and has emerged as a towering, multicolored confection. In place of old-fashioned horses are marvelously imaginative Seuss critters with serene smiles plastered across their goofy faces. Even if you have no interest in actually riding the thing, it's worth the time it takes to stop and admire this imaginative whirligig in full motion.

The *Caro-Seuss-El* is billed as the world's first interactive carousel. Here kids can ride on the back of a beautifully sculpted Seussian animal like Cowfish from *McElligott's Pool* or the Twin Camels from *One Fish, Two Fish*. There are seven different characters and a total of 54 mounts on the 47-foot diameter ride. The interactive part comes when you pull back on the reins and watch your steed's head shake, his eyes blink, his tail wag. Another fascinating feature of the *Caro-Seuss-El* is a special loading mechanism for wheelchairs that allows the disabled to experience the ride from their own rocking chariots.

If I Ran The Zoo

Rating: ★ ★ ★ +
Type: Interactive play area
Time: Unlimited
Kelly says: Fabulous fun for toddlers

This interactive play area is based on the charming tale of young Gerald McGrew who had some very definite ideas of what it takes to create a really interesting zoo. There are three distinct areas, each of which allows little ones a slightly different interactive experience. The first is filled with peculiar animals that appear over the hedges when you turn a crank or laugh when you tickle their feet. Little adventurers can also slide down the tunnels of Zambama-tant and crawl through the cave in Kartoom in search of the Natch before reaching a small island surrounded by a wading pool. There they'll be able to control bouncing globs of water and trap their playmates in cages made out of falling water. In the final area kids can stand over a grate where the Snaggle Foot Mulligatawny will sneeze up their shorts. Then they can squirt a creature taking a bubble bath, only to get sprinkled themselves when the critter spins dry.

All told there are 19 different interactive elements to keep your child giggling all the way through this attraction. Kids will dart about eager to try them all, which may be one reason the "Zoo Keeper Code of Conduct" at the entrance warns, "Keep track of adults, they get lost all the time."

And all the rest . . .

There are nooks and crannies of Seuss Landing that are easy to miss. These are not major attractions, to be sure, but if you take a fancy to this whimsical land, or if you have a young Dr. Seuss fan in tow, they might be worth seeking out.

Just through the woozy archway that marks the entrance to Seuss Landing from Port of Entry you will find, on your right, **McElligott's Pool**, a pretty little pond with a waterfall, some charming statuary, and some interloping ducks who have made it home. Just past this area, next to the Cat in the Hat shop, in a private courtyard with its own kid-sized entrance arch, lies

Horton's Egg. Climb atop the spotted egg (a sign invites volunteers to do so) for a great **photo op**.

The **Street of the Lifted Lorax** is a small walk-through area next to the *Caro-Seuss-El*. It retells the story from Dr. Seuss's book, "The Lorax," the moral of which is "Protect the environment!"

From time to time, there is a **Seuss Character Meet and Greet** held at the Seuss book shop. And don't forget to be on the lookout for the cat of "The Cat in the Hat," who makes frequent personal appearances on the street. He is fond of sneaking up on unsuspecting tourists and will gladly pose for photos.

Those elevated tracks you see snaking their way in and out of buildings and around and about Seuss Landing belong to a ride that never got off the ground. It was to be called *Sylvester McMonkey McBean's Very Unusual Driving Machines*, but after many postponements Universal quietly shelved plans to open the ride at all. Occasionally, you will see one of Sylvester's machines tootling along the tracks, giving a hint of what might have been.

Finally, if you are hurrying through Seuss Landing, you can save a few seconds by turning left at Green Eggs and Ham and following the path that circles behind the shops. This takes you through a broad open area next to the Inland Sea and beneath the tracks of *Sylvester McMonkey McBean's* ride and lets you out a few paces from the bridge that leads to The Lost Continent, thereby avoiding the crowds of kids that throng Seuss Landing's colorful main drag.

Eating in Seuss Landing

The eateries in Seuss Landing give new meaning to the term "fun food." The exteriors and interiors are every bit as ingeniously designed as the rides, with the same loopy, drooping, and dizzy details. Even the curlicue French fries mirror the "no straight lines" theme of the architecture. Dining here is strictly casual, with brightly colored plastic utensils.

Green Eggs and Ham Cafe

What:	Yummy fast food fare
Where:	On your left as you enter from Port of Entry
Price Range:	$

The exterior of this walk-up fast food stand is shaped like a giant green ham with an enormous fork stuck into it. A partially cut slice droops over to form a canopy for the two food service windows. It's a brilliant sight gag of a building.

The signature dish of this establishment — and a real winner — is the Green Eggs and Hamwich, scrambled fried eggs, thin slices of ham, and melted cheese served on a warm bun with spiral fries on the side. It makes for a yummy, if rather salty, meal. The eggs, it must be reported, are not all *that* green; a touch of pureed parsley has been added to give them a slight greenish tinge. The Green Eggs and Hamwich is just one of four Sam I Am Sandwiches ($6 to $7). The others are hamburger, cheeseburger, and fried chicken fingers.

Circus McGurkus Cafe Stoo-pendous

What: Large indoor cafeteria
Where: Across from the *Caro-Seuss-El*
Price Range: $ - $$

Under that enormous droopy big top is this humongous fast food emporium themed to a fare-thee-well with circus imagery a la Dr. Seuss. This is one of the most delightful restaurants in all of Islands of Adventure, clever, colorful, comfortable, and imaginative as all get out.

To one side are two complete cafeteria lines; to the other a series of booths disguised as a circus train transporting a weird variety of Seuss creatures, like the Amazing Atrocious, "a beast most ferocious." In between is a spacious seating area under the twin big tops from which swing a nutty trapeze artist and a spinning mobile of Seuss characters. There is also plenty of seating just outside the doors if you'd prefer to dine al fresco.

The food is designed with kids in mind, which means personal size pizzas, both pepperoni and cheese, and various pasta dishes served with bread sticks (all about $6 to $7). Grownups might prefer the Chicken Caesar Salad ($8) or the Fresh Cut Fruit and Chicken Salad ($6). Desserts ($2 to $3) include a yummy chocolate fudge brownie.

At one end of the room you'll see a small ice cream counter and above it a zany pipe organ where, from time to time, a costumed performer plays and conducts sing-alongs.

Hop on Pop

What: Ice-cream stand
Where: Across from Circus McGurkus
Price Range: $

The enormous ice cream cone that decorates this walk-up stand says it all. You can design your own "sundae on a stick" here for under $4. First it is dipped in your choice of chocolate, orange, peppermint, or peanut butter; then it is rolled in your choice of crushed peanuts, chocolate sprinkles, rainbow sprinkles, or candy daisies.

Among the more standard sundaes ($4 to $5), the Upside Down Sundae, a chocolate brownie topped with vanilla ice cream, caramel sauce, whipped cream, and an upside down sugar cone, is a standout. Regular old ice cream cones are also available here.

There is no seating right at the stand, but you can take your goodies around the corner to the Green Eggs and Ham outdoor seating area or even head across the street and into Circus McGurkus to eat in air-conditioned comfort.

Moose Juice Goose Juice

What: Frosted smoothies at an outdoor stand
Where: On your left as you exit to Lost Continent
Price Range: $

On closer examination, Moose Juice turns out to be a "turbo tangerine" fruit drink and Goose Juice is sour green apple. Either drink can be had fresh or frozen for about $3 to $4. Fruit cups, Jell-O parfait, and soft beverages are also available.

Shopping in Seuss Landing

If you failed to heed my sage advice to buy a library of Seuss books for the kids before coming to Orlando, don't worry. You'll be able to remedy that lapse here, as well as stock up on a wide assortment of other Seussian souvenirs.

Cats, Hats & Things

This cheerful little emporium celebrates the adventures of the Cat in the Hat and his good buddies Thing 1 and Thing 2. It's impossible to miss if you take the ride, but even if you don't, you might want to pop in for a quick look. Here you'll find the image of the Cat stamped, silk-screened, printed, painted, and embroidered on every conceivable piece of tourist souvenir. You'll even find the actual book that inspired the ride in both a full-sized version and a miniature edition sized just right to slip into a toddler's pocket. For adults there are silk Cat in the Hat pajamas ($70) and terry robes ($65). The Cat's trademark striped stovepipe hat runs $12.

Tip: If you visit the shop, don't forget to take a peek into the quiet back courtyard that houses Horton's Egg (see above).

Mulberry Street Store

This is the megastore of Seuss Landing, with its very own kid-sized entrance, and the tag line "Gizmos, Gadgets, Goodies Galore" pretty much sums it up. Here you'll find a large selection of Seuss wear for everyone in the family from the littlest tykes all the way to the grownups, who will find an even larger selection of silk p.j.'s here. There's also a nice denim jacket with

Seuss characters embroidered on the back for $70.

This is the place to come for the largest selection of plush toys in Seuss Landing. In addition to the Cat in the Hat and the Grinch, you'll find cuddly versions of Yertle the Turtle, Horton, and cute little Sneetches. At one end of the store is a display of day-glo wigs, feathery boas, and wacky hats. Tourists of all ages can regularly be seen here dressing up and taking photos; the staff doesn't seem to mind. Among the more intriguing gifts are some lovely limited-edition, hand-pulled Seuss lithographs ($325). Finally, there is every conceivable variety of inexpensive logo'ed souvenir, from key chains to coffee cups.

Photo Op: Outside there is a great spot where you can pose as part of a police escort that's whizzing by a reviewing stand filled with Seuss Landing dignitaries.

Dr. Seuss' All the Books You Can Read

Imagine! An entire bookstore devoted just to the work of a single writer! It should only happen to me. Still I can't begrudge the good doctor his success, and this happy, kid-scaled place is a great way to introduce your little ones to the magic of Seuss. Books range from about $7 to $15. You'll find videos and "read-along" book-cassette combinations as well, along with film and a nice array of t-shirts and games.

The shop offers plenty of kid-sized places to sit down and read. The big plastic-covered poufs scattered about make amusingly rude noises when you sit on them.

Snookers & Snookers Sweet Candy Cookers

This is a fairly standard candy and sweets-by-weight emporium ($2.25 per quarter pound) that also sells candied apples ($3 to $4) and other goodies. Some wonderfully whimsical Seuss mugs and glassware are also available.

THE LOST CONTINENT

From the color and fantasy of Seuss Landing, the intrepid adventurer plunges into the mystery of The Lost Continent, which in terms of sheer size (some 20 acres) is almost a theme park in itself. There are three distinct areas to be found here — the Lost City, an ancient Middle Eastern bazaar evoking 1,001 Nights, and Merlinwood which may remind some of Germany's Black Forest and others of Merrie Olde England.

Photo Op: The first thing you see, when you enter from Seuss Landing, is a statue of an armor-clad griffin. Another guards the entrance from Jurassic Park. These grim guardians have quickly become one of the favorite spots for tourists to pose for that "I was at Islands of Adventure" shot.

As you approach the Lost City, you glimpse over a craggy boulder an enormous hand holding an equally enormous trident. Only when you have walked a little farther do you realize that the boulder is an enormous head of the god Poseidon and what you are seeing are the remnants of a very large and very ancient statue that fell down eons ago. Just opposite is a brooding extinct volcano, with the faces of titans carved in its flanks. It hides Mythos, perhaps the most eye-popping restaurant in any Orlando theme park.

A bit further along you enter a Middle Eastern market filled with the clamorous activity of its many shops. Turn another corner and you are in Merlinwood, in a spacious plaza in front of the entrance to *Dueling Dragons*, Islands of Adventure's most spectacular coaster. Two huge statues of the battling dragons, Fire and Ice, frame the entrance. Facing these mortal combatants, across the plaza, is the enormous gnarled stump of an ancient tree of gigantic proportions. It sits atop the Enchanted Oak Tavern and it surely must be bewitched because it seems to be the weathered face of Merlin himself.

The grand scale and attention to detail in the architecture of The Lost Continent is unparalleled in any theme park I've ever seen. It's rare that theme park visitors pause just to take pictures of buildings but it happens here all the time. Add to the visual splendor a trend-setting dual roller coaster and what well may be the finest restaurant in any theme park in the world and The Lost Continent becomes a very special island indeed.

Poseidon's Fury

Rating: ★ ★ ★ +
Type: Special effects extravaganza
Time: About 25 minutes
Kelly says: Chaotic fun, but not everyone's cup of tea

Behind the ruins of Poseidon's statue lies his enormous temple, now cracked and crumbled by earthquakes, where his devotees once worshipped. Before entering, take a moment to drink in the scene. This is yet another of the park's triumphs of fantasy architecture. The scale alone is awe-inspiring. Check out the huge feet of Poseidon's now tumbled statue and the towering trident that stands nearby. Marvel at the once gorgeous mosaic floors now running with water diverted from its ancient course by long-ago earthquakes. Stare up at the towering facade, its massive columns seemingly ready to topple at any moment. The art direction that has created not just the iconography of an ancient and imaginary religious cult but its language as well is truly impressive. Any attraction inside has to be pretty darn good to meet the level of expectations conjured by this astonishing exterior.

With understandable trepidation, we step inside to something of a disappointment — a cool, dimly lit, snaking passageway. The overall design and the fragmentary murals on the crumbling walls are vaguely Minoan in appearance, but other than the flickering lights, some hard-to-read signage from "Global Discovery Group," and the ominous music there's nothing here to hint at what lies ahead, certainly no advancing "plot line" to keep visitors informed and entertained as the line inches forward.

When we reach the front of the queue line, we hear a static filled walkie-talkie transmission: "Get out of the temple! If you can hear my voice, get out of the temple!"

Then we are greeted by Taylor a very young and very nervous volunteer assistant to ace archaeologist, Professor Baxter. The prof seems to have disappeared along with everyone else on the dig while Taylor was on a lunch break. Too bad, because the professor had announced the discovery of a "secret message" but disappeared before he could tell anyone what it was. Taylor, played by a young guy or gal, gamely carries on with our tour of recent temple excavations.

The first chamber, which Taylor tells us is the Chamber of Sacrifices, contains an altar and ancient wall paintings documenting an epic struggle. Apparently, so Taylor tells us, legend has it that a high priest of the temple, Lord Darkenon, seized power from Poseidon sparking a battle in which all perished and that the spirits of those combatants still haunt the ruined temple. There is another, terrified transmission on the walkie-talkie from Professor Baxter after which all the lights go out.

Taylor grabs an ultraviolet lamp for illumination and in so doing reveals a hidden message written on the frieze that circles the chamber. Fortunately, the ancient Greeks had the foresight to write the message in English so Taylor can read it aloud. This turns out to be a big mistake because reading the message aloud awakens the spirit of Darkenon, who opens a secret passage to an undiscovered and cobweb-draped chamber filled with treasure and the skeletons of enormous warrior-guardians. We are facing a mysterious — and locked — portal when Darkenon seals us in and demands that Taylor find the trident of Poseidon or die. Taylor instead decides to try to pry open the door and, seeking something to use as a crowbar, unknowingly picks up...tah-dah!...Poseidon's trident.

This, in turn, wakens a goddess whose face appears above the portal. She can't grant Taylor's request to send us home but she can admit us to the heart of the temple and the portal begins to turn and open, revealing one of the niftier effects in the entire park — a gigantic vortex of roaring water that forms before our eyes. Taylor escorts us through this deafening tunnel to the third and final chamber, which seems to be yet another dead end.

I don't want to spoil it for you, so suffice it to say we soon find ourselves in the middle of a pitched battle between Poseidon, who uses water as his weapon, and Lord Darkenon, who responds with fire. We're talking heavy artillery here, with more than 350,000 gallons of the wet stuff and 25-foot exploding fireballs.

Just when our survival looks doubtful, a very thoughtful Poseidon steps in to save us. The entire audience is magically transported, almost literally in a puff of smoke, from this violent battlefield in the depths of the sea back to the surface.

I am a fan of this attraction but I should note that it has its detractors. Some people find the story line confusing and, in the heat of the battle, some of the dialogue does get hard to hear. Others just don't seem that impressed with the effects.

It is true that this is an immensely complex show from the technical standpoint. After repeated viewings I am still not sure whether I have seen all of the intended effects in any one show. Perhaps those who report being disappointed saw a show in which several of the more special effects weren't working properly. For many people, their enjoyment of the show will depend on how long they have waited to see it. Get a Universal Express pass if the wait seems too long to you.

The best seats in the house. The entire show is experienced standing up. In the second and third chambers, the audience stands on a series of steps set in a semicircle, with a guardrail on each level. In the first two chambers, it really doesn't matter where you stand. For the final battle scene, however, you will have a good deal more fun if you are in the very first row. I have found that most people instinctively climb the steps, not realizing that you can actually stand in front of the first guardrail, on ground level so to speak. That means that you can simply walk to the front as you enter. Despite being almost on top of the action, you won't get terribly wet, although some of those towering explosions of water find their way into the audience.

The Eighth Voyage of Sinbad

Rating: ★ ★ ★ ★ +
Type: Amphitheater show
Time: About 20 minutes
Kelly says: Staggering stunts and explosions galore

In a 1,750-seat theater we get to witness the eighth voyage of the legendary Sinbad (seven just weren't enough). This is a live-action stunt show that means to rival the Indiana Jones show over at that other movie studio park (no, not Universal).

Here Sinbad sets off on yet another search for riches untold, encountering along the way the inevitable life-threatening perils. It's an action-packed spectacular that features six "water explosions" and 50 — count 'em, 50 — of Universal's trademark pyrotechnic effects, including a 10-foot-tall circle of flames and a 22-foot high fall by a stunt person engulfed in flames.

Sinbad and his trusty sidekick, Shish Kebab, have traveled to a mysterious cavern filled with treasure and the bones of earlier adventurers. Here the evil sorceress Miseria holds the beautiful Princess Amora in thrall and only the Sultan's Heart, an enormous ruby with magical powers, can free her. It's Sinbad to the rescue, but first he must battle Miseria for the Sultan's Heart and the ultimate power that goes with it.

Sinbad fights valiantly on the Princess's behalf. But this is no wimpy maiden in distress. Amora is a princess for the postmodern age, with hair of gold and buns of steel, who can hold her own against evil monsters thank you very much. Together, the three heroes battle the forces of evil in its many grisly guises and (I don't think I'm giving anything away here) eventually triumph.

This is a terrific show, the best of the many stunt shows I have seen in the Orlando area. The set alone, with its dripping stalagmites and crumbling pirate vessels, is stupendous and the show takes advantage of every inch of it, including the wrecked prow of an ancient ship that seems to have run aground in the very middle of the audience.

The best seats in the house. If you enjoy getting wet, there are two "splash zones" in this show, one towards the front to the right of the audience and the other in the middle, to the left of the wrecked prow that juts into the seating area. Otherwise, every seat gives a good view of the action, which has very thoughtfully been spread all over the enormous set. I have found that sitting a few rows back, just to the right of the wrecked prow offers a particularly good perspective on the action, including some bone-crunching fights that happen almost on top of you.

Another good choice is the last row in front of either of the two arched entrances on the left and right. These seats give you a great panoramic view of the action, have a back rest, and offer a quick getaway at show's end. Another bonus, if you're sensitive to sound: the open archways behind you let the sound out instead of bouncing it back at you.

Tip: This show has an especially good warm-up act, a team of comic jugglers who would have done W.C. Fields proud. They start about ten minutes before the scheduled start time of the show listed in the Attraction & Show Times insert. By getting to the theater 12 or 15 minutes before showtime, you'll not only be guaranteed a good seat but you won't miss any of this entertaining prelude. Even if you *hate* stunt shows, it's worth coming just to see these two talented fellows fling scimitars and clubs at one another.

Unfortunately, the pre-show warm-up is dropped during slower periods. There is also the possibility that these gifted performers will have moved on by the time of your visit. If so, let's hope Universal replaces them with an equally entertaining act.

Dueling Dragons

Rating:	★ ★ ★ ★ ★
Type:	Twin roller coasters
Time:	1.5 minutes
Kelly says:	Aaaargh!

One reason The Lost Continent is so large is to house this immense inverted steel roller coaster. Actually, it's two separate roller coasters travelling along separate but closely intertwined tracks that diverge and then converge to terrifying effect.

You enter this experience near the Enchanted Oak Tavern, past two stone dragons standing as mute sentinels to a mysterious world of eerie chimes and chilling sounds. At the top of a winding path lies a brooding, ruined castle. When you enter, you discover that this was once a flourishing kingdom filled with happy and prosperous people until it was overrun by two ferocious dragons — the Dragon of Ice and the Dragon of Fire.

As you make your way slowly, slowly through the castle corridors — oh, let's face it, it's the waiting line for the coaster — you receive constant warnings to turn back before it's too late. Of course, you can hardly wait for it to be too late. It's a great way to keep people entertained during the wait and marks a new level of themeing in roller coasters. It must be said, however, that this is an extremely long queue line, so long in fact that some people begin to wonder if they will ever get to the coasters. A few people even turn back, convinced they've taken a wrong turn. If you find the line slowing down shortly after you enter the castle, you're in for a long, long wait. Leave and get a Universal Express Pass.

Tip: If the line is short and you find yourself whizzing through the castle, you might want to pause to watch the video that plays on the large stained glass window. It sketches in the story behind the ride.

Finally, you are confronted by Merlin himself who bellows that the time for cowardice is past and you must now choose which of the two dragons you will attempt to slay. There's even a special line for those brave nuts, er . . . knights who want to ride in the front.

This is an inverted coaster, which means that the cars, completely dressed to look like dragons, hang from a track over your head. Your feet dangle in the air below your seat. When the cars are fully loaded the passengers look as though they are hanging from the dragons' claws. Then it's off on a ninety-second ride through Merlinwood and over Dragon Lake, which is actually shaped like a dragon, a fact that few people who ride this attraction are likely to notice.

The two coasters share the same lift to the top of the first drop, but the Fire Dragon peels off to the left as the Ice Dragon swoops to the right. After that their separate trips are carefully synchronized so that, as they loop and swirl their way around Merlinwood, they meet in mid air at three crucial moments. A computer actually weighs each coaster and then makes the appropriate adjustments to get the timing just right. Perhaps the scariest close encounter comes when they come straight at one another on what is obviously a head-on collision course. At the last moment, they spin up and apart with the dangling feet of the riders coming within a foot or two of each other at nearly 60 miles per hour. At another point, both coasters enter a double helix, spinning dizzily around one another. All told there are three near misses in the 50 seconds or so it takes to travel from the first drop to the point where the coasters slow down to reenter the castle. If you've ever asked yourself what could be more terrifying than the current generation of high-speed steel roller coasters, ask no more.

Some people find this ride so extreme, the motion so violent, and the experience so short that they can't decide whether they liked it or not. Indeed, you'll notice many people exiting in stunned puzzlement.

Note: Lockers are provided to the left of the entrance for stowing excess or loose gear. The first 45 or 75 minutes are free with a $2 charge levied for each additional half hour. Since these lockers are electronic, the terms of rental can be changed at will and may be different when you visit.

Tip: If you'd like to get a preview of this ride, look for the exit. It's to your left as you face the entrance, behind The Dragon's Keep shop. A short way up you will find a viewing area behind a high metal fence; most likely a number of departing riders will have paused here for another look. This vantage point gives you a pretty good view of the twin coasters' routes. For those who have no intention of ever strapping themselves into this coaster, it's a pretty entertaining attraction in itself.

It's also possible to enter the queue line itself for a peek. Just a short way in is a spot where you can witness two of the ride's close encounters up close. You'll actually feel the wind rush through your hair as the coasters spiral past. If this dissuades you from venturing farther you can turn back. Don't worry: you'll see plenty of people doing the same thing.

The best seats in the house. The first row is the clear choice for the thrill seeker. Otherwise, the outside seats in each row give a better view (if you have your eyes open!) and are less likely to induce motion sickness. Seats farther back in the vehicle offer a different ride experience, partly because you can see what's coming and partly because the back rows snap about with a bit more zip. Finally, the Fire Dragon (the red one) is more "aggressive" than the Ice Dragon; that is, it has a few more spins to it and moves a bit faster at some points.

Tip: Dueling Dragons is the only ride with a "re-ride" door. If the wait is less than 15 minutes, ride attendants will open this door and let you get back on immediately.

A final tip: If your head is spinning and your knees quaking after this ride, look for the small Baby Swap area as you exit. You can sit here while you regain your composure.

The Flying Unicorn

Rating:	★ ★ ★
Type:	A baby roller coaster
Time:	Less than a minute
Kelly says:	Wee thrills for wee folk

Just past *Dueling Dragons* and just before you enter Jurassic Park, you'll find this cute little coaster tucked off to one side. The theme-ing is part Olde England, part Hobbit Shire, and altogether charming. Set in a gnarled and stunted wood, surrounded by a fence of crooked wood and twisted iron, the coaster looks like a survivor from another age. The eight tiny cars evoke medieval siege engines and the front car is decorated with a unicorn head in full battle armor.

After a slow climb to the first drop, the coaster glides briefly through a series of dips and swoops before returning to the crooked little shingled hut that serves as the station. Kids much over seven will find this ride beneath them. Smaller kids, though, seem to love it.

And All the Rest . . .

The Middle Eastern bazaar section, sometimes referred to as Sinbad's Village, houses a number of **carnival-style games**, much like those found along the Amity Boardwalk in Universal Studios Florida, just decorated differently. I made my feelings about this type of attraction abundantly clear in the preceding chapter, so I won't bore you by repeating myself here.

Far more entertaining than another game of ring toss is the mysteriously smoking and bubbling **Mystic Fountain** that sits in front of the central entrance to the Sinbad show's amphitheater. Once just an interesting added touch to the fun of Lost Continent, the fountain has been elevated to the rank of a full-fledged attraction in the Adventure Guide. It would appear to be dedicated to some ancient and mysterious oracle to judge by the open-mouthed face sculpted into it. Indeed, this fountain even talks to you. Although it seems friendly enough, beware. Its hidden agenda seems to be to get you very, very wet.

Nearby, in front of the Enchanted Oak Tavern, **The Swashbucklers** hold forth from time to time, usually during the warmer months. These three comic musketeers in bright colors put on a demonstration of sword fighting and cudgels accompanied by a steady patter of the sort of mildly off-color humor that will offend no one. One of the best bits involves tiny volunteers from the audience who play the part of fierce pirates in a mock battle between good and evil. You'll find a schedule of performances in the Attraction & Show Times insert.

Eating in The Lost Continent

The Lost Continent boasts the best restaurant in Universal Orlando's two theme parks — Mythos, which is possibly the best restaurant in any theme park in the world. On top of that, the Enchanted Oak Tavern has one of the coolest restaurant interiors. And for those who take a strictly utilitarian approach to food, there are walk-up stands offering a quick and filling bite.

Mythos Restaurant

What: Fine gourmet dining
Where: Opposite Poseidon's Fury
Price Range: $$$ - $$$$

This upscale restaurant is the feather in Islands of Adventure's culinary cap. In keeping with the unspeakably ancient theme of the island, it is housed (if that's the right word) in an extinct volcano with water cascading down its weathered slopes. Step inside and you've entered a sea cavern whose sinuous walls have been carved out and smoothed by centuries of surging waves. Eerie yet soothing music, of a provenance you just can't seem to place, tinkles through the air. In the main dining room, the cavern's roof vaults skyward and a large windowed opening gives out onto the lagoon and a spacious outdoor seating area. Subterranean streams run between the handsome seating areas, with seats upholstered in regal purple. The walls take on the shapes of long-vanished gods and their spirit minions. The effect is only a step or two this side of awesome.

The decorative magic is the work of architectural designer Jordan Mozer, a restaurant wizard who has created spectacular eateries around the world, including the American Grill at Vegas' Bellagio Hotel. Even the silverware, plates, glasses, and table decoration, some of which are the work of local Florida artisans, are special. Decor like this is a hard act to follow and you find yourself wondering if the food can rise to the level of your heightened expectations.

Not to worry. The cuisine produced under the direction of chef Mark Wachowiak pays homage to the hallmarks of contemporary cuisine — intriguing combinations of ingredients and flavors, dazzling presentations — and still manages to taste, well, just plain yummy. The menu changes every two months, with only a few very popular dishes repeated. So although I can't tell you exactly what will be available when you visit, I will try to whet your appetite.

Starters ($5 to $10) always include the Wood Oven Pizza of the Day. These are thin-crusted masterpieces that blend traditional cooking methods (there is a spectacular wood-fired pizza oven in clear view of the dining area) and eclectic ingredients that change with the seasons. One appetizer that has proven a perennial is the Tempura Shrimp Sushi, a miniature work of art served with a wasabi and soy drizzle. Soups are always included among the starters and the ones I have sampled have been ambrosial.

Salads ($5 to $15) range from deceptively simple bowls of mixed baby greens to elaborate entree-sized extravaganzas featuring chicken, shrimp, or fish. Pastas ($12 to $16), are meals in themselves. I especially liked a penne pasta with duck sausage, a bold and hearty combination of flavors that asserted their individuality and never descended to the level of mere "sauce."

Entrees ($10 to $22) range from a not so humble cheeseburger to lobster tail smoked with bacon and turkey osso buco. On another occasion, I enjoyed pan-roasted corvina, a deep-sea fish very accurately described by the maitre d' as a cross between swordfish and halibut. It was cooked to perfection and served over a bed of garlic mashed potatoes; a very special dish.

In addition to the pizzas, the menu always includes a Risotto of the Day and a superb rendition of those tortilla wraps that have become so trendy lately. You can also count on finding a salmon dish and a steak on the menu. There is a kids' menu ($6) featuring simple dishes for the less sophisticated gourmet.

You probably shouldn't have dessert after one of these filling meals, but a glance at the display case near the entrance showcasing the pastry chef's creations ($4 to $7) will convince you to find room anyway. The kitchen pulls out all the stops in presentations for these splendiferous tours de force. The Warm Chocolate Banana Gooey Cake looks like it's about to take off thanks to a fanciful helicopter-like arrangement of sugared fried banana strips. It's topped with a small dollop of handmade peanut butter ice cream, which struck me as an odd addition until I tasted it.

The restaurant features an intelligent and reasonably priced wine list of American varietals. Some suggested by-the-glass pairings are made on the menu, but feel free to ask for guidance.

The restaurant seats 180 with an additional 50 seats outdoors, many of them sheltered by the overhanging volcano. I'd try for an outdoor seat on a balmy night. Another tip: request the last seating on days when the park is open late. This will give you a chance to stroll through an almost deserted park on your way out.

Reservations are taken at Islands of Adventure's central reservations number, (407) 224-9255, but try the restaurant's direct line at (407) 224-4534 to feel like a regular. Mythos is open from 11 a.m. to park closing (although it may close as early as 3:30 during slow periods) and the menu remains the same all day.

Note: See *Good Things To Know About. . . Dining Passes,* above, for information on how to dine at Mythos without paying for park admission.

And after you've finished dining, it's just a short stroll to either the *Incredible Hulk* or the *Dueling Dragons* roller coasters. This could be the best meal you'll ever lose!

The Enchanted Oak Tavern

What: Indoor barbecue restaurant
Where: Opposite the entrance to *Dueling Dragons*
Price Range: $ - $$

The giant oak tree stump with the gnarled bark that bears an uncanny resemblance to the face of Merlin, is actually another beautifully designed restaurant. The interior is a masterful evocation of the inside of a vast and ancient oak that soars to a star-flecked skylight of mystical blue. The lighting, provided by hanging lamps and wall-mounted sconces is dim and spooky. In fact, the setting is so magical that Merlin himself sometimes puts in an appearance.

Along the gnarled and knotted walls you can find little nooks and crannies forming private booths. One of them even has a huge fireplace complete with cauldron. Out the back door, overlooking the jungles of Jurassic Park, is a spacious terrace dining area, much of it shaded and protected from the elements by a sturdy thatched roof. The atmosphere alone is worth a visit and, indoors or out, this is one of the nicest places in the park to eat.

The service here is fast food cafeteria-style and the food is "hickory-smoked" barbecue. Chicken, turkey leg, and rib platters run from $8 to $12 and come with fries, roasted corn on the cob, and a corn muffin, all of which can also be ordered as side dishes. Desserts are a bit under $3 and the Homemade Apple Pie is worth a try. The food is not quite up to the standards of Thunder Falls Terrace in Jurassic Park (see below), to which it bears some resemblance, but it is very good.

At the opposite end from the food counters is the **Alchemy Bar**, which has a separate entrance from the plaza outside. It is a full service bar serving very good Scotch, but its specialty is beer; over 20 brands of domestic micro-brews and imported premium brands are served. With its low ceiling and gnarled walls, it is a terrifically atmospheric pub.

Fire Eaters Grill

What:	Walk-up fast food stand
Where:	Near *Poseidon's Fury*
Price Range:	$ - $$

This stand offers "walking sandwiches," which is good because the nearby outdoor seating is limited and not very well shaded. The fare is vaguely Middle Eastern and on the spicy side, featuring Grilled Gyros and both Chicken Fingers and Fire Eaters Chicken Stingers ($7 to $8). A combo platter featuring gyro, fries, and a drink goes for $9. There are cookies for dessert and plenty of ice cold soda and beer to wash it all down.

Frozen Desert

What:	Walk-up ice cream stand
Where:	In the bazaar area near the Sinbad Theater
Price Range:	$

In addition to Frozen Mirage Swirls in cup and goblet sizes ($3 to $4), this ice cream stand also offers a Sultan's Sundae of vanilla and pineapple swirl topped with fresh pineapple ($4). Somewhat more traditional is the Treasure Chest Sundae ($4) of vanilla and strawberry. You can create your own delight by choosing from a selection of Turban Toppings (50 cents each). And if you insist on being healthy, there's a Lost Cargo Fruit Cup ($3).

Oasis Coolers

What:	Walk-up stand
Where:	In the bazaar area by the Mystic Fountain
Price Range:	$

Gatorade is the thirst quencher of choice at this stand hard by the talking fountain at the entrance to the Sinbad Theater. Other soft drinks are also available. On a recent visit, hot dogs (about $4) were the only "real" food you could order.

Shopping in The Lost Continent

In addition to the shops listed in the Adventure Guide, the Middle Eastern bazaar section of The Lost Continent has other specialty shops that change from time to time. Thus their omission here.

Treasures of Poseidon

You are not condemned to walk through this shop but you will pass it as you leave *Poseidon's Fury*. The "treasures" on offer include the usual souvenir t-shirts, baseball caps, and ceramic plates and mugs, along with costume jewelry, toiletries, and postcards. Sea shells, from tiny ones to large conch shells, and decorative shell-studded frames are featured.

Metal Melter

Looking for an item you won't find anywhere else in the park — or anywhere else in Orlando? You've come to the right place if your taste runs to things medieval. The shop sells handmade metal headdresses and jewelry, along with copper decorative items. Intricate hoods that can transform any woman into a lady of the realm cost from $95 to $575 but, if you ask, the owner will duck into the back room and produce a beautiful sterling silver version that goes for $1,500. Other, more modest, metal crafts are also on display. On a recent visit, an artisan was etching goblets and other glassware. Even if you don't want to buy, stop to watch these artisans at work.

The Coin Mint

The wares here are hand-minted medallions, made to order while you watch by an artisan who's garbed in Renaissance clothing and speaks in a simulation of a British regional accent. You specify the design for each side, and the master minter uses a heavily weighted guillotine-like device to slam the designs onto your choice of bronze, silver, or "gold layered silver" discs ($17, $42, and $59). The tented shop also sells sterling silver chains ($20 to $25) and crystal fantasy pendants ($10 to $30).

Shop of Wonders

This venue offers unicorn and dragon dolls in profusion. There are even some unicorn-shaped backpacks for very young children ($20). You will also find costumes and fancy headgear for little princesses and their knights, along with some nice decorative pieces. On a recent visit I saw beautifully decorated wooden boxes and "Meadow Fairy" figurines ($12 to $25).

Mystics of the Seven Veils

Entering this atmospheric tent transports you to a time before 900 numbers and the Psychic Friends Network. Here one of several fortune tellers will reveal your past and delve into your future — for a price. You can choose from sessions of 5, 10, 15, and 30 minutes for $10, $20, $30, and $50, respectively. There always seems to be a line of willing seekers here. Also to be found within the tent are assorted baubles, bangles, and crystals.

The Dragon's Keep

You'll find this shop hard by the exit to *Dueling Dragons*. It focuses on dragons, wizards, and magic potions. Magic tricks, puzzles, card games, and so on are on display along with t-shirts sporting fierce, brightly colored dragons and practical items such as sunglasses, film, and sunscreen lotion. There are some nice dragon figurines for $15 and up. Unicorn dolls here are $40.

JURASSIC PARK

If you've seen the movie *Jurassic Park*, you will recognize the arches that greet you as you enter. If you haven't, I would suggest you rent the original film from your local video store before coming. Knowing the film will help you understand a lot of the little details of Jurassic Park, including the frequent references to velociraptors.

Here, Universal's design wizards have re-created the theme park that the movie's John Hammond was trying to create before all prehistoric heck broke loose, and the lush and steamy jungle landscape they have devised fits in perfectly with Florida's humid summers.

As in the movie, we are asked to believe that we are in a park containing actual living dinosaurs, some which are quite dangerous, as the high-tension fences indicate. Periodically, roars are heard and bushes rustle ominously behind those fences. And those twists and dents in the metal may make you wonder just how safe you really are, for all this atmosphere can be surprisingly realistic. I've seen more than one child start in terror when an unseen critter growled in the underbrush.

Discovery Center

Rating:	★ ★ ★
Type:	Interactive displays
Time:	Unlimited
Kelly says:	Best for young dinosaur buffs

This is lifted almost straight from the film and houses a fast food restaurant, a shop and, on the ground floor, a children's "science center," which blends fantasy and reality in such a way that you might have to explain the difference to your more trusting kids. Kids will certainly recognize the huge T-Rex skeleton that perches menacingly on a rock outcropping and pokes its head through to the circular railing on the upper level.

A nursery carefully incubates dinosaur eggs. Nearby, kids can handle "real" dino eggs and put them in a scanner to view the developing embryo inside. Periodically an attendant appears and conducts a deadpan scientific show-and-tell as you watch an adorable baby raptor emerge from its shell.

Closer to reality is an actual segment of rock face from the North Sea area containing real fossilized dinosaur bits from the Triassic, Jurassic, and Cretaceous eras. A series of clever "neutrino data scanners" let kids move along the rock face looking for dinosaurs. When a fragment is found, the scanner analyzes it and then identifies and reconstructs the dinosaur from which it came. In somewhat the same vein is an exhibit of life-sized dinosaurs that lets you see the world as the dinosaurs saw it by looking through high tech viewfinders mounted periscope-style into the model dinosaurs' heads and necks and moving the creatures' heads around.

On the zany side is a DNA Sequencing exhibit which explains the cloning premise on which the movie is based and then lets you combine your own DNA with that of a dinosaur to create a saurian you. And completely over the top (but a lot of fun) is a quiz show with the rather naughty name, "You Bet Jurassic." Here you and two other tourists compete in a game of dinosaur trivia. But don't get your hopes up; the grand prize is a lifetime supply of Raptor Chow, which is apparently manufactured from losing contestants!

On the back wall of the lower level you'll find a large mural depicting life in the Jurassic era. If you entered the *Discovery Center* from the upper level, you might want to take a peek through the massive double doors in the middle of this wall. They open out onto a spacious park-like terrace that descends to the shores of the Great Inland Sea. This is one of the loveliest open spaces in the park and offers a stunning view back to the Port of Entry and the lighthouse that welcomes arriving guests.

Triceratops Discovery Trail

Rating: ★ ★ ★ ★ +
Type: Animatronic encounter with a dinosaur
Time: 5 to 10 minutes or longer if you wish
Kelly says: Astonishingly realistic

This is another never-before-been-done attraction of which Universal is justifiably proud. The conceit here is that, as a visitor to Jurassic Park, you are given a "walk-through opportunity" to visit one of several "feed and control" paddocks for an up close and personal visit with a real live triceratops. Here you meet a Jurassic veterinarian who will fill you in on the natural history and habits of this amazing beast and one lucky guest (usually a child) actually gets to pet it.

Lest you think that Universal has literally done the impossible, the triceratops is not a living, breathing critter but a remarkably clever counterfeit that takes the art of animatronics to a whole new level. Unlike most mechanically animated creatures, this 24-foot long, 10-foot high triceratops does not go through a fixed routine of motions, pause, then do it all over again for the next bunch of people passing by. This triceratops actually responds to stimuli provided by the guests, making each triceratops encounter a unique experience. Nor do they hedge the illusion by making you keep your distance. Once inside the paddock, you are remarkably close to the giant beast.

Your adventure begins as you enter the queue line, passing by a series of deserted research stations and tents. Television monitors offer a steady stream of reports from "Jurassic Journal," a Discovery Channel type show about the doings at Jurassic Park that leans heavily to interviews with park scientists and which is just ever-so-slightly tongue in cheek. How much of this you actually get to absorb will be a function of the length of the queue.

During slower periods, you will walk fairly quickly to a "dispatch palapa." Periodically, groups of about 18 to 20 people are sent off to one of three paddocks containing triceratops that have been brought in for routine physical exams.

There you come face to face and scarcely more than an arm's length away from a living, breathing triceratops named Sarah (or is that Cera?). She has a slight cold, apparently, and has been sedated so she can get a thorough examination. The vet banters good-naturedly with the visitors as the exam progresses and is happy to answer any questions you might have.

One person is chosen from the crowd to step forward and pet the triceratops. It's a very special experience, but be warned — there's a price to be paid! Barring "allergic reactions," the actual dinosaur encounter lasts about five to ten minutes and you may be asked to move along to make room for the next batch of guests. In slower periods, however, it may be possible to linger longer if you wish.

As mentioned before, the computer-controlled animatronic dinosaur employs a sort of "fuzzy logic" that allows the beast to respond to external stimuli in a fairly realistic manner. Just remember that triceratops are gentle creatures. If your group is quiet and respectful, she is likely to respond positively. However, if your group is loud and boisterous, she may display defensive behavior and your visit may be shortened.

Remember, too, that this triceratops — or more accurately the technology that animates her — is temperamental. Try not to be too disappointed if your visit is cut short or even cancelled altogether. The ranger will tell you that Sarah has had an "allergic reaction" or some other physical problem, but the truth is there's been a mechanical breakdown. Do try again later if you have the time.

I find this rather quiet experience to be remarkably realistic and one of the best things in the park. Some people complain that the dinosaur doesn't actually do all that much, but I find that adds to the realism. She is, after all, heavily sedated and if you've ever seen a large mammal in a paddock or other confined space they pretty much just stand there. One reason I didn't give this attraction a full five-star rating is the absence of a strong animal odor in the paddock area. Presumably, the designers decided that this would turn people off, but the powerful pong that invariably comes with any large beast would make the illusion absolutely convincing.

Frequent breakdowns of the animatronic mechanism are another problem. A long wait in line to see a motionless dinosaur can leave you positively cranky. Hopefully, the engineers will work out the kinks before your visit. Despite these caveats, if your kids are at that age when they are besotted with all things saurian, they will be absolutely enthralled. If you can suspend your disbelief, so will you.

The best seats in the house. You pretty much have the freedom to wander around as you view the triceratops, so I would recommend taking advantage of this to observe the critter from both the side and near the head. If you'd like your child to be picked for the close encounter, position him or her near its head; you should be able to spot the place where the low metal fence will swing forward to allow a closer approach to the beast's beak.

Jurassic Park River Adventure

Rating: ★ ★ ★ ★
Type: Water ride
Time: 5 minutes
Kelly says: Terrific fun

Amazing as the *Triceratops Discovery Trail* may be, this is the attraction that will draw people to Jurassic Park. Those who have experienced the current Jurassic Park ride at Universal Studios California know what to expect. This version contains some "enhancements" but it is essentially the same ride.

The pre-ride warm-up plays it straight. Video monitors in the queue line emphasize proper boarding procedures and ride safety, just as you would expect in the "real" Jurassic Park. The result: it's nowhere near as entertaining as the *Jaws* warm-up at USF.

River Adventure itself is an idyllic boat ride that gives you an opportunity to view from close range some of Jurassic Park's gentlest creatures. Unfortunately, on the trip you take with 25 other guests, things go very, very wrong. Your first stop is the upper lagoon, where you meet a 35-foot tall mama ultrasaur and her baby. Then you cruise past the park's north forty where you glimpse stegosaurs and the playful hydrosaurs. Too playful, unfortunately.

Before you know it, you're off course in the raptor containment area and on the lunch menu. In a desperate attempt to save you, the boat is shunted into the environmental systems building, that huge 13-story structure at the back of Jurassic Park. It is in this vast, dark, and very scary setting that the ride reaches it climax. After narrowly escaping velociraptors and those nasty spitting dinosaurs, you come face to face, quite literally, with T-Rex himself. After that, the 85-foot plunge down the "longest, fastest, steepest water descent ever built" in pitch blackness will seem like a relief.

This is a great ride to experience at night, especially once you enter the main building. The bright Florida sun tends to give away the approach of the final breathtaking drop; at night it comes as a real surprise.

Note: Lockers are provided near the entrance for stowing gear you might want to keep dry. The rental rate is $1 an hour to a maximum of $10. Since these lockers are electronic, the terms of rental can be changed at will and may be different when you visit.

The best seats in the house. Clearly the first row of the boat is where you thrill seekers want to be; just be warned that you *will* get wet. Of course, you'll probably get wet no matter where you sit, although seats in the center of the craft are a little more protected. The ride attendants are more likely to accommodate a request for a seat that gives you some protection from a drenching than they are to put you in the front row. However, if you come early in the day or late at night, you may be able to pick any seat you want.

Camp Jurassic

Rating:	★ ★ ★ ★
Type:	Interactive play area
Time:	As long as it takes
Kelly says:	Terrific fun for pre-teens

This 60,000 square foot interactive kids' play and discovery area is about four times the size of *Fievel's Playland* over at Universal Studios Florida and will appeal to a slightly older age group, although kids of all ages will find plenty to keep them occupied. The place is a minor masterpiece of playground design and even adults will enjoy sampling its pleasures.

Camp Jurassic transports you to a jungle on the slopes of an ancient active volcano. The roots of banyan trees snake around ancient rock outcroppings and an old abandoned amber mine offers exciting networks of rope ladders and tunnels, as well as subterranean passageways, to explore. There are corkscrew slides, cascading waterfalls, secret hideaways, and a place where kids can do battle with water cannons made up to look like the deadly spitting dinosaurs from the film.

Aside from the water cannons, all the fun here comes from kids burning off energy and exercising their imaginations as they run, climb, and slide their way through this intricate and imaginative maze of a prehistoric environment. Don't be surprised if your kid gets lost in here for an hour or so and don't be surprised if you find yourself enjoying it just as much.

Pteranodon Flyers

Rating: ★ ★ ★ +
Type: A mild, hanging coaster
Time: 80 seconds
Kelly says: Fun, but not worth a wait
Note: Universal Express is not available for this ride.

Taking off from the back of *Camp Jurassic* is this "family" ride that glides gently around the camp's tropical perimeter for an enjoyable but all-too-brief soaring experience. The ride vehicle consists of a pair of swing-like seats, one behind the other, that dangle from a metal pteranodon. Pteranodons, you might remember, were flying dinosaurs with long mean-looking beak-like faces and hooks on their leathery wings. These pteranodons are not at all threatening and, in fact, you hardly notice them once you are seated.

Your vehicle glides rather than rides along the overhead track, taking you on a journey that lets you survey *Camp Jurassic* below and the Great Inland Sea in the distance. This ride is a little more "aggressive" than the sky rides you may have encountered at other parks and offers a few mild "thrills" as the flyers bank and curve.

The main problem with this ride is that it accommodates so few riders. Universal has tried to remedy this situation by imposing a 56-inch maximum height requirement; if you are taller than this, you must be accompanied by a child. This has helped somewhat, but compared to all the other rides in the park, its hourly "throughput" is still laughably low. The result is that the line forms early and lasts a long, long time. I am not alone in thinking that an hour and a half wait for an 80-second ride is a tad on the long side. So if you think this is the kind of thing you'll enjoy, plan on coming first thing in the morning. The wait also tends to be more reasonable shortly before the park closes.

Be aware that some children, especially those with a fear of heights, might find this ride terrifying. And if they do, they won't have Mommy or Daddy to cling to since the two seats are quite separate.

And All the Rest...

From time to time, there is **live street entertainment** in Jurassic Park. I have spotted a steel-drum ensemble outside Jurassic Park Outfitters, for example. Behind the *Discovery Center* you'll find a beautifully terraced **park** that leads down to the Great Inland Sea. With its tropical foliage, it's secluded and romantic at night. And to *really* get away from it all late in the day, descend the stairs to the dock area once used by Island Skipper Tours.

Eating in Jurassic Park

Jurassic Park offers another stunningly beautiful restaurant, Thunder Falls Terrace, where the service is cafeteria style but where you dine on nice plates with real knives and forks in a beautifully designed space.

For the rest, there are a number of fast food options and a great outdoor bar for the drinkers in your party.

Thunder Falls Terrace

What: Grilled cuisine with flair
Where: On your left as you enter from Toon Lagoon
Price Range: $ - $$

This restaurant takes wonderful advantage of the *Jurassic Park River Adventure*, using it as both backdrop and entertainment. After you've taken your own harrowing journey on the ride, you can repair here, sit in air-conditioned comfort, and gaze through the picture windows at other happily terrified tourists as they emerge from the final 85-foot drop. There is an outdoor seating area that receives the cooling mist from the thundering waterfall next door. The luxurious jungle-lodge atmosphere also contributes to the experience. There are two spacious circular dining areas under soaring conical roofs held aloft by massive log beams and dominated by a large hanging black metal chandelier with amber colored glass panels and cutouts of dinosaurs.

The food is casual and it's served cafeteria style. But it's served on real china plates with real silverware, which makes eating here a pleasure. (On some occasions, unfortunately, they switch to disposable plates and utensils.) The food is also very good. The menu was designed by the same chef who created Mythos (see Lost Continent) and careful attention has been paid to both quality and presentation.

The menu consists of unusually well prepared backyard barbecue staples such as chicken, ribs, beef kabobs, and chicken wings ($8 to $12). The platters are served with roasted rosemary-tinged potatoes or yellow rice and black beans. The corn on the cob is especially nice. The corn is fresh from nearby Zellwood and roasted to perfection, with the peeled-back husks adding a festive touch to the platter. Thunder Falls also dishes up a serviceable conch chowder and two tasty entree-sized salads. The desserts are equally appealing. All in all, this is the best "fast food" style restaurant in the park. With a full meal running about $17, it's a real bargain for the quality.

The Burger Digs

What: Walk-up indoor fast food counter
Where: On the top level of the *Discovery Center*
Price Range: $ - $$

This fast food eatery opened on an adventuresome note by putting alligator meat on the menu, but found few takers. Now you'll have to be content with hamburgers, cheeseburgers, and grilled chicken sandwiches ($7) served with fries and a help-yourself fixin's bar laden with lettuce, tomato, chopped onions, and other burger enhancers. For the grownups there's beer.

You'll find plenty of indoor, air-conditioned seating just a few steps away from the serving windows, in a spacious dining room decorated with murals depicting life in the Jurassic age. There is also a lovely balcony with a palm-fringed view of the Inland Sea – a great place to sit on a balmy night. Clearly the seating area here was designed with corporate events and private parties in mind. For the casual tourist, it means plenty of room to spread out, even to gain a modicum of privacy and peace on a hectic day.

Pizza Predatoria

What: Walk-up outdoor fast food stand
Where: Near *Triceratops Discovery Trail*
Price Range: $

Pizza by Pizza Hut ($6 to $7) is the signature dish here. There are also large hoagie-style sandwiches (meatball and Italian sausage) for about $6. Sweets, soft drinks, and beer round out the menu choices.

All seating is at nearby umbrella-shaded tables, but you could conceivably take a short stroll to The Burger Digs in the *Discovery Center* and eat your pizza in air-conditioned comfort.

The Watering Hole

What: Outdoor full-service bar
Where: Near the *Discovery Center*
Price Range: $

Rather unusual for a theme park is this walk-up bar specializing in exotic drinks that pack a prehistoric wallop. The main feature is Island Coolers in a variety of flavors, from piña colada to electric blue raspberry, for $5 or about $3 without the alcohol.

If you really want to get a buzz on, choose the Triple Threat of Extinction, a mixture of tangerine, strawberry, and piña colada for a bit less than $6, or about $4 without the alcohol. There's also beer and a full bar for those who prefer a more straightforward drink. You won't find much food here other than nachos for $4.

Shopping in Jurassic Park

Dinostore

Located on the top level of the *Discovery Center* opposite Burger Digs, this small shop actually has some redeeming educational value. There are wooden dinosaur skeleton kits, books about dinosaurs aimed at the younger set, videos and DVDs of the movies, and copies of the Michael Crichton novel that started it all. There is also a more subdued and upscale selection of Jurassic Park clothing here, including some very sleek $300 jackets.

My eye was caught by the genuine prehistoric amber with insects trapped inside. Small pieces with barely visible bugs are $20 while larger, framed specimens are in the $200 range.

Jurassic Park Outfitters

This is the gauntlet you run after splashing down on the *River Adventure* ride. As you might expect, you will find the Jurassic Park logo on every conceivable surface from t-shirts ("I Survived Jurassic Park, the Ride!") to mugs. Of particular interest are some quite nice jungle adventurer hats ($30 to $34), boxer shorts covered with velociraptors, and Jurassic Park beach towels, which you actually might need. Best of all are the framed photos taken of you and your fellow tourists plunging screaming down the last drop of the ride. You can get them for $17 to $24 (depending on size).

TOON LAGOON

After the intensity of Jurassic Park, the zany, colorful goofiness of Toon Lagoon is a welcome change of pace. Many of the characters you have come to know and love through the Sunday funnies in your hometown newspaper can be spotted here — some appear in blow-ups of their strips, some have been immortalized in giant sculptures, and some will actually be strolling the grounds and happy to pose for photos. A visit here offers a unique opportunity to live out a child's daydream of stepping into the pages of the comic strips and exploring a gaudy fantasy world filled with fun and laughter.

Toon Lagoon's main drag is **Comic Strip Lane**, a short street of shops and restaurants, including those described below, that is an attraction in itself. Nearly 80 comic strip characters call this colorful neighborhood home, including Beetle Bailey (on furlough from Camp Swampy no doubt), Hagar the Horrible, and Krazy Kat. The concept makes for all sorts of serendipitous juxtapositions. Hagar's boat hangs over a waterfall that falls into a big pipe that bubbles up across the way at a dog fountain where all the dogs from the various comic strips hang out.

Turning off Comic Strip Lane is the zany seaside town of **Sweet Haven,** a separate section of Toon Lagoon containing a variety of Popeye-inspired rides and attractions. Water is a recurring theme in Toon Lagoon and you can get very wet here. See *Good Things To Know About … Getting Wet* in the introduction to this chapter for a strategy to follow.

Dudley Do-Right's Ripsaw Falls

Rating: ★ ★ ★ ★
Type: Log flume ride
Time: 6 minutes
Kelly says: Laughs and screams

In Dudley's hometown of Ripsaw Falls, as you might expect, Nell is once again in the clutches of the dastardly Snidely Whiplash. That's all the excuse you need to take off on a rip-roaring log flume ride that, like so many other attractions in this park, takes the genre to a whole new level.

The build-up takes us through a series of scenes in a "moving melodrama" in which the much-loved characters unfold a typically wacky plot that includes not just Dudley, Nell, and Snidely but Inspector Fenwick and Horse, too, as our six-passenger log-boats rise inexorably to the mountainous heights where Snidely has his hideout. Along the way we pass animated tableaux that advance the tie-her-to-the-railroad-tracks plot. The landscape is dotted with signs that echo the off-the-wall humor of the old cartoons. At one point the boat detours into the abandoned Wontyabe Mine, at another we pass a billboard advertising Whiplash Lager ("made with real logs"). Of course, Dudley triumphs almost in spite of himself. Anticipating victory a bit too soon, he strikes a heroic pose with his foot on a dynamite plunger, precipitating a plunge through the roof of a TNT storage shack which blows to bits as the riders are shot beneath the water surface only to pop back to the surface 100 feet downstream. This is the first log flume to pull off this little bit of wizardry and how they manage it I'll leave you to discover. Another nice touch is that the final drop is curved rather than a straight angle; the result is that, as the angle steepens, you could swear you're hurtling straight down.

This is one ride that just may be as entertaining to watch as to take. If you'd prefer not to take the plunge and actually go on the ride, you can stand and watch others take the steep 60-foot drop into the TNT shack, which shatters to smithereens before your eyes. Its constituent parts fly skyward, hang there in cartoon-like suspended animation for a moment, and then fall back on themselves, miraculously reassembling the shack for the next bunch of riders.

Tip: If you're coming from Marvel Super Hero Island, you can take a shortcut to *Ripsaw Falls.* Just turn left at Betty Boop's piano!

Popeye & Bluto's Bilge-Rat Barges

Rating:	★ ★ ★ ★ +
Type:	Raft ride
Time:	About 5 minutes
Kelly says:	Super soaking good fun

You may get spritzed a bit on the *Jurassic Park River Adventure* and on *Dudley Do-Right's Ripsaw Falls*, but for a really good soaking, you have to come to Sweet Haven, home to Popeye, Olive Oyl, and the gang. The barges of the name are actually circular, 12-passenger rubber rafts that twirl and dip along a twisting, rapid-strewn watercourse.

Just as Dudley has his Snidely, Popeye has Bluto. Their lifelong enmity and rivalry for the affection of Miss Olive form the basis for the theme-ing on this ride, which involves Olive, Wimpy, Poopdeck Pappy, and all the rest. Water splashes into sides of the raft in the rapids and pours in from above at crucial junctures. And at least one person in your raft is sure to get hosed by the little devils (actually someone else's kids) manning the water cannons on *Me Ship, The Olive* (see below) before the raft is swept into an octopus grotto where an eight-armed beast holds Popeye in its tentacled grip, preventing him from reaching his lifesaving spinach. Before it's all over, the hapless rafts have been spun into Bluto's fully operational boat wash, which is just like a car wash except it's for boats.

This is the spiffiest raft ride I've ever taken and the ride to take at the hottest, stickiest part of the day. Because the free-floating rafts spin and twist as they roar down the rapids, how wet you get is somewhat a matter of luck; you certainly will get damp and you may be drenched. The rafts have plastic covered bins in the center in which you can store things you'd rather not get wet. They do a pretty good job, too. Many people are smart enough to re-move and stow their shoes and socks since plenty of water sloshes into the rafts along the way.

Tip: The heavier the raft, the faster the ride. So if you want a little extra oomph in your ride, get in line behind a bunch of weight lifters or opera stars.

Me Ship, The Olive

Rating:	★ ★ ★
Type:	Interactive play area
Time:	Unlimited
Kelly says:	Nice but can't beat *Camp Jurassic*

Resist the temptation to come here after the raft ride and throttle the little darlings who were squirting you with the water cannons. Instead let your littlest kids loose in this three-story interactive play area representing the ship Popeye has named after his one true love. Older kids will find this spot of limited interest.

The ship theme is clever and well executed but makes for cramped spaces. Still there are some good reasons for at least a brief visit. The top level offers some excellent views of *Dueling Dragons*, all of Seuss Landing, and an especially good angle on the *Hulk Coaster*. Videographers and photographers will definitely want to take advantage of these **photo ops**. Also on the top level is a tubular slide that will deposit little kids on the middle level where they will find, on the starboard side, four water cannons they can aim at hapless riders on the *Bilge-Rat Barges* ride — and they're free! Also on this level is a "Spinach Spinnet," a cartoon piano that little kids will enjoy banging on. Yet another corkscrew tubular slide takes your tykes to the bottom level, where they can play in Swee' Pea's Playpen. For those who cannot climb the many stairs of *Me Ship, The Olive*, a small elevator is thoughtfully provided.

Xtreme Xventure

Rating: ★ ★ ★ ★
Type: Amphitheater stunt show
Time: About 20 minutes
Kelly says: Non-stop, razzle-dazzle action

This show elevates hip-hop skateboard culture to the realm of high art in a razzle-dazzle, helter-skelter display of acrobatic artistry by a talented band of inline skaters, skateboarders, and bikers. Eight guys and two gals, accompanied by a throbbing rock soundtrack and the occasional burst of pyrotechnics, zip, slide, soar, and tumble up ramps, through the audience, and back and forth across the stage, striking poses and doing stunts that are literally breathtaking.

At first, it seems like the show is pure pandemonium (indeed, that is the name of the amphitheater in which it takes place), but you soon realize that this beehive of activity has been carefully choreographed to prevent the numerous midair collisions that would otherwise result. There is an endearing three-ring-circus aspect to the show and, at times, you don't know where to look next. But wherever you look there is something worth watching going on. A girl skater is pulled aloft to do an aerialist act, or a boy-girl duo do an adagio routine that is straight out of an ice show. But the real stars are the skateboarders and the bikers on their specially modified BMX dirt bikes. They zip back and forth on a huge, U-shaped "half pipe" at the back of the stage almost disappearing into the lighting equipment at the top of each run or pausing to do a gravity-defying handstand. Amazing!

The best seats in the house. Periodically the performers zoom out into the audience, fly up a short ramp, and come to a deft stop right in front of the first row of the upper section of seats, making this the prime seating location.

This show is "seasonal," meaning summer, Christmas, and Spring Break. If it's on during your visit, I highly recommend checking it out.

And All the Rest...

Toon Lagoon's Comic Strip Lane offers some terrific **photo ops**. There are cut-outs that put you in the comic strip and many of the palm trees are mounted with comic strip speech balloons. You pose underneath and get a nice shot of you saying things like, "It must be Sunday...We're in color!" or "Don't have the mushroom pizza before you ride *Ripsaw Falls*."

My favorite is a trick photo involving Marmaduke, that playful Great Dane. You'll find it on the facade of Blondie's restaurant (see below) and a nearby sign tells you exactly how to set up the shot.

If you turn to the right at *Me Ship, The Olive* and follow the path over the raging rapids of the *Bilge-Rat Barges* ride, you'll find yourself in a delightful snarl of walkways along the Great Inland Sea, another of the park's wonderful get-away-from-it-all spots.

The plaza in front of the Pandemonium amphitheater is the venue for the **Toon Lagoon Beach Bash Show**, an interactive session of fun and games in which your host, Sandy Beach (can that be her real name?), leads audience volunteers through a series of silly dance games, followed by a surfer dance routine featuring Beetle Bailey, Zero, Popeye, Olive Oyl, Bluto, and Woody Woodpecker. The show wraps up with a limbo involving about eight or so kid volunteers. The characters hang around afterwards for **photo ops** and autographs. The area from the plaza to the entrance to Marvel Super Hero Island is also home to a collection of so-called Games of Skill.

Eating in Toon Lagoon

Blondie's

What:	Overstuffed sandwich shop
Where:	On the plaza near the entrance to Sweet Haven
Price Range:	$

This one comes with a subtitle, "Home of the Dagwood." It's a sandwich of course, and for those who don't know, it's named after Blondie Bumstead's hapless hubby, who made comic strip history with his colossal, 20-slice, clear-out-the-fridge sandwich creations. The sandwiches here don't quite live up to the gigantic depiction that graces the entrance to the joint, and they sprawl across the plate rather than tower above it as they do on the signage. But you'll likely find them pretty good nonetheless.

Pride of place among the "Side-Splitting Sandwiches," as they are called, goes to The Dagwood ($7), consisting of ham, salami, turkey, bologna, Swiss and American cheese on several slices of hearty white bread. Other choices are less fully packed and less expensive. A hot dog is a bit over $5, or $6 with chili. Soups, salads, and Alarm Clock chili are also served here ($3 to $7). The Lunch Pail kids' meal consists of a bologna and American cheese sandwich, with potato salad or coleslaw and a small drink for less than $6. Indoor seating is limited.

Wimpy's

What:	Walk-up burger joint
Where:	In Sweet Haven across from *Bilge-Rat Barges*
Price Range:	$

Popeye's pal is as closely associated with hamburgers as it's possible to be, so it's good to see him here serving up the apotheosis of the all-American burger. Burger and chicken finger meals are about $7, with hot dogs a bit less. A "Sweet Pea" kids' meal is about $6. Soft drinks are served and draft beer ($4 to $5) is available to slake that deeper thirst.

Service is from walk-up but shaded windows in a building that serves as a portside supply shack. All seating is outdoors, only some of it shaded. Perhaps the best spot to grab a table is in the shaded area over the raging rapids of the *Bilge-Rat Barges* ride.

Comic Strip Cafe

What:	Multicultural cafeteria
Where:	On Comic Strip Lane
Price Range:	$

This large, loud, and boisterous space houses four separate fast food counters arranged in a row along the back wall. Reading from left to right they are Fish, Chips & Chicken; Chinese; Mexican; and Pizza & Pasta. All of them have about three or four entrees in the $6 to $7 range and complete kids' meals for about $6. The selections are not terribly imaginative and are about what you would expect for their genres: beef and broccoli and a lo mein dish at the Chinese stand; beef and chicken tacos and fajitas at the Mexican; and spaghetti and lasagna at the Italian stand. Salads ($4 to $7) are also available. Desserts ($2 to $4) are the same at every stand and include flan and cheesecake. If everyone in your party can't agree on a cuisine, be prepared to stand in several lines; each counter has a separate line and cashier.

The room itself is bright and garish in a self-consciously postmodern way. The high ceiling, with its exposed air-conditioning ducts and pipes, is painted a matte black, but the walls are brightly striped and covered with blown-up panels and cutouts from a variety of Sunday funnies comic strips, providing a bit of light reading for those dining alone. There's plenty of table and booth seating indoors and a fair amount of al fresco seating as well.

Cathy's Ice Cream

What: Walk-up stand
Where: On Comic Strip Lane, near the Comic Strip Cafe
Price Range: $

In the comics, Cathy is constantly worrying about her weight. She must have taken leave of her senses, not to mention her scale, when she opened this place. The stand takes the form of a huge container brimming with a hot fudge sundae topped not by a cherry but by the bewitchingly bikini-ed Cathy herself. The slogan here is "Home is where the hot fudge is," a sentiment to live by. Hot Fudge sundaes are just under $5; other toppings are available. Cones are $3 to $4 or so.

Shopping in Toon Lagoon

Gasoline Alley

If your Florida vacation is going to include a trip to the beach, you can stop here to stock up on baggy t-shirts, cover-ups, Hawaiian shirts, beach hats, beach towels, sandals, sunscreen, and the like. Clothing prices are in the $18 to $50 range for the most part.

WossaMotta U

This shop, which takes its name from one of America's great institutions of higher learning, is dedicated to Rocky and Bullwinkle and the other characters created by Jay Ward. There are plenty of inexpensive souvenirs here that won't strain a kid's allowance. Rocky and Bullwinkle plush dolls run about $20. WossaMotta U t-shirts are $16, sweatshirts are $28. They screen videos of the old Rocky and Bullwinkle TV show here but when I last visited, they weren't selling any. Too bad.

Betty Boop Store

Tucked away under Betty Boop's piano is the entrance to this shrine to the original boop-oop-a-doop girl. Collectible dolls in a variety of sizes and outfits range from $5 to $40. There are t-shirts, of course, but the silk sleepwear ($35 to $65) is a classier choice. An eight-volume video collection of Boop cartoons goes for $90. There are plenty of Boop souvenirs, too, ranging from cheap key rings to expensive figurines ($180).

Toon Extra

This large store is not well marked, but you can enter it through Beetle

Bailey's tent, under Flash Gordon's rocket, or through those huge rolled up Sunday funnies that serve as columns for the zany building in which it is housed. This is another Islands of Adventure shop that's worth popping into just to gawk at the decor.

Clothing of the casual t-shirt and polo shirt variety, much of it for kids ($14 to $32), is the main stock in trade here, and some of it is quite nice. Infant t-shirts are about $12. In addition, you will find the usual souvenir mugs and such, along with a selection of plush toys.

At one end, under a sign that says "Photo Funnies," are two self-service photo booths that put your smiling face on a sheet of 16 little stickers with a Woody Woodpecker or Jurassic Park design. The cost is $5 per sheet and the machines accept $1 bills.

MARVEL SUPER HERO ISLAND

It's still a comic book world, but this one is considerably darker and a lot scarier than the one you just left. Here, in a glitzy but gritty cityscape that bears some resemblance to Manhattan, Good is locked in a never ending battle with Evil. As in the Marvel comics, the facades of the brightly colored buildings bear simple declarative signs: Bank, News, Store, Fruit. The smaller food kiosks have names like Chomp and Krunch. Adding to the fun, enormous cutouts of your favorite Marvel characters loom overhead.

Those from another planet may not know that Marvel is the name of a comic book company that revolutionized the industry way back in the sixties with a series of titles showcasing a bizarre array of super heroes whose psychological quirks were as intriguing as their ingeniously conceived superhuman powers. As might be expected, this cast of characters offers rich inspiration for some of the most intense thrill rides ever created.

After the extensive theme-ing of the other islands, Marvel Super Hero Island can seem a little, well, flat. Some people suspect, erroneously, that Universal was cutting corners or had run out of money when it came to designing this section of the park. Not at all. Marvel Super Hero Island is, in fact, a brilliant evocation in three-dimensions of the visual style of the comic books that inspired it. Marvel used strong colors and simple geometric shapes to create a futuristic cityscape with an Art Deco flavor. Against this purposely flat backdrop, they arrayed their extravagantly muscled and lovingly sculpted heroes. Marvel Comics had a profound effect on American visual design, not to mention its effect on contemporary notions of the body beautiful.

But enough art history. What you've come here for are the thrill rides and Marvel Super Hero Island has some of the best examples of the genre you're likely to find in Central Florida.

The Amazing Adventures of Spider-Man

Rating:	★ ★ ★ ★ ★
Type:	3-D motion simulator ride
Time:	4.5 minutes
Kelly says:	The new state-of-the-art in a new category of thrill ride

Universal's publicity powerhouse trumpets this as "the next threshold attraction," the one that takes theme park entertainment to a new level, just as *Back to The Future. . . The Ride* and *T2* did when they opened.

Visitors step into the offices of the "Daily Bugle" only to discover that the evil villain Dr. Octopus and his Sinister Syndicate have used an antigravity gun to make off with the Statue of Liberty and other famous landmarks as part of a plot to bring the New York City to its knees. Since cub reporter Peter Parker and all the rest of the staff are mysteriously absent, crusty editor J. Jonah Jameson drafts his hapless guests into a civilian force with the mission of tracking down the evildoers and getting the scoop on their nefarious doings. Guests board special 12-passenger vehicles and set off through the streets of the city, where they discover Spidey is already on the case. What ensues is a harrowing high-speed chase enhanced through a variety of heart-stopping special effects.

The vehicles are simulators, much like the ones in *Back To The Future*. Underneath they have six hydraulically operated stalks that can be used to simulate virtually any kind of motion. But these cars can also move through space and they do, along tracks that allow for 360 degrees of rotation. The combination of forward motion, rotation, and simulator technology creates startling sensations never before possible.

Further heightening the experience is the environment through which the cars move. This is the world of Marvel comics sprung vividly to life and startlingly real. Intermixed with the solid set elements (that include enormous chunks of a cut up Statue of Liberty) are almost undetectable screens on which three-dimensional films are projected to add an extra measure of depth and excitement: both villains and heroes seem to leap directly at you. At several points, various villains and Spidey himself drop onto the hood of the vehicle with a thud and a jolt. They are insubstantial three-dimensional cartoons, of course, but the effect is amazingly real.

As your ill-fated journey proceeds, it is your bad luck to keep interrupting the evildoers at awkward moments and they do their utmost to destroy you, with deadly bursts of electricity, walls of flame, and deluges of water. They narrowly miss each time, sending your vehicle spinning and tumbling to its next close encounter with doom.

Finally you are caught in the irresistible force of an antigravity ray that sucks the vehicle ever upward as Spider-Man struggles valiantly to save you. The ride culminates with a 400-foot drop through the cartoon canyons of New York to almost certain death on the streets below. It's quite a ride.

The big question, of course, is "Is *Spider-Man* a better ride than *Back To The Future*?" Personally, I find *Back To The Future* far more intense, although some people disagree. I also find that the story line in *Back To The Future* is a lot clearer, which adds to the excitement. The *Spider-Man* "plot" is almost impossible to follow, except in broad outline, unless you ride several times and pay very close attention. And the pre-ride buildup in the queue line doesn't help much; often it is completely drowned out by the large and chattering crowds. *Back To The Future* has the advantage of isolating small groups of riders to explain the setup to them.

In fairness, however, it's something of an apples and oranges comparison. The track on which the *Spider-Man* vehicles ride, the 3-D effects, and the claustrophobia of the narrow streets and subterranean tunnels of a nightmare New York all add forms of excitement which *Back To The Future* can't provide. *Spider-Man* is very different and very much its own experience. Any way you slice it, and despite some minor carping on my part, it still adds up to another 5-star attraction.

The best seats in the house. Logically, the first of the three rows in the vehicle should be the best, since you don't have the heads of fellow passengers in your field of vision. Yet I find the other rows, because they are slightly farther from the screens, provide better 3-D effects.

Tip: For a post-ride chuckle, pause to read the newspaper at the ride's exit. Few people do.

Doctor Doom's Fearfall

Rating: ★ ★ ★ ★
Type: A free-fall ride with oomph
Time: 30 seconds
Kelly says: Gulp!

Near the Bugle building is Doom Alley, a part of town that has been completely taken over by the bad guys of the Sinister Syndicate: Dr. Octopus, The Hobgoblin, and The Lizard. Here the archfiend Doctor Doom has secreted his Fear Sucking Machine, in which he uses innocent, unsuspecting victims (that's you in case you hadn't guessed) to create the Fear Juice with which he hopes to finally vanquish the Fantastic Four.

The payoff is a fiendish twist on the freefall rides that have long been a staple of amusement parks and which were artfully updated in Disney's *Tower of Terror*. But whereas those rides take you up slowly and drop you, *Doctor Doom*, in the true Universal spirit, takes things to a whole new level.

Sixteen victims, I mean passengers, are strapped into seats in small four-person chambers. Only then do they learn the hideous fate Doctor Doom has in store for them as the chamber fills with smoke and the Doctor's eyes glow a menacing green. Suddenly they are shot upward 150 feet at a force of four G's. There is a heart-flipping moment of weightlessness before the vehicles drop back, bouncing a few times before returning to terra firma.

Most people scream on freefall rides, but this one happens so quickly (less than 30 seconds) and registers such a shock that many riders won't remember to scream until the ride is over.

The Incredible Hulk Coaster

Rating: ★ ★ ★ ★ ★
Type: Steel coaster
Time: 1.5 minutes
Kelly says: Aaaargh!

In the scientific complex where Bruce Banner, a.k.a. the Incredible Hulk, has his laboratories, you can learn all about the nasty effects of overexposure to gamma radiation. No, it's not more edutainment, it's the warm-up for another knock-your-socks-off roller coaster.

In a high-energy video pre-ride show, you learn that you can help Bruce reverse the unfortunate effects that have so complicated his life. All you have to do is climb into this little chamber which is, in fact, a 32-seat roller coaster. This is no ordinary roller coaster, however, where you have to wait agonizing seconds while the car climbs to the top of the first drop. It seems to get off to a fairly normal start, slowly climbing a steep incline, but thanks to an energizing burst of gamma rays you are shot at one G 150 feet upwards, going from a near standstill to 42 miles an hour. From there it's all downhill so to speak as you swing into a zero-G roll and speed toward the surface of the lagoon at 58 miles per hour. This is no water ride though, so you whip into a cobra roll before being lofted upwards once more through the highest (109 feet) inversion ever built. After that it's under a bridge — on which earthbound (i.e. "sane") people are enjoying your terror — through a total of seven inversions and two subterranean trenches before you come to a rest, hoping desperately that your exertions have, indeed, helped Bruce out of his pickle.

Here's an interesting note for the technically minded: The initial thrust of this ride consumes so much power that, if the needed electricity were drawn directly from Orlando's electric supply, lights across town would dim every time a new coaster was launched. So Universal draws power at a steady rate from the city's power grid and stores it in a huge flywheel hidden in the greenish building by the Inland Sea labeled "Power Supply." This enables them to get the power they need for that first heart-stopping effect without inconveniencing their neighbors.

Tip: This can be a very discombobulating experience. If you feel a bit weak in the knees as you step from the ride vehicle, look for the Baby Swap area on your right. Here you can sit down in air-conditioned comfort for a few minutes to regain your composure before striding out pridefully into the Florida sun.

Note: Lockers are provided near the entrance for stowing excess or loose gear. The first 45 or 75 minutes are free with a $2 charge levied for each additional half hour. Since these lockers are electronic, the terms of rental can be changed at will and may be different when you visit.

And on your way out, don't forget to check out the photo of your adventure. The high-speed cameras capture each of the eight rows of the coaster as it zooms past, so one of the frames is likely to have a good shot of you. If you'd like to have a record of your triumph over (or surrender to) terror, it'll set you back $16 for a framed 8x10 or $19 for two 5x7s.

Storm Force Accelatron

Rating: ★ ★ ★
Type: Spinning cup ride
Time: 1.5 minutes
Kelly says: A standard amusement park ride

Tucked behind the Hulk coaster and Cafe 4, under a futuristic purple and blue dome, is this Marvelized version of a fairly standard amusement park ride. A large circular spinning platform contains four smaller circles that spin independently. Each of these small circles holds three cup-like cars that also spin independently. When the whole thing gets up to speed, there are three levels of spin. An added bit of oomph comes from the circular control in the center of each car that allows the riders to control just how fast their car spins.

The cars are designed to hold four adults but with kids aboard the number can increase; I am told the record is eight passengers in a car. The spin control works quite well and with some vigorous turning you can add quite a bit of momentum to your brief spin cycle whirl. Even if you skip the ride, it's worth strolling back here to take a peek at the back end of Hulk.

Tip: To get the full effect of the strobe lights that represent Storm's lightning, ride this one at night.

And all the rest...

Kingpin's Arcade, I am forced to admit, seems less out of place here than its equivalents elsewhere. That's because the world of video games is, after all, a comic book world and some of the machines in here represent the current state of the art in this genre. The games run on tokens, which you can obtain from a vending machine. $1 gives you 4 tokens, $5 nets you 20, $10 gets you 40, and $20 gets you 80. No refunds are given so you're forced to use them all, which might not be all that much of a challenge since some of the fancier games require six tokens. If you ride *Doctor Doom's Fearfall*, you will exit through this incredibly loud emporium. For your added convenience, a hole has been thoughtfully blasted into the wall here to give you access to Cafe 4, and vice versa.

Several times a day, according to a schedule listed in the Attraction & Show Times insert, there is a **Meet and Greet** in the plaza opposite the entrance to the *Spider-Man* ride. Several characters from the X-Men comics — Rogue, Storm, and Wolverine — appear to give autographs and pose photogenically with your kids. Unlike the costumed cartoon characters encountered elsewhere, these heroes will actually talk to you.

Eating in Marvel Super Hero Island

In keeping with the style of Marvel Comics, the food choices here are pared down and straightforward. There are two cafeteria-like restaurants and a few outdoor stands serving very limited menus of snacks and sweets.

Cafe 4

What:	Italian food cafeteria style
Where:	Straight ahead as you come from Port of Entry
Price Range:	$ - $$

That huge gizmo that dominates the center of Cafe 4 and looks like a gigantic prop from a laboratory in a sci-fi movie beams colorful floating images of the Fantastic Four onto the curved ceiling above. The colorful mural behind the gizmo serves as a fitting welcome to this spacious, ultramodern cafeteria.

Judging by the menu, the Fantastic Four must be Italian food fans. Personal sized pizzas are about $7. The BBQ chicken and Boursin pizza is especially tasty. You'll also find standard pasta dishes for about $7 and subs and hoagies for about $6. A spaghetti meal for kids 11 and under is $6 and includes breadsticks, fruit, and a small beverage. Minestrone soup and Caesar salads round out the Italian theme. Desserts are $2 to $4. Draft beer is served here along with the usual array of soft drinks.

There's plenty of indoor seating but it can get loud when it's filled with noisy kids. There's also a fair amount of outdoor seating that can also get loud because of the screams from *Incredible Hulk* riders. A hole torn in the wall leads to the video game arcade (see above).

Captain America Diner

What: All-American diner fare
Where: Near *Spider-Man*
Price Range: $ - $$

The food here is perfectly themed: All-American Burgers and Super Hero Sides. The burgers, which are pretty good actually, range from about $6 to $7 and a "price-buster combo" offers a cheeseburger, "frings," and a medium soda for under $9. Frings, by the way, are a combination of French fries and fried onion rings. Chicken fingers and sandwiches are $7.

Any diner worth its salt should serve milk shakes and this one does, chocolate and vanilla for plus or minus $3. For dessert there is Homemade Apple Pie for under $3; add a buck and you get it a la mode.

The decor is techno-modern, with steel seats and metal benches in the booths and huge mural-like depictions of characters from the Captain America comics looming overhead. There are two circular dining areas with tall walls of windows looking out to the Great Inland Sea. A small outdoor seating area is right on the Sea and makes a great place to eat, if you don't mind the occasional freeloading bird. These seats not only look out to the Lost Continent but also offer one of the best vantage points for watching riders on *Hulk*.

Chill Ice Cream

What: Walk-up stand
Where: Near the entrance to Toon Lagoon
Price Range: $

The big sign that says "Ice Cream" is self-explanatory. A Deep Freeze Sundae is under $5 and Ice Cap Cake Cones are under $3. Root beer floats and waffle cones are under $4. Soft drinks are also served here.

Frozen Ice

What: Walk-up stand
Where: Near the entrance to *Spider-Man*
Price Range: $

"Island Coolers" are the stock in trade of this walk-up counter. They are available only in nonalcoholic versions ($3 and $3.50) and flavors include Coca Cola, raspberry, cherry, and Sprite. Regular soft drinks are also served.

Fruit

What: Walk-up stand
Where: Across from *Spider-Man*
Price Range: $

Fresh fruit cups are $3 here and individual pieces of fruit, apples and the like, are $1, but mostly they serve soft drinks and juices at the usual prices.

Cotton Candy

What: Walk-up stand
Where: Across from Cafe 4
Price Range: $

This dome-shaped building topped by a huge cutout of the Silver Surfer serves up exactly what the name implies for about $3. Cinnamon churros, a Mexican fried pastry, are about $2, and there are soft drinks to wash it all down.

Shopping in Marvel Super Hero Island

Comics Shop

Here's your chance to fill in that unfortunate gap in your literary education by immersing yourself in the Marvel universe. Colorful wall displays feature the last two or three issues of virtually every title in the Marvel comic line. You can also get large format paperback collections and novelizations based on popular characters. For collectors without the big bucks needed to acquire the real thing, there are hardbound, full-color volumes of the first ten issues of The Avengers, X-Men, Spider-Man, and other popular titles ($35 to $50). Paperbound collections in black and white are $15. T-shirts, videos, model kits, and the standard Marvel souvenirs round out the offerings here.

Oakley

This vest-pocket shop sells high-end sunglasses and watches, most of them bearing the ultra-hip Oakley brand for $75 to $400. (There's a price to be paid for being on the cutting edge of fashion.) They also offer shoes and backpacks just in case you have any money left.

Spider-Man Shop

You can't miss this one unless you're foolish enough to skip the *Spider-Man* ride. (If you're entering from the street, look for the "5 & Dime" sign.) T-shirts form the bulk of the merchandise on display with prices ranging from $16 to $26; nice polo shirts are $32 and sweats are $30 to $45. Best of all, are the striking dress shirts with huge, colorful Spidey figures ($48). Guaranteed to appeal to the adolescent male sensibility are the Marvel boxer shorts adorned with images of a superhero plus one bold word, along the lines of "Incredible" or "Amazing" ($16). Those who really identify with Spidey can pick up a Spider-Man costume for $48 ($36 for kids). You can also pick up some original art signed by Stan Lee for astronomical prices, or settle for something from the vast collection of mugs, action figures, and other small items.

The Marvel Alternaverse Store

This shop, identified on the facade simply as "Store," is the largest on the island and is sort of a Giorgio Armani boutique for 13-year-old boys. In other words, this is Marvel t-shirt central, and if you're into this sort of thing, the assortment is fabulous. Prices range from $16 to $26 for the really colorful homages to Spider-Man and Captain America.

For the well-to-do kid, there are figurines (up to $300), signed posters, and even animation cels from Marvel cartoons ($850). More affordable are videos, mugs in the shape of the heads of various Marvel characters ($5), and toys and action figures for younger kids.

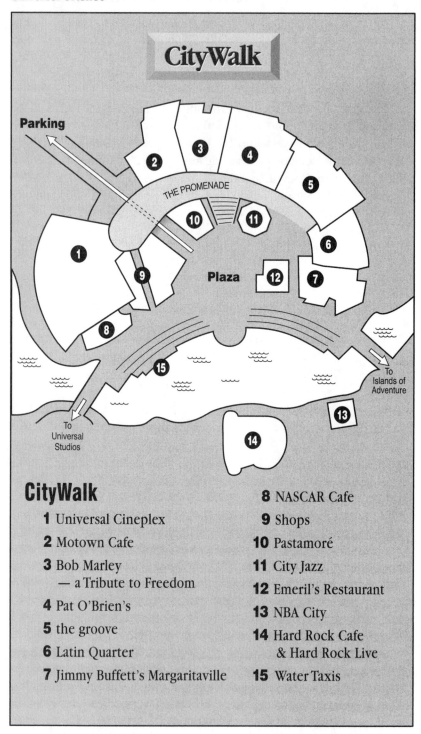

CityWalk

1 Universal Cineplex	**8** NASCAR Cafe
2 Motown Cafe	**9** Shops
3 Bob Marley — a Tribute to Freedom	**10** Pastamoré
4 Pat O'Brien's	**11** City Jazz
5 the groove	**12** Emeril's Restaurant
6 Latin Quarter	**13** NBA City
7 Jimmy Buffett's Margaritaville	**14** Hard Rock Cafe & Hard Rock Live
	15 Water Taxis

CHAPTER FOUR:

CityWalk

"Get a nightlife!" the ad campaign advises and this is most definitely the place to do that. CityWalk is a happening enclave of heavily themed restaurants, nightclubs, shops, and movie theaters that rocks long after the nearby theme parks have closed up for the night. Cynics might say it is Universal's attempt to mimic Pleasure Island and Downtown Disney. But then again other cynics might point out that Pleasure Island was an attempt to mimic Orlando's original sophisticated adult entertainment venue, Church Street Station. Who cares? The bottom line is Orlando has yet another top-notch entertainment district to satisfy its visitors' seemingly bottomless appetite for things to do.

Orientation

The layout and setting of CityWalk is ingenious. It is a 30-acre lozenge-shaped area plopped right down between Universal Studios Florida and Islands of Adventure. It is impossible to get from your car to either of the parks, or from one park to the other, without passing through CityWalk. On top of that a river runs through it — or rather a man-made waterway that separates most of CityWalk from the theme parks and links CityWalk to the Hard Rock and Portofino Bay Hotels, and the Royal Pacific Resort.

Most of the buildings in CityWalk are arrayed along the perimeter closest to the parking structures, facing in towards the waterway. To mask the backs of the buildings and their service areas, the park's designers created an immense steel latticework that curves up and over CityWalk. The idea was that climbing vines and other plants would cover it in a camouflaging green cocoon. So far it hasn't worked. Mostly what you see is the latticework.

There are three major streets, a straight avenue that leads from the parking structures, a curving boulevard that leads from Universal Studios to Islands of Adventure near the waterway, and the Promenade that runs past the major nightclubs. Smaller streets wind between CityWalk's few freestanding buildings; one of these is "Lombard Street," a zigzag stairway that descends from the upper exit of the Cineplex to the waterway. Along the waterway runs an esplanade in the middle of which is an outdoor performance space for special concerts and other events. Also along this esplanade is a dock where you can pick up an elegant complimentary motor launch for the short trip to the resort hotels.

Smack dab in the middle of CityWalk is a large open space called simply the Plaza. On one side, a series of grass and stone platforms descends toward the water, forming a seating area for the performance space at water's edge. On the other, a stage sits over a sloping, waterfall-like fountain. Here you are likely to encounter a team of young comedians who kibitz with the crowd, lure folks on stage for what might be called "stupid guest tricks," and keep up a lively patter about the many attractions and special events CityWalk has to offer. They also hand out coupons that offer two-for-one drinks and free appetizers at various clubs and restaurants. From time to time you may see other off-the-wall entertainers — jugglers, stilt-walkers, and the like — roaming the grounds spreading smiles and good cheer.

Also in the Plaza is a street-level "fountain" consisting of several rows of hidden water jets that send up columns of water of various heights, at various times, in various patterns. It is seldom without a crowd of young kids and adults old enough to know better dodging and weaving through its liquid columns getting thoroughly drenched.

With one exception, the nightclubs in CityWalk are located along the Promenade, which rises gradually from Plaza level, curving behind the Plaza, to the upper exit from the Cineplex. This clever arrangement makes the nightclub area a separate and easily policed enclave within an enclave. The exception is Hard Rock Live (a concert hall more than a nightclub), which is connected to the Hard Rock Cafe and lies across the waterway along the short walk leading from the gates of Universal Studios Florida to those of Islands of Adventure.

Getting Information

There are a number of ways to get information about what's going on at CityWalk prior to your visit. On the Internet, you can get information on upcoming events by visiting www.citywalkorlando.com. CityWalk advertises prominently in the *Orlando Sentinel*'s Friday Calendar section, which also carries listings of many CityWalk entertainment events. The main City-

Walk number for "reservations and additional information" is (407) 224-3663. You can also dial (407) 363-8000 and follow the prompts through an extensive inventory of recorded announcements about CityWalk's various restaurants and clubs.

Arriving at CityWalk

You arrive at CityWalk just as you would arrive for a visit to the theme parks. You park in the same parking structures and pay the same parking fee (see *Chapter One*). If you arrive after 6:00 p.m., parking will be **free**. If you are arriving just for lunch and plan to stay for less than two hours, valet parking is free with restaurant validation (see below).

You enter CityWalk itself down a long broad avenue that passes by the Cineplex on your right and Motown Cafe on your left (see map, page 164). That bridge you pass under is the Promenade and it leads from the upper exit of the Cineplex past CityWalk's string of nightclubs. An escalator to the bridge is available if you just can't wait.

Note: If you are arriving by motor launch from one of the resort hotels, you will disembark at a dock just below the NASCAR Cafe.

Also by the bridge and the escalator is a kiosk called **Dining Reservations and CityWalk Information**. Here you can peruse menus of the various CityWalk restaurants, but despite the name you can't really make reservations for CityWalk restaurants except for Emeril's (see below). You *can* make priority seating requests, however, (a process described below) and get pretty decent advice on how to plan your evening. Two brochures worth picking up here are **CityGuide**, a colorful if hard to read map of the enclave and **CityMonth**, an extremely helpful calendar of events at the various clubs. You can also pick up maps and show schedules for the two theme parks here, although they sometimes run out.

Just past the bridge, on your left, you will see the Guest Services window; come here with questions and problems and to purchase tickets. A short walk brings you to the Plaza, CityWalk's broad open center. From here you proceed straight ahead to Islands of Adventure, turn right to head to Universal Studios Florida, or turn left to make your way to the Promenade and the nightclubs.

The Price of Admission

Officially, there is no admission to CityWalk, but that's only partially true. First, if you are coming to Universal Orlando just to visit CityWalk, there's the parking fee to consider — unless, of course, you arrive after 6:00 p.m., which is the perfect time to begin a visit to what is primarily a nighttime attraction. More importantly, CityWalk's biggest draws, the nightclubs, all levy a $5 cover charge for the live evening entertainment. The exception is The Latin Quarter, which charges anywhere from $5 to $10 depending on a variety of factors that I have yet to decipher. Hard Rock Cafe never charges a cover, even when there's entertainment, and Hard Rock Live is not really a nightclub, so cover charges don't apply there. Of course, the cover charge at a given club could rise dramatically depending on the caliber (or at least the presumed popularity) of the performers inside. If Brittney Spears ever plays CityWalk, all bets are off. The Cineplex also charges admission.

If you are coming simply to enjoy the pleasures of CityWalk, you have a choice of paying each cover or admission charge individually or purchasing a one-day **CityWalk Party Pass**, which is sort of an "open sesame" to all the entertainment venues except Hard Rock Live, which always charges its own, separate admission. It costs $9.49, including tax; annual passholders receive a 20% discount. If you have purchased a FlexTicket or a two- or three-day pass to the theme parks (a very likely scenario), then you already have seven consecutive days of access to CityWalk's clubs, starting on the day you first use your ticket or pass.

Be aware that the Party Pass will not be honored at clubs with special events and the Latin Quarter sometimes levies an additional cover charge on Party Pass holders.

To purchase your Party Pass, turn left at the Plaza and look for the box office windows outside the groove discotheque. If these windows are closed, check with the Guest Services window between the Endangered Species store and the Pastamoré Market Cafe.

From time to time, CityWalk will make combination offers such as the **Meal and Party Deal** ($18 including tax), which combines a meal at your choice of CityWalk restaurants (except Emeril's) and the Party Pass. This would be a better deal if the selection of entrees offered wasn't so limited and so boring; cheeseburgers and lasagna is about as exciting as it gets. Before you go for this deal, remember that many entertainment venues serve food, some of it quite good. The **Meal and Movie Deal** ($18 including tax) combines the same simple meals with a movie and strikes me as an even less attractive proposition. Offers like this may or may not be available when you visit. There is also a **Movie Plus Party Pass** ($12.77 including tax), which combines the standard Party Pass with a movie at the Cineplex. With this deal the incremental cost of a flick is just $3.28.

What's The Best Price?

If you purchased a multi-day theme park pass, then price is not a consideration. Go. Boogie. Enjoy. Otherwise, you may want to spend a few moments considering your options. If you plan on visiting most, if not all, of the clubs on a single night, the Party Pass is a fabulous deal. Personally, I think that's insane. But even if you only visit two, the Party Pass is a good deal.

However, be aware that it is possible to visit two clubs and pay only one cover charge. It works like this: The cover charge clicks in at a certain hour, which varies from venue to venue, but they don't go around from table to table to collect the cover from those already in the club. So you could arrive at, say, Marley's half an hour before the cover takes effect, grab a good seat and catch the first show. Then you could move on to, say, CityJazz, paying the $5 cover there. If you call it a night then, you've only spent $5 in cover charges and saved a little money.

On the other hand, the additional cost of a Party Pass is so small that why not go for it, at least once? That way you can satisfy your morbid curiosity about clubs you otherwise wouldn't try. And who knows? You might discover a place you really love.

Good Things To Know About . . .

Discounts

Your Universal Orlando Annual Pass is good for a 20% discount for up to four people on the CityWalk Party Pass. Your Annual Pass also may get you a 10% discount on food and beverages at select full-service restaurants and clubs from Sunday through Thursday. I say "may" because discount policies change frequently. Members of the American Automobile Association (AAA) may be eligible for some discounts in CityWalk, most likely at the shops. In fact, which card gets what discount where is subject to constant change, so the best policy for the traveling tightwad is to ask about discounts every time you have to pay for something.

Drinking

The legal drinking age in Florida is 21 and the law is strictly enforced in CityWalk. The official policy is to "card" (i.e. ask for identification) anyone who appears under 30. So if you fall into this category make sure to bring along a photo ID such as a driver's license or passport to prove your age. Once you've passed muster, your server will attach a plastic bracelet to your wrist, which absolves you from producing identification for the rest of the evening.

Alcoholic beverages are sold quite openly on the streets of CityWalk and from walk-up stands at the various clubs along the Promenade. To prevent those over 21 from purchasing drinks for underage friends, a standard policy is to sell one drink per person. Just to make sure, CityWalk maintains a very visible security presence (see below).

First Aid

And speaking of drinking, if you fall down and injure yourself, or have another health problem, there is a first aid station located near Guest Services. Just follow the passage to the restrooms and look for the door at the end of the passage.

Happy Hour

Most restaurants and clubs in CityWalk have a generous happy hour that runs from 3:00 to 7:00 p.m. when draft beers are $1.50 and well drinks $2. NASCAR Cafe frequently has a happy hour that runs all day. The bar in Cigarz, however, does not offer a happy hour.

Money

There is an ATM on your left as you enter CityWalk, near the Guest Services window. There is another just outside the upper exit from the Cineplex, near Cigarz.

Private Parties

Most of CityWalk's restaurants have facilities for private parties. The central number for information is (407) 224-CITY (2489).

Reservations

Of the restaurants and nightclubs, only Emeril's officially accepts (indeed, demands) reservations, which can be made up to six months in advance by calling (407) 224-2424 or faxing (407) 224-2525. Most others officially operate on a first-come, first-served basis. You may have to stand on line for admittance but some restaurants take your name and give you a silent pager (it vibrates) to alert you when your table is ready.

However, there is a way around this no-reservations policy. If you dial (407) 224-3663, between 8:00 a.m. and 4:00 p.m. on the day you wish to dine, you will reach the "Priority Seating Request Line." You can also make a request at the information kiosk you see when you enter CityWalk. Priority seating is available at Motown, Pastamoré, Hard Rock Cafe, Margaritaville, and when it's busy, Bob Marley's and Pat O'Brien's.

Note: If you are a guest at a Universal Orlando resort hotel, you can make a priority seating request through the concierge desk.

Priority seating is subtly different from a reservation. A reservation, in theory, guarantees you a seat at the specified hour, because the maitre d' holds it for you. Priority seating, on the other hand, carries no such guarantee. It means that the restaurant will give you the first table that will accommodate your party that becomes available at or after the time you requested.

That can mean immediate seating or a long wait; still, a priority seating request should make the wait less lengthy than it would be without it.

Restrooms

Most restrooms are inside the restaurants and nightclubs. You'll find "public" restrooms in CityWalk tucked away down corridors next to Guest Services and near The Latin Quarter on the Promenade.

Security

CityWalk's security is so pervasive and so visible that some people might wonder if there's something to be worried about. In addition to the in-house security staff with their white shirts emblazoned with the word "SECURITY," you will see armed members of the Orlando police force. What you won't see are the undercover security personnel that mingle with the crowds. The primary mission of all these security elements is to prevent any abuse of state liquor laws. For example, while you can stroll around CityWalk with your beer or cocktail, you are not allowed to carry it back to your car or into the parks.

Valet Parking and Validation

Most restaurants will validate your valet parking ticket during lunch hour (11:00 a.m. to 2:00 p.m. Monday through Friday only). A two-hour stay is free. Emeril's validates anytime including Saturdays and dinner.

Volume

The overall sound level at CityWalk ranges from ear-piercing to head-splitting. This is equally true for the outdoor entertainment and the various clubs. Sometimes, of course, damaging decibels are part of the "art," as in the more antisocial veins of rock and roll. In other cases, the choice seems peculiar. An eleven-piece orchestra in the Latin Quarter or just about any group in the intimate confines of CityJazz would scarcely seem to require any amplification. Someone clearly disagrees and the volume is regularly pumped up past the threshold of pain.

If you're hard of hearing you may find this a thoughtful gesture. If you're a teenager who thinks that losing your hearing is a sacred rite of passage, you'll love it. If you're a liability lawyer, you'll probably start gathering names and addresses for a class action suit. If you're a reasonably normal adult, however, you may find the sound level so painful that enjoying CityWalk will be impossible. I have seen people fleeing the nightclubs with their fingers in their ears, and staffers in the entertainment venues admit that they get complaints.

In fairness, I should note that excessive volume is not invariably a problem. I have enjoyed entertainment at Bob Marley's, Pat O'Brien's, Margaritaville, and City Jazz that, while loud, was not painful. However, if you have any doubts about your ability to withstand an all-out aural assault, pack earplugs. And if you want to enjoy a meal at one of the restaurants that features live entertainment, especially if you wish to carry on a conversation, do so before the entertainment begins.

The Talk of the Town

Just as the theme parks have their five-star attractions, there are some very special things in CityWalk. I have not attempted a star rating system for CityWalk but instead offer this highly subjective list of my personal favorites.

Best food. Emeril's has to be the choice here with the Latin Quarter running an extremely close second.

Best bar. The funky bar at the back of Cigarz, a cigar shop near the upper exit of the Cineplex is hip and hidden. The bar at Hard Rock Cafe with its spinning Caddy takes second prize.

Best food value. When you factor in what you pay for what you get, Pat O'Brien's comes out on top, with the Latin Quarter again running a very close second.

Best place to take the kids. The NASCAR Cafe, with the Hard Rock Cafe the runner-up.

Friendliest service. NBA City, with NASCAR Cafe the runner-up.

Best burgers. The Hard Rock Cafe. Have yours with a chocolate milk shake.

Best dessert. The Latin Quarter's Crepas Rellenas wins this prize, with Emeril's elaborate creations the clear second choice.

Best for the midnight munchies. Finding food after midnight is not always possible, but if Pat O'Brien's is serving late, that's the clear winner. Otherwise, check out the "grazing" menu at Jimmy Buffett's.

Most romantic. If you're idea of "romantic" is letting your date know you're dropping a bundle on the meal, then Emeril's is the place for you. Otherwise, you'll have to travel to Delfino Riviera at the Portofino Bay Hotel for truly romantic dining.

Most fun. Jimmy Buffett's Margaritaville, with its wild and wacky decor and exploding volcano, wins the prize here.

Best decor. The Hard Rock Cafe. Never has the teenage wasteland looked so elegant.

Coolest. The exquisitely designed CityJazz is one of the hippest, most sophisticated rooms I've seen in a long time.

Universal Cineplex

This is the mall multiplex writ large and it's hard to miss because it's the first thing you see on your right as you arrive from the parking lots. Given its 4,800 seats in 20 theaters on two stories, it's unlikely you have anything quite like it at home.

The soaring lobby is decorated with giant black and white banners depicting cinema heartthrobs, and escalators whisk you past them to the nine theaters upstairs. The theaters range in size from an intimate 150 seats to nearly 600. Unfortunately, 20 theaters does not mean 20 films. Expect the usual assortment of first-run features with the very latest releases playing in multiple theaters and, on weekends, midnight screenings of cult favorites. If you live in or near any moderately sized city in the United States, chances are all the films playing at the Cineplex are playing back home; it's just that here they're all under one roof. Of course, all the theaters here have stadium seating with plush high-backed seats that rock gently, and the screens are about twice the size of those you are probably used to. Every theater is also equipped with Sony Dynamic Digital Sound (SDDS), touted as "the most advanced digital cinema sound system in the marketplace today." So all in all, catching a movie here is a viable option for a rainy Florida afternoon.

Admission for adults is $7.25 (tax included) for evening shows. Bargain matinees (all shows that start before 6 p.m.) are $5.25, as are tickets for seniors (62+) and students (any age, with school ID) at all times. Children 2 to 11, pay $4.25 at all times. Annual Pass holders get a $1.25 discount in the evenings.

In addition to the regular box office windows, there are three vending machines to your right that allow you to skip the line and purchase tickets, at no extra charge, using your credit card. You can book and pay for tickets over the phone, with a credit card, by calling (407) 354-5998 and using the automated system; there is a 75 cents service charge per ticket. More detailed information can be obtained from a human being by calling (407) 354-3374.

You can check the Cineplex's current schedule of films on the Internet at www.enjoytheshow.com/locations/fl. If Loews is running any special events or promotions at the theaters, as they do from time to time, the web site should have that information, too.

Don't worry about going hungry while you watch. There is the usual array of soft drinks, popcorn, and candy, all at inflated prices. More interesting are the mini-pizzas, nachos, and hot fudge sundaes. There's even a coffee bar if you crave a latte and another bar serving up beer and wine coolers.

Tip: If you are coming to see a movie before 6:00 p.m. you will have to pay for parking. But if you show your parking stub at the concession stand, they will deduct up to $8 from the cost of your food and drink purchases.

A major disappointment, in my view, is the lack of a "revival house" — a theater dedicated to showing classic films. Since Universal Studios produced films by Mae West, W.C. Fields, and the Marx Brothers, among many other greats, this would be a logical addition to the Cineplex. It would also be a terrific way for Universal to help educate the next generation of filmmakers who have precious few opportunities to see the great films of the past as they were meant to be seen, on the large screen, in the dark, with an audience.

Tip: You may want to exit on the upper level, even if you are seeing a film on the Cineplex's bottom level. From there you can either descend Lombard Street, a narrow zigzag street lined with shops, or stroll along the sloping Promenade, home to City Walk's row of restaurants and nightclubs.

Restaurants at CityWalk

I make a distinction between City Walk restaurants and City Walk nightclubs, although some don't. The difference is somewhat hazy in practice, since some restaurants offer terrific entertainment (usually at night, usually with a cover charge) and some nightclubs serve excellent food. The main distinction seems to be that "restaurants" open early in the day and serve full meals, while "nightclubs" open in the late afternoon or early evening and serve only a limited food menu. Among the restaurants, Jimmy Buffett's Margaritaville and Latin Quarter turn into nightclubs, with cover charges, in the evenings. NASCAR Cafe offers the occasional entertainer in its al fresco dining area and NBA City screens great moments in basketball history all day. All the others are strictly dining establishments.

Most restaurants serve the same menu at the same prices all day. The exception is Emeril's. The menus for some — but not all — City Walk restaurants, along with other helpful information, can be found on the Internet at www.citywalkorlando.com.

Hard Rock Cafe

What: American casual cuisine
Where: Across the waterway
Price Range: $$ - $$$
Hours: 11:00 a.m. to midnight (kitchen closes at midnight)
Reservations: None
Web: www.hardrockcafe.com

The huge structure across the water, with the peculiar hodgepodge architecture, the Caddy sticking out of the facade, and the huge electric signs, is the world's largest and busiest Hard Rock Cafe. Those who have visited other Hard Rocks will know what to expect — just expect more of it. For the uninitiated, the Hard Rock Cafe is a celebration of rock and roll history and lifestyle that has become an international marketing and merchandising phenomenon. From its auspicious beginnings in London's Mayfair section, Hard Rock has grown to a mega-chain, with restaurants in virtually any city that has pretensions to world-class status.

The Hard Rock's primary claim to fame is its extensive and ever-growing collection of rock memorabilia that is lovingly and lavishly displayed. As befits the largest Hard Rock in the world, the Orlando outpost has some spectacular mementos, including the actual bus used in the Beatles' film *Magical Mystery Tour*, reportedly, it is the single most expensive piece of rock memorabilia ever purchased. (It sits outside, in front of Hard Rock Live.)

After your meal, take the time to wander about and drink it all in. The staff won't mind; they're used to it. In fact, they run free 30-minute **tours** every half hour from noon till 7:00 p.m. You'll find the tour impressive indeed. There is dark paneling and deep carpeting on the floors and winding wooden staircases. There are rich gold frames on the photos, album covers, gold records, and other memorabilia that fill every inch of wall space. "Rock and roll is here to stay," they like to say. "We've got it screwed to the walls!" Upstairs, take note of the two circular rooms, one at each end, dedicated to the Beatles and the King. There's even an elegant wood-paneled library.

At the heart of the restaurant, downstairs, is a circular bar open to the second level. A magnificent 1961 pink Cadillac convertible spins lazily over the bar and above that is a splendid ceiling mural straight out of some domed chapel at the Vatican. Except that here the saints being serenaded by the angels are all dead rock stars, most of whom died from drug overdoses. To one side is a trio of towering stained glass windows paying homage to Chuck Berry, Elvis Presley, and Jerry Lee Lewis. All in all, this expansive Hard Rock has the look and feel of a very posh and very exclusive men's club — which I suppose is what rock and roll is, after all.

Tip: If your party is small, the bar is an excellent place to eat. If the place is crowded, you may be seated sooner. They serve the full menu there and it gives you an excellent vantage point from which to soak up the ambiance. If the downstairs bar is full, there is another upstairs.

The Hard Rock Cafe is also justly famous for its American roadhouse cuisine, which gives a nod to the black and southern roots of rock. Burgers, barbecue, and steak are the keynotes, with sweet and homey touches like milk shakes, root beer floats, and outrageous sundaes. It's no wonder the place was an instant hit when it opened in the midst of London's culinary desert. The menu also reminds us that, in its heyday, rock's superstars were scarcely more than kids. This is teenybopper comfort food prepared by expert cooks for people who can afford the best.

Probably the heart of the menu is the selection of barbecue dishes ($10 to $16), with the chicken and ribs combo a popular favorite. For those who prefer their barbecue Carolina-style, there is even a pulled pork pig sandwich. A decided step up in sophistication is offered by the "Hard Rock Cafe Specialties" ($10 to $22) like the Texas T-Bone and the succulent Honey Bourbon New York Strip.

Of course, if you're still a teenager at heart, you'll order a burger ($8 to $9). My favorite is the Hickory BBQ Bacon Cheeseburger, but there's also a Veggie Burger to keep Sir Paul happy. The fries that go with them are very good, too. Lighter appetites can be satisfied with one of the appetizers ($6 to $14) or a salad ($7 to $10), while bigger appetites can order a small Caesar salad to go with their entree. But save room for dessert ($4 to $7) because the HRC Hot Fudge Brownie lives up to its fabled reputation. Shakes, malts, and root beer floats are listed with the desserts, but if you want to return to your pre-cholesterol-crisis youth, you'll have one with your burger.

Your meal comes complete with a soundtrack, of course, and the excellent choice of songs leans heavily to the glory days of rock in the late sixties and early seventies. Television monitors dotted around the restaurant, and gold-framed like the rest of the memorabilia, identify the album from which the current track is taken. The volume has been turned up (this is rock and roll, after all) but not so high as to make conversation impossible.

No self-respecting Hard Rock Cafe would be without a shop hawking Hard Rock merchandise, and this one has two. With admirable truth in advertising they are labeled simply **Merchandise** in big bold letters. Believe it or not, the shops sometimes have lines just like the restaurant and they are handled the same way, with a roped-off queue filled with people who can't wait to add another Hard Rock shot glass to their growing collection.

NBA City

What:	American casual cuisine
Where:	Across the waterway
Price Range:	$$ – $$$$
Hours:	Sunday through Thursday 11:00 a.m. to 11:00 p.m.; Friday and Saturday to 11:30 p.m.
Reservations:	None
Web:	www.nbacity.com

This modern mélange of weathered brick, steel, glass, and concrete is almost dwarfed by the statue of a dribbling basketball player that graces its entrance. Both the building and its interior evoke the ambiance and mystique of a classic 1940s-era basketball arena, and devotees of the game will find much to enjoy here.

The two-level dining area, dubbed the CityWalk Cage, seems intimate but it holds nearly 375 people at capacity. The floor is that of a highly polished basketball court filled with tables. In fact, this is a regulation half court that can be cleared of tables and booths so that visiting NBA stars can hold clinics with eager youngsters, while fans watch from the upper level. Two massive projection screens flank the hoop and multiple monitors dot the walls. A constant stream of taped highlights from championship seasons past plays during your meal, with the volume thoughtfully turned up for the hard of hearing. There is the occasional nod towards women's professional basketball, but the emphasis is plainly on the guys.

This is hardly the place for a quiet business discussion or a romantic tête-à-tête. But if your idea of a good time is watching your hoop heroes' finest moments while you drop food into your lap, you'll love it here.

If you'd like some relief from the general din, try the **NBA City Club**, a bar and lounge on the second level, to the front of the building. Its decor is that of a posh sports club with leather chairs and sofas and, if you wish, they will serve your meal here. The NBA City Club also offers an extensive menu of specialty drinks ($6 to $11). The drinks, as well as a modest wine list ($20 to $65), are available in the main restaurant. There is another quiet refuge on the second level, a glassed-in wedge of a dining area but, alas, that is set aside for VIPs and private parties.

The food is good enough to deserve a little attention of its own. The cuisine, which might be described as upscale sports bar, is very good and the portions seem to have been designed to fill up those eight-foot-tall basketball behemoths. Eating a starter and an entree may well force you to skip the scrumptious desserts. Many people will find a starter plenty big enough for a satisfying meal.

Appetizers ($7 to $13) include such standards as chicken wings, bruschetta, and quesadillas. The Pecan Chicken Tenders could make a full meal, with a biting mustard sauce worthy of the name. For the lighter appetite, entree salads ($10 to $14) are offered, with side salads ($4) also available.

The main entrees ($13 to $25) lean heavily to hearty meat and fish dishes like salmon, pork chops and steak. Pastas ($13 to $15) tend to feature chicken and fish with some daily specials priced slightly higher. Sandwich offerings ($8 to $11) include a Reuben and a Cajun-spiced grilled mahi mahi. Ten-inch personal pizzas ($9 to $11) round out the menu. A "Rookie Menu" for kids features a small choice of entrees and a drink for about $7.

Among the desserts ($5 to $7), the star is an NBA City original, the Cinnamon Berries. Exquisitely ripe strawberries are dipped in batter, flash fried, coated in cinnamon sugar, and elegantly displayed in a circle on a bed of vanilla cream filigreed with strawberry sauce; a dollop of vanilla ice cream topped with another fresh strawberry forms the centerpiece. It may sound a little weird but it's delicious.

Tip: The food and drink are only part of the fun here. In fact, you don't have to have a meal to enjoy NBA City. The entrance is flanked by a display of bronze basketballs bearing the handprints of basketball greats. If you've ever wondered why you're not in the NBA, losing your own hand in these massive prints will give you a hint. Inside, before you enter the dining room, you'll find the **NBA City Playground,** a place where you can test your free-throw skills and, if you're good enough, get some fleeting fame on the electronic scoreboard. There is also a shop filled with NBA-branded clothing, personalized jerseys, and novelty items. This area stays open for about an hour after the restaurant stops serving.

Jimmy Buffett's Margaritaville

What:	Casual food with an island flair
Where:	Near the bridge to Islands of Adventure
Price Range:	$$
Cover:	$5 after 9:00 p.m. Thursday through Sunday
Hours:	11:30 a.m. to 2:00 a.m. (full menu until 11:00 p.m., snacks until 1:00 a.m.)
Reservations:	None
Web:	www.margaritaville.com

After crossing the bridge from Islands of Adventure and the NBA Restaurant, this is the first place you encounter in the main section of CityWalk, and a welcoming joint it is. Owned by singing star Jimmy Buffett and reflecting the easygoing themes of his popular songs, Margaritaville is a hymn to the laid-back life of the Parrot Head.

The various sections of the bar-restaurant are decorated to reflect Jimmy's various interests and the songs he wrote about them. The Volcano Bar answers once and for all the question, "Where you gonna go when the volcano blows?" Every 45 minutes or so the volcano that tops the bar rumbles ominously to life and spews out bubbling margarita mix that cascades down the slopes into a huge blender on the bar.

In the restaurant section, the booths are styled to evoke the back end of a fishing boat. Look up and you'll see a model of the Hemisphere Dancer, Jimmy's amphibious flying boat. Huge whales and hammerheads "swimming" overhead decorate another bar section. Outside, facing Islands of Adventure, is a verandah seating area that frequently features its own entertainment. Buffett fans will enjoy spotting the insider references scattered through the decor while others will be having too much fun to care.

The "Floribbean" cuisine draws its inspiration from all aspects of

Buffett's life story, from his Gulf Shore roots to his Caribbean island-hopping. The food also reflects the atmosphere of the ultra-casual off-the-beaten-track island bars where Buffett used to perform and chow down.

There's a heavy emphasis on fresh seafood and the conch chowder ($4) is quite good. Those who are serious about their food will probably find their best choice the ever-changing Catch of the Day, prepared to order. The rest of the menu runs heavily to salads, sandwiches, and junk food (in the best possible sense of the term). There are nachos, conch fritters (super!), and fried calamari, and the servings are generous to a fault. Prices are moderate and only a couple of choices are over $15.

I found that the spicy Louisiana-inspired dishes fare best. For those who like their food extra spicy, a selection of Caribbean hot sauces is available. I looked forward to sampling the Cheeseburger in Paradise ($8) but found it to be merely a large but otherwise undistinguished example of the genre. Far better is the Shrimp Cobb Salad ($11) which appears on the menu as a special when they have all the ingredients on hand. There's good news on the desserts ($5 to $6). The key lime pie is a winner and the Chocolate Banana Bread Pudding is to die for.

Beer drinkers will appreciate the wide selection of premium bottled brews (about $4). For those who like their drinks on the sweet side, the specialty drinks run about $7 and are available in non-alcoholic versions for less.

A restaurant by day, Margaritaville transforms itself after the dinner crowd thins out into a cross between a nightclub and a full-fledged performance space showcasing bands and live performers that reflect in one way or another that certain indescribable Jimmy Buffett style. The house bands I have seen here are very good, alternating between Buffett standards and a mix of calypso, easy going rock, and country-western. Every great once in a while, Buffett himself drops by. I had the great good fortune to be there on an occasion when the master himself sat in with the house band. That night, Margaritaville became the hottest spot in all of Florida.

Jimmy Buffett has been very savvy in marketing himself, so it's no surprise that there's a very well stocked gift shop, the **Margaritaville Mini-Mart**, attached to the restaurant with a second entrance from the Plaza. Here Parrot Heads can fill in the gaps in their Buffett CD collection or buy one of his books (he's a pretty good writer it turns out). In addition, there are plenty of t-shirts, gaudy Hawaiian shirts, and miscellaneous accessories that the well dressed beach bum simply can't afford to be without.

Latin Quarter

What: Nuevo Latino cuisine
Where: Next to Jimmy Buffett's

Price Range:	$$ – $$$$
Cover:	After 9:00 p.m. Thursday through Sunday
Hours:	Monday through Wednesday 5:00 p.m. to 10:00 p.m.; Thursday and Friday 5:00 p.m. to 2:00 a.m.; Saturday and Sunday noon to 2:00 a.m. (kitchen closes 10:00 p.m. daily)
Reservations:	None
Web:	www.thelatinquarter.com

This ambitious restaurant/nightclub salutes one of the newer ethnic groups to get stirred into the cultural menudo that is the United States — the natives of the 21 Spanish-speaking nations that lie south of the border. It does this most notably through its "Nuevo Latino" (or "new Latin") cuisine. If you're thinking of Tex-Mex cliches with their heavy leaden sauces, think again. The Nuevo Latino style draws its inspiration from traditional recipes but reinterprets them in very modern fashion, placing the emphasis on simple fresh ingredients expertly prepared. It also exults in flamboyant presentations that make this food as fun to look at as it is to eat.

The large, two-level space with its arching blue walls creates the illusion of a sultry tropical night in the ruins of an ancient city. The first-floor stage is flanked by two massive Aztec gods and backed by what surely must be the Andes. Upstairs, a balcony seating area looks down on the spacious dance floor in front of the stage.

The food here is very good indeed, making the Latin Quarter second only to Emeril's in CityWalk's gourmet food sweepstakes. It is an excellent choice for a big, blowout meal. Just make sure to pack a hearty appetite.

The menu is huge and varied and filled with unfamiliar terms like "boniato" and "garlic mojo." Fortunately, there's a glossary to explain it all. Among the appetizers ($5 to $11), the crab meat layered with fried plantain strips is a real winner. The pork tamal on a bed of black bean puree is also quite tasty. Salads ($4 to $11) are delicious and make an excellent lunch choice. Try the chicken breast or the grilled Chilean salmon over greens.

The "Platos Fuertes" ($14 to $25) were designed with the he-man meat-lover in mind. The Churrasco a la Parrilla takes the humble skirt steak to new heights, rolling it up into a tower and serving it over a bed of garbanzos, ham, and chorizo. The Gaucho a la Parrilla is a massive T-bone steak served with roasted garlic boniato mashed potatoes; it may well be the best meat dish to be found anywhere in CityWalk. Among the seafood entrees ($17 to $26) the broiled red snapper with chorizo "scales" is a standout, as is the Parrilla de Mariscos, a mélange of shellfish served over yellow rice.

The desserts ($5 to $6) include a sort of key lime pie served amusingly in a large martini glass. But the real winner is the Crepas Rellenas, two crepes filled with a vanilla cream, bathed in a dark rum sauce, topped with banana slices, and set off by a scoop of vanilla ice cream. It's worth visiting the Latin Quarter just to luxuriate in this splendiferous creation.

Portions are generous and the flavors intense. A standard three-course meal will have you groaning in distended pleasure. Plan accordingly. A full meal, without drinks, can easily top $40. Prices are slightly higher at dinner. To ease the strain on the family pocketbook, a kids' menu featuring $6 meals is also offered. The Latin Quarter adds a 17% gratuity to all checks.

Drinkers have their choice of a lengthy menu of specialty drinks that salute various Latin American countries. Mixed drink enthusiasts could do worse than set a goal to sample them all. For the less adventuresome, beer is also served and it makes an excellent accompaniment to most of the dishes. A small wine list is offered.

In the evening, on Thursday through Sunday, tables are cleared from the dance floor and the focus turns from food to entertainment, with an emphasis on dancing and audience involvement. If you'd like to delve a little deeper into Latin culture, check to see if the Latin Quarter is offering dancing lessons during your visit. This is a great opportunity to learn to salsa. These "happy hour" sessions usually take place on Saturday at 6:30 p.m. and are **free**. Also offered from time to time are cooking demonstrations.

The musical menu is almost as extensive as the dinner menu and varies from night to night. The entertainment mix includes a solo sax player, the Latin Quarter Dance Troupe serving up a tightly choreographed (and oh so sexy) floor show, fiery flamenco dancers, and a 13-piece orchestra playing dance music from the Spanish-speaking Caribbean. Even if you are too shy to try out your salsa skills, you'll have fun watching those who grew up with these dance steps strutting their stuff, for the music quickly fills the dance floor. Just one word of warning: the sound level can be painful, but that seems to be the current fashion in el Mundo Latino.

The entertainment usually starts around 9:00 p.m. The cover varies from $5 to $10 depending on the entertainment and the day of the week.

Emeril's Restaurant Orlando

What:	Gourmet dining
Where:	On the Plaza
Price Range:	$$$$+
Hours:	Lunch 11:30 a.m. to 2:00 p.m. Dinner 5:30 p.m. to 10:00 p.m. Sunday through Thursday, to 11:00 p.m. Friday and Saturday
Reservations:	Mandatory. Call (407) 224-2424; fax (407) 224-2525
Web:	www.emerils.com

Emeril Lagasse, the popular TV chef and cookbook author, brings his upscale New Orleans cuisine to Orlando in this lavish eatery decorated (if that's the word) with over 10,000 bottles of wine in climate-controlled glass-walled wine cases. This is an extremely handsome restaurant that evokes and improves upon Emeril's converted warehouse premises in the Big Easy. The main dining room soars to a curved wooden roof and the lavish use of glass on the walls facing the Plaza makes this a bright and sunny spot for lunch. The exposed steel support beams contrast with the stone walls and rich wood accents, while stark curved metal chandeliers arch gracefully overhead. It's a hip, modern look that matches the food and the clientele.

The cuisine is Creole-based but the execution is sophisticated and the presentation elaborate. Many dishes follow a standard Emeril architectural template: A layer of hash, relish, or puree is topped by the main ingredient, which in turn is topped by an antic garnish of potatoes, onions, or some other vegetable sliced in thin strips and flash fried; the plate is then decorated with a few swirls or dots of various sauces, sprinkled with spices and greenery, and delivered to the table with a flourish. Many dishes are based on home-style comfort foods like barbecue, fried fish, or gumbos and there's an unmistakable spiciness to much of it. The result is a cuisine that is fun and festive with only the occasional tendency towards self-conscious seriousness, making Emeril's a great choice for a celebratory blowout.

Despite its noisy, bistro-like atmosphere, this is a first-class restaurant where dining is theater and a full meal can last two and a half hours, with the per-person cost, with drinks and wine, easily rising to over $100. In the European fashion, Emeril's closes after lunch (11:00 a.m. to 2:00 p.m.) to allow the kitchen a chance to catch its breath and ready itself for a different and more extensive dinner menu.

Appetizers ($9 to $13 at lunch and dinner) include such homey touches as fried green tomatoes, spicy Cajun-style andouille sausage, and fried calamari along with sophisticated creations like wild mushrooms over angel hair pasta that is absolutely terrific and a heavenly white truffle potato soup. Soups and salads ($6 to $13) enjoy their own section on the menu and include a sturdy gumbo of the day and some artfully presented and deceptively simple green salads.

Entrees are in the $19 to $24 range at lunch, $20 to $38 at dinner. They include the odd sounding but delicious andouille-crusted Texas redfish at dinner (a pecan-crusted version is offered at lunch). Also worth inquiring about is the grilled fish of the day, perfectly prepared and attractively presented. And Emeril's grilled half chicken, available at lunch, is a fanciful take on downhome cooking.

Desserts (about $8) are equally elaborate, although it says something about the chef that his signature dessert is a homey banana cream pie served with chocolate shavings on a latticework of caramel sauce.

Dining here is a special experience. Emeril's is not the kind of place where you will feel comfortable in full tourist regalia even though the management officially draws the line only at tank tops and flip-flops. Stop back at your hotel to change and freshen up.

Tip: If you are dining alone or there are just two of you, you might want to try the "Food Bar," a short counter with stools that looks into the kitchen. The primo dining location is the L-shaped dining area by the windows; VIPs are seated here, so reserve well in advance if it's your preference.

For those who take their sybaritic pleasures seriously, there is a wine room and a separate cigar room for after-dinner drinks and a good smoke. An upstairs dining room can be reserved for private dining. Mr. Lagasse is very much the hands-on chef, I am told, so if you're lucky you might have your meal prepared by the master himself.

Emeril's, by the way, is strictly a restaurant; there is no entertainment. For most people, the eye-catching, tongue-tingling food will be entertainment enough.

Special note on reservations: Let me stress again that reservations are mandatory. Emeril's accepts reservations six months in advance and often books up completely several months in advance. So if you are planning on visiting at a busy time or are planning a special-occasion meal here, you will be well advised to book as early as possible. A day or two before your visit, the restaurant will call you to remind you of your reservation. Even so, you **must call** the restaurant **to confirm** the day before or up to 3:00 p.m. the day of the reservation. If you don't call, you **will** lose your reservation. By the way, the concierges at Universal's resort hotels have no special pull with Emeril's.

So how do you get seats at the last minute? Most often you don't, but your best shot is to call at 3:15 p.m. on the day you want to dine. If all else fails (and this may, too), show up early and ask for a seat at the main bar, where people are seated on a first come-first served basis and can order from the full menu. Generally, it's easier to come by a table on short notice at lunch.

Pastamoré

What:	Home-style Italian
Where:	On the Plaza
Price Range:	$$ - $$$
Hours:	5:00 p.m. to 11:00 p.m.
Reservations:	None

This cheerful and noisy Italian eatery blends contemporary decor with the homey touch of that old neighborhood Italian restaurant you loved as a kid. The decor is trendy postmodern with terra cotta colored walls and blue banquettes. Decorative accents are provided by Roman stone heads and words like "cucina," "pizza," and "antipasto" spelled out in cursive red neon. The menu features the kind of comfortable Italian dishes that won't have you reaching for your Italian-English dictionary.

Appetizers and salads ($4 to $7) include fried calamari, stuffed portobello mushrooms and Caesar salad. Pasta dishes ($10 to $12) are familiar trattoria staples like spaghetti with meatballs and lasagna. Penne Puttanesca is about as adventuresome as it gets. They also serve up some very tasty personal pizzas ($7 to $9) from a wood-fired pizza oven in the open kitchen at the back.

Meat and poultry dishes ($13 to $20) include such Italian staples as veal parmigiana, chicken piccata, and chicken marsala. A standout is the steak served over rosemary potatoes and sweet peppers and topped with bubbling Boursin cheese. Among the seafood entrees ($15 to $19) the Clams Cresta di Gallo is a standout. Vegetable side dishes ($4 to $5), include a wonderful broccoli with roasted garlic and lemon.

Desserts ($3 to $5) are of the standard Italian variety and for about $12 you can pig out on your choice of three of them.

Because everything is a la carte the bill can add up quickly. Pastamoré has an attached deli and espresso bar that opens early and is covered in the Fast Food section, below.

Motown Cafe

What:	Upscale soul food
Where:	At the entrance to City Walk
Price Range:	$$ - $$$
Cover:	$5 after 10:00 p.m. on Friday and Saturday
Hours:	11:00 a.m. to midnight, to 2:00 a.m. on Friday and Saturday (kitchen closes around 10:00 p.m.)
Reservations:	None

Downhome cooking and an infectious backbeat is the winning combination at this loud and glossy eatery celebrating the Motown sound and Motown stars. In Hard Rock Cafe fashion, the walls are lined with photos and memorabilia of the label's greats. There's less of it here than at Hard Rock, but what's here is fun to peruse, including many of the outrageously colorful costumes that were a Motown signature.

There are three levels with a central atrium that soars aloft to a huge 45-rpm record tilted at a rakish angle. From the ground floor, a curving staircase, the "Stairway of Success," its risers decorated with gold 45s, leads to the second-floor dining area, which also has an entrance from the Promenade. These are the dining areas. The third level houses **The Big Chill Lounge**, something of an after-hours club that opens on Friday and Saturday nights at 10:00 p.m. Tucked away under the eaves up here is a vest-pocket radio studio for the occasional live broadcast. Step outside onto a spacious balcony that looks out to the Hard Rock Cafe and Islands of Adventure for a great late night vantage point.

The cuisine could be classified as soul food, but it wanders all across the African-American experience, from southern fried chicken to Philly steaks, and it varies in quality from so fine to so-so. Among the appetizers ($5 to $14), the shrimp and sweet potato fritters with honey pecan butter is a standout. Sandwiches ($8 to $10) include the aforementioned Philly cheese steak, sliced barbecued pork, and portabello mushroom.

Entrees ($12 to $22) include standards like ribs, deep-fried catfish, and combo platters. Desserts ($4 to $6), if you have room, are over-the-top versions of shortcake, bread pudding, and other homey indulgences.

If the food has inspired you, step into the **SuperStar Studios** on the second level (opens between 5:00 and 6:00 p.m.) and record your very own Motown hit. Here you sing along to your choice of songs, which range from Motown to country and western ($14 for a cassette, $21 for a CD). Or create your own singing group for an additional $6 per person. You can add a second song to the same cassette or CD for $9. A word of warning, however. The recording booths have glass walls that make you visible (and perhaps risible) to the crowds on the Promenade.

There is a constant soundtrack of Motown music, as you might expect, but there is not much in the way of live entertainment here. A DJ plays nightly after 10:00 p.m. and a cover kicks in at that time on Friday and Saturday nights. Earlier in the evening, the restaurant employees dance and try to lure guests into joining them in a conga line. Once a month there is a special event that you will find listed on the CityMonth calendar.

The **Motown Shop**, on the ground floor to your right as you enter, has the usual assortment of Motown t-shirts, denims, shot glasses and other trinkets. Best of all, however, they have boxed sets of CD compilations of Motown hits, a great way to reacquaint yourself with this chapter of pop history.

NASCAR Cafe

What:	Southern country cooking
Where:	Near the bridge to Universal Studios Florida
Price Range:	$$ - $$$
Hours:	11:00 a.m. to 11:00 p.m.

Reservations: None

Web: www.nascarcafe.com

Just by the bridge that leads to Universal Studios, the large building that houses the NASCAR Cafe is an ode to speed. It swoops and leans and looks for all the world as if it's doing 120. In front of the main entrance (a two-story-tall evocation of a checkered flag) sits the latest winning car from NASCAR's Winston Cup series. Inside, the world of NASCAR roars to life around delighted diners.

NASCAR, in case you don't know, stands for National Association of Stock Car Automobile Racing, the organization that sets the rules for stock car racing and owns the tracks on which hard-driving, good-old-boy folk heroes are created. Stock car racing is a distinctly American sport, with roots in the rural and blue-collar south. NASCAR and the Cafe it has created reflect these roots. Along with the fun and fast cars, there's a healthy dose of old-fashioned American pride in flag and country. Fans of NASCAR racing will need no introduction and no urging to visit here. But even those with no knowledge of or feeling for stock car racing will find a meal at NASCAR Cafe a lot of fun, especially if they have young kids in tow.

Forget the standard restaurant vocabulary here. Tables are cars, tablecloths are car covers, the kitchen is the garage, and the check is the damage to your vehicle. It's a full-service sit-down restaurant and priority seating "reservations," or "pole positions" (see above) are taken. You might need them, too. Expect the restaurant to be crowded, with long waits for a table, and plan accordingly.

You could while away the wait by wandering through the memorabilia and displays on the ground floor. Laid out like a racetrack, and making lavish use of steel poles and wire fencing as decorative motifs, this floor is sort of a NASCAR museum and information center. It's filled with displays on the cars and their famous drivers and provides information about the latest races. In addition, there are plenty of race-themed video games ($1 to $1.50) and a 16-seat race car simulator to help you work up an appetite. If you try out the simulator, here's a tip: try to ride with only three or four others; the lighter load means a peppier ride. The ride costs $4 and lasts about four and a half minutes.

A **NASCAR shop** will help you get rid of some of that extra cash. There's plenty of themed clothing here including some very nice men's shirts ($40 to $60), but the flashiest items are the colorful "limited edition" lambskin jackets with a price tag ($1,000) larger than many drag race purses.

The downstairs centerpiece, smack in the middle of all that memorabilia, is a bar set on 55-gallon oil drums. It's topped with a real race car and lit with lamps in racing helmets. Also downstairs is an outdoor shaded terrace that looks out over the canal to the Hard Rock and serves a limited food menu consisting of the sandwiches and salads offered in the main dining room. The shading won't protect you from the afternoon sun, but after sundown it's a pleasant place to sit and drink or snack. Occasionally there is free country music entertainment here.

The dining room upstairs is decorated with more race cars hanging from the ceiling. The walls are plastered with the same sponsor logos that decorate the cars, and large projection screens are filled with races that begin about every 20 minutes with the deafening sound of masses of stock cars revving their engines and screaming off at the wave of the checkered flag. This is obviously music to the ears of many diners, as the smiling faces in the crowd will attest. Those with their fingers in their ears have obviously wandered into the wrong restaurant.

Oh, by the way, there's food, too. The centerpieces of the racing-themed menu are steaks and chops, with prices in the moderate to expensive range. Starters and salads are in the $4 to $10 range, with entrees running $9 to $20. Sandwiches are $8 to $9 and desserts are $5 to $7.

Fish lovers should check out the Catch of the Day. If it is grilled salmon with your choice of lemon pepper or Cajun spices, go for it. The Chicken Pot Pie is not so much a pie as a tower of flaky puff pastry smothered in creamy chicken chunks and peas. Side dishes ($2) are homey and delectable. The sweet potato souffle is studded with pecan sugar chunks and the broccoli has a rich garlic tang to it.

On balmy evenings, request a table on the outdoor balcony. It has a nice view across the canal to the Hard Rock and the two theme parks. NASCAR Cafe also boasts some of the friendliest waiters and waitresses I have encountered in CityWalk. Young, enthusiastic, and very knowledgeable about stock car racing, they will be happy to instruct the neophyte in the fine points of the sport.

Fast Food at CityWalk

There are a few less elaborate, less costly dining choices in CityWalk for those looking for morning coffee, a quick bite, or a budget-saving alternative to a full-course, full-price blowout meal.

Pastamoré Marketplace Cafe

> **What:**   Italian snacks, sweets, and wine
> **Where:**   Between the Cineplex and the Plaza
> **Price Range:** $

This annex to the Pastamoré restaurant opens bright and early (at 8:00 a.m.) to serve strong coffee and strength-building pastries to the crowds arriving for a busy day at the theme parks. They also have "breakfast pizzas" that are worth a try. At lunch, the emphasis turns to Italian-style panini, pizza, pasta, and antipasto salads. Finally, late in the day, you can stop by again for dessert or a glass of wine. Indoor seating is limited and the few outdoor tables let you survey the passing scene.

Cinnabon

What:	Cinnamon buns and ice cream
Where:	Between the Cineplex and the Plaza
Price Range:	$

Across the street from the Pastamoré Marketplace Cafe is this branch of the nationwide chain famous for its oversized, gooey and delicious cinnamon buns at moderate prices. Ice cream and a small selection of desserts are also available. Seating is very limited and all outdoors. This place opens early to snag the breakfast crowd.

Starbucks

What:	Coffee, latte, and light snacks
Where:	On the Promenade near upper entrance to Motown
Price Range:	$

The best thing about this airy coffee shop is the view over the plaza and the crowds below. Otherwise, it's pretty much like every other Starbucks you've ever been in, which I guess is the point. If you like the jolt of Starbucks, note that this one opens at 8:30 a.m. and stays open late.

Big Kahuna Pizza

What:	Walk-up pizza window
Where:	On the Promenade near Motown
Price Range:	$

Nicely framed by gaudy pizza-themed surfboards, this simple stand serves up personal sized pizzas courtesy of Pizza Hut. Cheese, pepperoni, and "supreme" versions are all $5 or under. Wash it down with draft beer ($4) or a soft drink.

Latin Express

What:	Walk-up snacks
Where:	On the Promenade near the Latin Quarter
Price Range:	$

Most of the nightclubs along the Promenade have walk-up windows dispensing specialty alcoholic drinks, but the Latin Quarter also serves up some tasty and inexpensive munchies for about $4 to $7. Choices include Cuban sandwiches and flan. There are even empañadas for just $2. Latin Express has irregular hours, but is generally open Wednesday through Sunday evenings.

Galaxy

What:	Walk-up bar
Where:	Near the Latin Quarter
Price Range:	$

No fast food, just fast booze. This walk-up full-service bar has a small seating area in the plaza framed by the groove, the Latin Quarter, and Emeril's. A nice place to sit and survey the passing scene.

Nightclubs at CityWalk

As mentioned earlier, nightclubs at CityWalk are those entertainment venues that open only in the evening and serve either no food at all or a limited food menu. Fortunately, the food served in the clubs is very good food indeed. The latest information on performance schedules as well as food menus for the nightclubs can be found online at www.citywalk.com.

Hard Rock Live

What:	Rock performance space
Where:	Across the waterway next to Hard Rock Cafe
Tickets:	$15 and up, depending on the act
Hours:	Most shows start at 8:00 p.m.
Web:	www.hardrocklive.com

The Orlando Hard Rock Cafe may be the world's largest but what really makes it special is its next door neighbor, Hard Rock Live, the chain's first live performance venue. Underneath that retro take on Rome's ancient Coliseum is a cutting edge rock performance space loaded to the gills with sound, light, and video technology, including two video walls flanking the stage. In its standard configuration the joint holds 1,800. If they pull out the seats and turn the first floor into a mosh pit they can pack in 2,500, which still makes it "intimate" by rock standards. At the other end of the spectrum, they can use flywalls and props to shrink the performance space to the size of a truly intimate club.

The large stage (60 feet wide and 40 feet deep) offers bands plenty of room in which to rock and the computerized lighting system, strobes, and fog machines create the kind of dazzling effects that rock fans used to have to roll up and bring with them. Most important for the true aficionado, the sound system answers the burning question, "What does it sound like at ground zero of a nuclear explosion?" Like, I mean, the place totally rocks.

Given the limited capacity, it's unlikely that the real giants of rock will be able to play here (at least not too often), but Elton John has fluttered like a candle in the wind here and hemi-demi-semi-stars both rising and falling are booked here with some regularity, including thus far the likes of Sheryl Crow, Weird Al Yankovic, the Pet Shop Boys, Indigo Girls, and Elvis — Costello, that is.

If the music isn't blowing you away, you can repair to one of six bars and, depending on the show, you may be able to get something to nosh on from the Hard Rock Cafe kitchen, like foot-long hot dogs, wood-oven pizzas, or nachos.

Ticket prices are moderate, with most acts checking in at between $15 and $30 and the occasional show rising to $50. Elton John commanded a $150 ticket price, but it was a charity event. Every once in a while you can catch an evening of rocker wannabes for as little as $6. Tickets can be purchased at the box office or, for an additional fee, from TicketMaster at (407) 839-3900. Tickets for some events can also be purchased online at www.hardrock.com/live. Most shows begin at 8:00 p.m., with the box office opening at 10:00 a.m. Information about upcoming events is available by calling (407) 351-5483 or online at the address just given.

Bob Marley — A Tribute To Freedom

What:	Reggae club
Where:	On the Promenade
Cover:	$5 beginning at 8:00 p.m.
Hours:	3:00 p.m. to 2:00 a.m.; Friday through Sunday, 2:00 p.m. to 2:00 a.m.
Web:	www.bobmarley.com

Reggae fans will appreciate this salute to Bob Marley, the Jamaican-born king of reggae, where the infectious backbeat of Marley's lilting music mingles with the spicy accents of island cooking. Created under the watchful eye of Marley's widow, Rita, who has contributed Marley memorabilia for the project, this venue is as much a celebration of Marley's vision of universal brotherhood as it is a restaurant or performance venue.

When Marley first hit the U.S. scene, he was regarded as something of a dope-smoking revolutionary barbarian. Like many black artists, he suffered the indignity of having his songs "covered" by white artists (like Barbra Streisand!). But music hath charms to soothe the conservative as well as the savage breast and Marley's infectiously charming music gradually became domesticated, despite his occasionally radical-sounding lyrics. Today, his lilting "One Heart" is the unofficial national anthem of Jamaica, made universally familiar through the magic of television commercials.

Sadly and ironically, his too-early death of cancer at age 36 probably helped turn Marley, who was once described by *The New York Times* as "this wiry, spindle-shanked singer, this self-styled black prince of reggae," into the sort of cuddly pop icon who could be enshrined in a family theme park.

Marley was a member of the Rastafarians, a religious sect with roots in 1920's Harlem, that believes in the divinity of the late Emperor Haile Selassie and the coming of a new era in which the African diaspora will return in glory to the Ethiopian motherland. "Rastas" shun alcohol, adhere to a vegetarian diet, and smoke copious quantities of ganja, or marijuana, which is seen as a gift from God and something of a sacrament. The nightclub that bears his name violates all those principles; there's plenty of booze, meat on the menu, and no ganja.

One thing close to Marley's heart that does get full expression here is the theme of universal brotherhood. It is preached by the MC and practiced by the patrons, making Bob Marley's perhaps the most multicultural entertainment venue in Orlando, a place that turns up the volume and lives out the words of Marley's most famous song: "One love. One heart. Let's get together and feel all right."

The exterior is an exact replica of 56 Hope Road, Marley's Kingston Jamaica home. Inside you will find two L-shaped levels, each with its own bar, opening onto a spacious palm-fringed courtyard with a gazebo-like bandstand in the corner. Because both levels are open to the courtyard, Marley's is not air-conditioned but fans do a good job of keeping a breeze going.

The predominant color scheme is yellow, red and green, the national colors of Ethiopia; the lion statues evoke Haile Selassie's title of Lion of Judah, a motif that is repeated in the mural on the bandstand. The walls are covered in Marley memorabilia and the sound system pumps out a steady stream of Marley hits.

The nighttime entertainment, which kicks off at about eight, typically consists of a house band of skilled reggae musicians performing a mix of Marley hits, other reggae classics, and the occasional pop standard adapted to the reggae beat. From time to time, a name group will appear, boosting the cover charge.

The music of the house bands is good, but not so good that it makes you forget how much better Bob Marley and the Wailers were. Still, their main job is to get people out onto the dance floor and they accomplish that task easily. After a few drinks and once you are gyrating with the crowds, you'll find no reason to quibble.

The "Jammin' Drinks" ($5 to $6) are non-alcoholic. However, the "Wild Side of Tings" and "Extreme Measures" ($6 to $8), fueled with island rum and other potent potables are designed to help get you past your inhibitions and onto the dance floor. Of course, Red Stripe, Jamaica's favorite beer is also available.

The food is designed more as ballast for the drinks than anything else, but it is quite good and a nice introduction to Jamaican fare for the uninitiated. The portions are about appetizer size, so you could well sample several in the course of a long evening. Marley's Munchies ($5 to $8) are well named, consisting mostly of plates of nibbles that can be shared around the table. Stir It Up is a cheese fondue laced with Red Stripe and served with vegetables for dipping; Jammin' is an island version of chips and salsa. There is more substantial fare as well. The Ocho Rios fish sandwich ($11) is a good choice, marinated in "jerk" seasoning (a sort of all-purpose Jamaican marinade), grilled, and served with a pineapple salsa. Another jerk specialty is the "Catch a Fire" chicken skewers ($9), which come with a creamy cucumber dipping sauce. There are also both meat and vegetarian versions of Jamaican patties ($8 or $9), filled flaky pastries. Several dishes are served with yucca fries, which look deceptively like French-fried potatoes but have a taste and texture all their own. Jamaican cuisine tends to be spicy but, for those who find the dishes here too bland, Cashioux's Gourmet Mango Hot Sauce is on every table.

Desserts ($5 to $7) are worth sampling, with the Is This Love coconut cake in a shortbread crust especially good. Fresh fruit on a skewer is also available.

A small shop counter in a downstairs corner hawks Marley t-shirts and polos ($20 to $48) as well as Marley CDs. This is probably as close as you'll get to finding the complete Marley discography in one place, a perfect chance to fill in the gaps in your collection. There is also a small selection of books on reggae and Marley for those who would like to learn more.

Bob Marley's is a popular joint and on weekends can spawn long lines of people waiting for one of the 400 spaces inside to open up. Even early in the week, space can be hard to come by for those who don't arrive early. If you want to be in the thick of it, you'll definitely want to be downstairs. If you're not the dancing type, a row of stools along the railing of the upstairs balcony offers excellent sightlines to the stage. For a change of scenery, you can take your drink onto a second floor balcony that looks out over the Promenade.

Anyone looking for a fun evening of dancing and drinking and infectious music to go along with it will find little to complain of here. True Marley devotees will find everything they are looking for.

Everything but the ganja.

Pat O'Brien's

What:	The original dueling pianos, plus New Orleans cuisine
Where:	On the Promenade
Cover:	$5 beginning at 9:00 p.m. in piano bar only.
Hours:	4:00 p.m. to 2:00 a.m.
Web:	www.patobriens.com

Step into Pat O'Brien's and you'll believe that you've been magically transported to the Big Easy. At least you will if you've ever visited the original Pat O'Brien's in New Orleans' French Quarter, because CityWalk's version is virtually a photographic reproduction. This is the first attempt to transplant the O'Brien's experience and word is that when O'Brien's owner visited CityWalk he marveled that Universal's design wizards had captured the place "right down to the cracks in the walls."

There are three main rooms at Pat O'Brien's. The Piano Bar houses the famed copper-clad twin baby grand pianos that are an O'Brien's trademark. This is strictly a bar, its brick walls and wooden beams hung with dozens of gaudy German beer steins that let you know this is a place for serious drinkers. Here a steady stream of talented pianists keeps the ivories tickled almost constantly as patrons sing along, pound on the tables, and shout requests. In fact, Pat O'Brien's is credited with inventing the "dueling pianos" format that has been copied so often. The word seems to have gotten around that this is a great place to bring a bunch of old friends (or perhaps new acquaintances from the latest convention to blow through town) to drink and blow off some steam.

O'Brien's draws a somewhat older crowd than Marley's or Buffett's. If you're old enough to remember when popular music meant songs with lyrics you could actually understand, you'll probably have a good time here, especially if you can carry a tune and aren't shy about singing along.

Across from the Piano Bar is a smaller version, called the Local's Bar, minus the pianos but with a jukebox and large-screen projection TV that always seems to be tuned to some sporting event. Out back is a delightful open-air patio dining area. Here, at night, the ambiance is highlighted by yet another O'Brien's trademark — flaming fountains.

Upstairs is given over to private party rooms, but you can mount the stairs and find your way to a narrow balcony overlooking the Promenade. It's a great place to sip a drink and survey the passing scene.

And speaking of drinks, Pat O'Brien's (for those who don't know) is the home of the Hurricane, a lethal and lovely concoction of rum and lord knows what all else that has made the place famous worldwide. In fact, the original New Orleans location pulls in more money than any other bar its size in the world.

As wonderful as the atmosphere is, as good as the music may be, I find the real attraction here is the food. Devotees of New Orleans' spicy Creole- and French-influenced cuisine won't be disappointed even though the presentation and service are decidedly casual. Your meal arrives in little fake skillets lined with shamrock dotted wax paper. Plates and utensils are black plastic. But the offhand presentation belies the sophistication of the cuisine. Best of all, the prices are extremely reasonable, with nothing on the menu over $10, except the combo platter designed for sharing ($12).

The Jambalaya is a spicy medley of shrimp, chicken, andouille sausage, and rice flecked with vegetables. Perhaps best of all is the Cancun Shrimp, with its coconut-flecked frying batter and sweet, fresh fruit salsa. It's served over Pat O'Brien's signature French fries, dusted with paprika and ever-so-lightly spiced with cayenne before being fried to the perfect texture. The Shrimp Gumbo comes in a small portion just right for the lighter appetite (or choose it as an "appetizer" if you really want to chow down).

The Po' Boy sandwich is a New Orleans signature dish. It's the Big Easy's version of the heroes and hoagies from up north. Pat O'Brien's version is a heaping portion of spicy fried shrimp served on an open-faced baguette with a rich Cajun mayonnaise on the side. Eating it as a sandwich is a bit of a challenge, but worth it as the bread, veggies, shrimp, and rich Cajun sauce play off each other very nicely indeed. It's served with those magnificent spicy French fries.

The Crawfish Nachos sounds better than it tastes. For me, the delicate flavor of crawfish etouffe (very nice on its own) doesn't stand up well against the tortilla chips, melted cheese, and sour cream. For dessert (about $5) choose from the Strawberry Hurricane Cheesecake or Pat O's Bread Pudding, redolent of nutmeg and cinnamon and served with a whisky sauce that packs a 100 proof wallop. There is also a kids menu, offered before 9:00 p.m., featuring simple meals for about $6. At 9, all kids must leave.

Out front, facing the Promenade, you'll find a small gift shop offering Pat O'Briens souvenir glassware and other gewgaws.

the groove

What:	High-tech, high-gloss disco
Where:	On the Promenade
Cover:	$5 cover always charged, except on Teen Nights
Hours:	9:00 p.m. to 2:00 a.m

the groove (the lower case is intentional) is CityWalk's dance club and it sets out to compete head to head with the legendary nightspots that have caught the public imagination in urban centers like New York, Chicago, and Los Angeles. It is also the only venue that does not come with a recognizable brand name. No Jimmy Buffetts or Bob Marleys to give this place instant name recognition. This joint stands or falls on its own merits.

It succeeds remarkably well by providing a place where a mostly young crowd (you must be at least 21 to enter) can come and boogie the night away in a cacophonous atmosphere that duplicates big city sophistication. The main difference is that here you will be let in even if you don't meet some snotty doorman's idea of what is currently cool and hip. Intimate it's not, with a maximum capacity of 1,277 on multiple levels, but with crowds comes excitement.

The design conceit is that you are in a century-old theater that is in various stages of renovation, but the dim lighting and pulsing light effects negate much of the intended effect. The various areas of the club have been designed to provide ample space for those who want to thrash and writhe under pulsating lights to ear-splitting music while offering some refuge to those who just want to watch.

The main dance floor is dominated by a soaring wall of video monitors that operate separately and then coalesce to form a single image. Patterns of light swirl across the floor to disorienting effect. There is a small stage for visiting groups but I've never seen any here. Most nights the nonstop sound assault is provided by a DJ. The music is eclectic; typically the evening starts off with the more widely popular forms of dance music, with the mix changing gradually as the night wears on.

Late at night, the music is predominantly "progressive house." If you don't know what that means, take it from me, you probably won't like it. But those who know it love it.

There are occasional "Teen Nights" ($10), alcohol-free dance parties for 13- to 19-year-olds, lasting from 8:00 p.m. to midnight. Parents get a Party Pass as part of the teen's admission and teens get the first soft drink **free**. On these nights, the groove reverts to adult form at the witching hour. Teen Nights are more frequent during the summer months and are listed on the CityMonth calendar.

Fortunately, there are some relatively quiet corners (50- to 80-seat bars actually) where you can get better acquainted with that special someone you just met on the dance floor. These are the Red, Blue, and Green Rooms, respectively, and each is decorated differently. The Red and Green Rooms are dim and deliciously decadent but the Blue Room is lit with a ghastly pallor that will flatter only Goths and vampires and seems designed to convince you you've had too much to drink. When it all becomes too much, you can repair to a balcony over the Promenade and look down on the latecomers standing in line.

CityJazz

What:	Jazz club
Where:	On the Promenade
Cover:	$5 beginning at 9:00 p.m.
Hours:	Sunday through Thursday 8:00 p.m. to 1:00 a.m.; Friday and Saturday 7:00 p.m. to 2:00 a.m.

Located in an octagonal building almost at the geographical center of CityWalk, CityJazz celebrates that most American of all musical forms, the forerunner of rock, soul, and reggae, and the one musical form that bridges the gap between popular and serious music.

The club's two-story design combines the intimate ambiance of a true jazz club with the great sightlines of a conventional theater. The color scheme of soothing browns and jazzy purples, along with the plush banquettes, creates an aura of ultra-cool sophistication. Memorabilia from *Downbeat* magazine's **Jazz Hall of Fame** pays tribute to the greats, from the founding fathers, to the red hot mamas, to the eclectic cool jazz of modern times. Fascinating relics of the greats are displayed along the walls with giant colorized and cutout photo blowups. The overall effect is at once festive and laid back. CityJazz is easily the handsomest performance space in all of CityWalk. The space has also been designed to serve as a state-of-the-art recording facility, an additional draw for big-name acts looking to do a live album.

CityJazz lends itself to small-combo sophisticated jazz groups, but they must be in short supply because the management has also taken to booking hyper-amplified, blow-your-brains-out blues and rockabilly groups that would be better suited to the larger confines of Hard Rock Live. My recommendation would be to save a visit here for an evening when the act on stage matches the ambiance.

Of all the "nightclubs" at CityWalk, CityJazz stays closest to the old-time, big-city definition of what a nightclub should be — an intimate, hip venue with small tables each offering a great view of the stage. The food and beverage service follow the formula, too. You can have the bartender pour the usual well drinks for about $5, but since this is a classy joint, you can also ante up a few more bucks for premium brands that are listed at some length in a small but elegant padded menu. There's 15 year old bourbon and 18 year old single malt scotch as well as the super trendy brands of vodka.

Food is served in portions that match the postage stamp size of the tables, but the mostly appetizer-sized dishes ($6 to $12) are very good and lend themselves to serial nibbling. If you come here hungry, you can put together an impromptu "menu de degustation" during the course of the evening. Among the more interesting choices are the tricolored chips with two salsa dips and the beef tenderloin sandwich.

The cover charge can rise with the fame of the performers inside. City-Jazz opens for dining and entertainment at 8:00 p.m., but you can usually get in at 6:00 p.m. to browse through the Hall of Fame memorabilia.

Shopping in CityWalk

The designers of CityWalk had a difficult challenge when it came to creating retail spaces that would both complement and enhance their entertainment district. How do you create an upscale shopping experience that has the strength and credibility of major "brands" without offering "the same old thing," familiar big-name shops just like the ones holiday-goers have back home? And to hold its own against the entertainment venues, the shopping has to be pretty entertaining in its own right, without overwhelming CityWalk's prime reason for being. By and large, management has met the challenge.

The shopping here is fun without being overbearing, and the range of goods for sale fits in very well with the peculiar circumstances of the customers who come here — people on vacation, bent on having fun rather than purchasing necessities. There's probably nothing here that you can't live without, but there's also plenty of stuff you'd love to have, either as a special treat for yourself or as a gift for friends and family who couldn't make the trip with you. Prices, on the whole, are surprisingly moderate. Oh sure, you can drop a bundle if you want, but there's plenty here to appeal to a wide range of budgets.

Need another souvenir?

As you've probably noticed by now, nearly every entertainment venue has its gift shop selling branded souvenirs. So it comes as a relief that the major retail spaces do not simply repeat the merchandise themes you found in the theme parks. The one exception is the **Universal Studios Store** that, with its towering and colorful exterior signage, dominates the CityWalk Plaza. Here you will find a tasteful selection of touristy trinkets, with an accent on nicely designed (and, hence, moderately expensive) clothing. The merchandise mix here changes frequently to take advantage of seasonal fads or the latest Universal film venture in need of targeted promotion. It's not as large as its sister store in Universal Studios Florida but if you are in desperate need of something to remind you of your visit to either of the theme parks, you should be able to find something suitable here.

All-Star Collectibles is also something of a souvenir shop, but with a difference. Professional sports is the motif here and odds are you'll find a cap, t-shirt, or jersey emblazoned with the name of your favorite baseball, football, basketball, or hockey team. What makes the shop special, however, are the beautifully framed and displayed autographed photos and other memorabilia of famous sports stars of today and yesterday. Even if they're out of your price range (they sure were out of mine!), it's worth a visit here just to gawk.

Clothe thyself

Clothing, the kind that doesn't advertise anything, can be found at several locations. **Fresh Produce**, a large airy shop on the Plaza, features women's, girls', and infants' casual clothing in a limited palette of vibrant pastels. Many dresses and blouses are imprinted with bold and simple floral or animal motifs, for a sort of summery backyard feel. The designers, twin sisters from Colorado, describe their products as "make you feel good clothing." What will also make you feel good are the prices, which are surprisingly modest for the obvious stylishness of the clothes. Many ensembles can be put together for well under $100. There are a few polo shirts and unisex shorts for the guys. But this is really a woman's store. Mothers and young daughters should have great fun picking out coordinating outfits here.

More casual clothing, this time with the emphasis on men's wear, can be found at **Quiet Flight Surf Shop**. It is easy to spot on your right, near the Cineplex, as you enter CityWalk; the display window framed by the huge curling wave is the tipoff. In this window, you will see from time to time a craftsman shaping a high-end surfboard. Although you can actually buy a surfboard here, the selection is small and most of the space is devoted to casual clothing designed to make you look like a well-heeled surf bum. There are wildly colorful print shirts for men and equally colorful "baggies," the capacious swim trunks favored by surfers. Women get almost equal time with a goodly selection of swimwear and casual poolside attire. Here you will also find the kind of accessories no well-dressed surfer should be without, from ultra-hip sunglasses to waterproof watches.

Photo Op: Before you move on, check out that curling fiberglass breaker one more time. There's a riderless surfboard perfectly positioned in the curl. Step aboard for a nifty souvenir photo.

Still more casual clothing can be found at the **Endangered Species Store**, which is to your left as you enter CityWalk. The shop's exterior has the look of some long-lost Southeast Asian temple complex, with the doorway flanked by twin elephants and guarded by a huge stuffed toy gorilla. The merchandise isn't quite that exotic, however. There are animal themed t-shirts here as well as more dressy (and gaudy) examples of the genre. There is also a small selection of practical gear, like safari hats, for the adventuresome traveler. For the rest, it's a mixed bag of animal-themed gifts, figurines (some of them quite handsome), and bric-a-brac along with some stuff that was obviously chosen just because it's fun.

Baubles, bangles and canned watches

A staple of holiday shopping is jewelry and upscale fashion accessories. What better way to cap off that honeymoon or anniversary trip? What better way to reward yourself when your better half won't? CityWalk offers several intriguing opportunities to buy the perfect bauble.

Silver is a small shop near the Endangered Species Store. True to its name, it specializes in sterling silver jewelry, as well as accessories such as frames and watches. Most of it is for women but there are a few rings for men. Look for the twin Art Deco statues of the guys holding large silver spheres.

Farther along, on the Plaza, is **Fossil**, where the branding seems to be just as important as the merchandise. The stock consists of moderately priced, and nicely designed, watches, leather handbags, and sunglasses. But it's the packaging that's eye-catching. Watches come packaged in small tin cans, like the kind grandpa used to hold pipe tobacco. These are decorated in the style of 1940s magazine advertising. Nice merchandise, odd concept.

Guys who want to impress that special girl and still afford to eat will find much to applaud at **Elegant Illusions**, located on Lombard Street, a narrow shopping arcade that descends from the upper level exit of the Cineplex to the NASCAR Cafe. Fake diamonds, as well as emeralds and sapphires, are for sale here in a variety of imposing sizes and flashy settings. This stuff ain't cheap but it's a good bit less than the real thing.

What on earth was I thinking?

Another recurring theme of holiday shopping is the irresistible pull of the "novelty item." Otherwise sensible people, when far from home and in an expansive mood, will buy the darndest things, and CityWalk has some wonderfully offbeat shops along Lombard Street that cater to this urge.

Dapy, at the top end of Lombard Street, offers a dizzying variety of novelty toys, gizmos, gadgets, and miscellaneous thingies, many of them linked to current films. Can't remember the sixties? The interior of **Glow!** might seem vaguely familiar. Here you'll find lava lamps and an impressive variety of glow-in-the-dark tchotchkes, all displayed under blue light. **Captain Crackers**, at the bottom of Lombard Street, with the huge shaggy dog peering from its roof, is a small video and game arcade. No souvenirs, but a fun place to visit.

Finally, at the top of Lombard Street is **Cigarz at CityWalk**, which doesn't quite fit into any category. Most obviously it is a cigar store wonderfully decorated to evoke an old Cuban cigar factory, complete with sheaves of tobacco leaves hanging from the corrugated tin roof. A walk-in humidor holds the good stuff, while the rest of the shop offers exotic cigarettes and a variety of paraphernalia for the serious cigar buff. Best of all, at the back is a compact and cozy bar where smokers, preferably cigar smokers, can repair for quiet conversation, a warming scotch, and a fine cigar. A separate room offers more seating, including some super-comfy leather sofas. This is one of CityWalk's few hidden corners where you can actually get away from the noise and the crowds. It's not surprising that it has become a favorite hang-out for Universal employees.

CHAPTER FIVE:

The Resort Hotels

In the hospitality industry, the word "resort" refers to a hotel that offers not just a high standard of luxury and extra amenities, but special recreational opportunities, either natural or man-made. Well, two world-class theme parks surely qualify as a recreational opportunity.

Of course, if the visionaries at Universal had done nothing more than add Islands of Adventure and CityWalk to the existing Universal Studios Florida they would have had a vacation destination that could challenge Disney World in appeal and popularity. Fortunately for us they set their sights much higher than that, seeking to turn Universal Orlando into a true resort destination with five distinctively themed hotels surrounding the theme parks. To accomplish that they have partnered with Loews Corporation to provide the hotel part of the equation.

If you've never heard of Loews hotels, you're forgiven. There are only 18 of them worldwide. Loews has forgone the current craze of hotel consolidation, with larger chains devouring smaller chains to create ever larger chains, to concentrate on operating a small portfolio of one-of-a-kind hotels of the four- and five-star variety that seek to become the dominant hotels in their marketplace. The plans for Universal Orlando Resort fit in perfectly with that strategy and Loews has made a $560 million commitment to see the vision through.

The Portofino Bay Hotel, Hard Rock Hotel, and the Royal Pacific Resort, described in this chapter, are the first of the five planned hotels. The fourth and fifth hotels are reportedly in the development stage. They do not yet have names or announced themes (although an Egyptian-themed hotel has tested well in focus groups according to some reports).

Honored Guests

Staying at one of the Universal Orlando hotels has some obvious advantages. For one thing, you will be staying almost literally at the gates to the theme parks. None of the first three hotels is more than a ten-minute, complimentary boat ride from the parks and some are much closer. For another, these are very nice hotels, far superior to the usual run of tourist hotels that ring Universal Orlando and continue down the tacky environs of International Drive. But there are other, less obvious advantages to being a Universal hotel guest.

Staying at an on-property hotel confers certain VIP privileges unavailable to the average run-of-the-mill tourist.

- *Universal Express Priority Access.* Perhaps the greatest perk of all is that resort guests get priority access at most of the rides and attractions in the theme parks. (The exceptions are the line for front row seating for the roller coasters and *Pteranodon Flyers* and *One Fish, Two Fish* in IOA and the water slide at *Fievel's Playland* in USF.) Simply use your room key to get immediate access to the Universal Express entrance to the ride. According to the fine print on the park maps, this privilege can be used only once per ride per day, but the the most recent information I have suggests that hotel guests are allowed Priority Access to a given ride once an hour. Of course, this may change in the future, so don't count on it. Check with the concierge when you arrive.

  You can get a separate room key for everyone in your party when you check in, which will allow your family to split up and still get Express access. If you tour together, however, a single key will typically gain access for four, sometimes five people.

  This perk is sometimes referred to as "Front-of-the-Line" or FOTL and perhaps because of this some people think it means they are supposed to quite literally be the very first person in line. Not so. What it does mean is that your wait to ride will be cut to under 15 minutes, usually well under. It is just like the "normal" Universal Express system with the important difference that you can pop into a ride or attraction as the spirit moves you instead of making an appointment to ride later.

  If you are wondering whether or not to ante up for a stay at one of the resort hotels, consider for a moment the time and hassle this perk will save you. Many people say that after experiencing the priority access perk, they cannot imagine visiting Universal Orlando again without staying on site.

- *Priority seating.* This perk gets you the best seats for some shows and priority seating Sunday through Thursday nights at some restaurants in CityWalk and the theme parks. Check with the hotel concierge to see which shows and restaurants are offering this perk at the time of your visit.

- *Package delivery.* Any park visitor can get some shops to deliver their purchases to the front gate for later pick-up, but Universal hotel guests can have their purchases sent directly to their rooms, provided they are staying over till at least the next day. Packages are delivered the day after your purchase.

- *Charge privileges.* You can use your room key (which looks much like a credit card) to charge purchases in park shops and restaurants that accept credit cards. You pay just one bill at checkout.

- *Length-of-stay tickets.* Resort guests can purchase park passes valid for however long they are staying at the hotel. These tickets are usually booked as part of a package. They don't represent any great savings on park admission but they have the beneficial effect of giving you a better room rate. They can also come in handy if the length of your stay doesn't match one of the standard pass options. If you wish to purchase length-of-stay tickets once you have checked in, see the concierge.

- *Character Dining reservations.* Some resort hotel restaurants play host to characters from the Universal stable of stars. Typically, these events happen a few times a week during the evening meal. As a hotel guest, you will have priority when making reservations for these popular events. Check with the concierge for the nights and restaurants involved in the Character Dining experience during your stay.

Additional perks may be added. It's also possible that some may be changed or discontinued. So make sure to ask the concierge for the latest information when you check in. You are paying a premium to stay in such style so close to the parks, so you should take advantage of the privileges conferred by your status as an honored guest.

Room Rates At A Glance

The hotels follow similar patterns when it comes to rooms and rates. Two hotels have "standard" rooms and larger, pricier "deluxe" rooms. In all hotels, the view from the room also affects the rate, with "pool" or "bay" views costing more. Some hotels have a Club floor offering special amenities and perks for a price. Next come the suites. Two hotels have "Kids' Suites," specially designed for families. For high rollers, there are larger, more elaborate suites with suitably larger, more elaborate price tags.

I wish I could tell you exactly what your room will cost, but I can't. Hotel rates are notoriously volatile, rising and falling with the seasons, leisure travel patterns, and a variety of market conditions that are impossible to forecast. My hope here, is to provide some general guidelines about the "going rate" that will prove useful in considering your Universal Orlando resort hotel choices. Then you can use the tips offered in *Getting A Good Deal* (below) to zero in on the best rate for the room you want. The prices given are the low season to high season range for 2002. Expect prices to rise modestly in all categories in 2003.

Room Rates

Portofino Bay Hotel

Garden view	Bay view	Deluxe
$249-$299	$285-$339	$305-$359

Hard Rock Hotel

Garden view	Pool view	Deluxe	HR Club
$199 -$249	$219-$279	$259-$309	$299-$359

Royal Pacific Resort

Garden view	Pool view	Royal Club
$159-$199	$179-$219	$249-$299

Suite Rates

Portofino Bay Hotel

Kids' Suites	Parlor Suites	Super Luxury
$450-$525	$625-$900	$1,400-$2,100

Hard Rock Hotel

Kids' Suites	King Suites	Super Luxury
$395-$475	$345-$495	$1,250-$1,575

Royal Pacific Resort

King Suites	Royal Suites	Super Luxury
$279-$329	$599-$699	$1,000-$1,200

Getting A Good Deal

While the resort hotels offer excellent value for the money, they are not precisely cheap. But the advantages of staying on site are so attractive that figuring out a way to make a stay at one of these great hotels fit into your budget will be worth the effort. Here, then, are a few suggestions on how to get the best possible deal on your resort hotel room rate.

Book a package. Ask your travel agent about a package that includes an on-site hotel, theme park tickets, and perhaps airfare and car rental. You will probably wind up paying less than if you had booked all the elements separately.

Entertainment Card. To get the Entertainment Card, you must purchase a "book" of discounts to merchants in your local area ($20 to $30, plus $5 shipping). The card that comes with the book entitles you to discounts of up to 50% off rack rate (the highest rate charged) at the resort hotels. Those outside the United States should purchase a book for the Orlando area. Log on to www.entertainment.com for details, and be sure to allow plenty of time for delivery.

AAA. Members receive a 20% discount.

Purchase an Annual Pass. Annual passholders to the theme parks receive a discount of about 30% off regular rates and are eligible for periodic special offers.

Loews First. Membership in Loews First, the hotel chain's frequent lodger program, does not get you any discounts, but it qualifies you for some nice perks like a complimentary bottle of wine or fruit basket at check-in, a newspaper delivered to your door, free use of the fitness centers, frequent flier miles on American and Midwest Airlines, and room upgrades at check-in based on availability. You can enroll online at www.loewshotels.com or call (800) 23-LOEWS to have an application mailed to you.

Go on the Internet. As a supplement to some or all of the above ploys, I recommend checking out a site called The DISBoards.com. The "DIS" in the name stands for Disney Information Station but the site has a discussion group devoted just to Universal Orlando. You will have to register to post messages, but it's free and there are no strings attached. On the DISBoards home page, scroll down until you see the link to "Universal Studios/Islands of Adventure Forums" and click there.

When you get to the USF/IOA board look for a permanent thread near the top called "What's Your Date and Rate?" This is where members post information on when they are going to the various resort hotels, the rate they got, and how they got it. This is invaluable intelligence for the budget-conscious traveler.

Making Reservations

If you are not using a travel agent to book a package vacation, you can do so yourself by calling Universal Orlando Vacations at (800) 711-0080 or (888) 322-5537. For the hearing impaired, there is a TDD line at (800) 477-

0672. If you are calling from overseas or are already in Orlando, call (407) 363-8000 and ask to be transferred.

If you are interested in booking a room only, you can call Loews central reservations number toll free at (800) 23-LOEWS. Those calling from Orlando or overseas can dial (407) 503-1000 for Portofino Bay, (407) 503-ROCK for the Hard Rock, and (407) 503-3000 for Royal Pacific Resort.

Good Things To Know About...

Access for Non-Guests

The resort hotels are tucked away in corners of Universal Orlando, carefully masked from the nearby streets, with grand entrance gates that have an air of exclusivity about them. That may be why many people mistakenly assume the resorts are closed to all but hotel guests. In fact, anyone can drop in for a visit and, if your vacation schedule affords the time, you should by all means come for a meal at one of the restaurants and a stroll through the very special grounds and public areas of the hotels. You can come by boat or on foot from the parks or you can drive in. If you drive, you can choose between valet and self parking.

Non-guests must use the main entrances to the hotels since other entrances (like the pool areas) require a room key for access.

Business Centers

All resort hotels have a "business center" for those who need to photocopy or fax something or use a computer. Most are conveniently located, although at the Royal Pacific Resort, the business center is a good hike away in the adjoining conference facility. The fees charged won't surprise the average business traveler but might make others gasp.

Concierge Service

All of the hotels offer concierge service. The concierge desk staff is extremely knowledgeable, not just about all things Universal, but about Orlando in general. They can offer tips on what else to see in the area, where to shop, and where to find a baby sitter or get the perfect birthday cake for your kid. You can even stop by the concierge desk for information about and tickets to most local attractions. Although they stock plenty of brochures about Walt Disney World and can arrange transportation to get you there, Disney does not allow them to sell Disney tickets.

Did You Forget?

All hotels offer a service aimed at the forgetful among us, so if you forgot your toothbrush or razor you can call Star Service (see below) for a complimentary replacement.

Drugs

No, not that kind. I'm talking about medicine, the kind your doctor prescribes. The Loews resort hotels have partnered with a nearby pharmacy to provide 24-hour prescription service. It's even possible to arrange delivery. For more information, call (407) 248-0315.

Golf

None of the resort hotels offers a golf course, although Royal Pacific has a well-manicured putting green. Earlier plans for an on-property golf course have been shelved apparently, but golfers needn't despair. The facilities of the Keene's Point Golf Club in nearby (and very posh) Windermere are available to all guests. Greens fees vary with the seasons but are over $100 for 18 holes. To make a reservation for a tee time, the best strategy is to call the hotel prior to your arrival and let them do it.

Hotel Hopping

Guests in the hotels are encouraged to visit the other on-site properties and take advantage of their restaurants, amenities, and special events like Dive-In Movies. Your concierge will make dining reservations. Your hotel key will not work in the gated areas of other hotels, so if you want to check out the pool at another property show your key to an attendant who will grant you access.

Kids

Loews has a soft spot for kids. Kids under 18 stay free in a room with their parents and the hotels frequently run special promotions, such as one that offered special perks for kids with A's on their report cards. Check when you make reservations to see if there are any special deals going on during your visit. Loews also sponsors a "Generation G" program designed for kids traveling with their grandparents; it offers some nice special amenities and is worth checking out if it applies to you.

When you check in, be sure to ask about Character Dining, special mealtime appearances by costumed characters from the Universal stable, and Character Wake-Up Calls, tape-recorded telephone messages for your kids. All of the hotels have special children's playrooms with supervised activities (see below) and the Portofino and Hard Rock have special "Kids' Suites" designed to give families a little extra room.

Kids' Activities

All the resort hotels have special supervised activities programs for children aged 4 to 14. These center around large, colorful playrooms filled with fun things to do, from computers with educational CD-ROMs, to computer games, to arts and crafts, to movies shown on large screen TVs. The programs also take advantage of the hotel grounds for outdoor fun and games when appropriate.

These are typically evening programs, designed to let Mom and Dad go off to enjoy more adult nighttime entertainment knowing that their little darlings are being looked after and well entertained. So expect the programs to run from about 5:00 p.m. to 11:30 or so, a little later on weekends. During busier periods and school holidays, hours can expand. On some occasions, typically on weekends, these programs will run from 10:00 a.m. to midnight. During slow periods, the program at one hotel might close altogether, but since a guest at one hotel can use the program at any other hotel, this should not pose a problem.

Pricing varies from hotel to hotel and is subject to change without notice. $10 per hour for the first child and $8 per hour for any additional kids in the same family is fairly common, but some programs will charge a flat fee of $45 for the first child and $35 for each additional. I have also seen special "Happy Hour" rates of $25 for two hours. In short, if you think you might be interested in these programs, you will have to check with the hotel at check-in or shortly before arrival to ask about the current schedule and pricing arrangements. The concierge will be able to provide you with a flyer containing complete information on activities offered, hours, and pricing. In the sections on the individual hotels, I will provide information about locations and how to contact that hotel's kids' program.

Private child care services provided by reputable outside agencies can also be arranged. Ask the concierge for assistance.

Parking

Each resort hotel has its own parking lot. Self-parking is $6 per day for hotel guests, unless you take advantage of the valet parking service, in which case there is a $12 per day fee (plus tips, of course). For non-guests, the rates are as follows: $6 for up to two hours, $8 for two to four hours, $10 for four to six hours, and so on to a maximum of $15 for 24 hours. If you come for a meal, ask to have your parking ticket validated at the restaurant and three hours of parking will be free.

Pets

Loews is a pet-friendly hotel chain and your furry friends are not only welcomed but pampered. A number of rooms in each hotel have been designated as pet rooms and a separate room service menu offers first-class pet dining for about $10. Maps provided by the hotels point out areas in which you can walk your pets. People with allergies should alert the hotel when making reservations to avoid being inadvertently placed in a pet room.

Star Service

All the hotels offer "Star Service," a one-stop, one-phone-call solution for just about any need that might arise during your stay. It even has a special button on your in-room phone. The folks at Star Service seem to pride themselves on providing speedy answers to all your questions.

Transportation to the Parks

The hotels are linked to CityWalk and the theme parks by complimentary water taxi and shuttle bus. Each hotel has its own water taxi that runs between the hotel and a dock just below the NASCAR Cafe; from there, it's a short walk to either park. If you want to go from hotel to hotel by water, you will have to change boats at CityWalk. Shuttle buses run about every half-hour from each hotel to the bus stop area near the entrance to City-Walk, but walking or taking the water taxi is a far quicker and more scenic way to get to the parks. If you prefer the bus, check with the concierge for details.

Transportation Elsewhere

Complimentary bus shuttle service is also provided from all hotels to Wet 'n Wild and SeaWorld. Typically, there are three departures in the morning and, in the evening, three returns from SeaWorld and two from Wet 'n Wild. Check with the concierge for more precise schedule information.

Mears Transportation operates on-demand shuttle services to and from Orlando Airport to the resort hotels, as well as scheduled shuttle service to and from each of the Universal Orlando resort hotels and the Disney World parks. Check with the concierge for schedules and the minimum advance notice required for pick-ups. Limousine and towncar services are also available through the concierge.

If you prefer to do the driving yourself, all hotels have Hertz rental cars available. They can be reserved ahead but, if you decide you need a car at the last minute, chances are they will be able to accommodate you. Cars can be returned to the hotel or, for an additional fee, the Orlando Airport.

PORTOFINO BAY HOTEL

An eight-minute ride aboard a gracious nineteenth century motor launch takes you from CityWalk to one of the favorite getaways of Europe's fabled jet set — Portofino, Italy.

Well, okay, it's not really Portofino, Italy, but a near photographic replica of the picturesque Ligurian fishing village that has long been a retreat for the rich and famous. And while you don't have to be famous to stay at this Portofino, it might help to be rich because the room rates place this property in the super-luxury range. If it's any consolation, staying at the Hotel Splendido (yes, that's its name) in the real Portofino will set you back $600 or $700 a night, while a room can be had at this Portofino Bay for well under $300.

If you're familiar with the real Portofino, you'll be amazed at how closely the architects and designers have come to re-creating the ambiance. If you're not, you might think the designers have cut corners by painting architectural details on the facades. Not so. This is exactly the way it's done in Portofino, Italy. It's called "trompe l'oeil," French for "trick the eye," and it's considered quite posh. Indeed, Loews brought in Italian artists and local scenic design wizards to cover the hotel's public spaces with a wide variety of trompe l'oeil effects and colorful murals at a reported cost of $70 a square yard. The real trompe l'oeil accomplishment, however, is that what looks for all the world like a quaint fishing village made up of scores of separate homes, shops, courtyards, churches, palazzos, and alleyways is in fact a state-of-the-art luxury hotel whose 750 rooms have been artfully hidden behind those picturesque facades.

If you arrive by boat, you will walk from the dock to the large central piazza with all of Portofino arrayed before you. If you arrive by car, you will drive around the Bay to arrive at a portico entrance where you can turn your vehicle over to a valet and step into a sumptuously appointed marble lobby. Either way, it's a spectacular introduction to a very special experience.

Orientation

Portofino Bay Hotel is located at the corner of Kirkman and Vineland Roads, but it turns its back to those streets and looks out on its own artificial harbor and across to Universal's Hard Rock Hotel and the theme parks beyond. The sole vehicular entrance is on Universal Boulevard near the Vineland Road entrance. You can also arrive by boat from CityWalk or walk onto the hotel property either from CityWalk and the Hard Rock Hotel or from Universal Boulevard.

The hotel wraps around "Portofino Bay," a small manmade harbor dotted with fishing boats and dinghies. A large open piazza faces the Bay and forms the focal point for the entire establishment. Most of the eateries and many of the shops face the piazza and the Bay.

The hotel's East Wing runs down one side of the Bay and the West Wing occupies the other forming a rough "U." The section at the bottom of the "U" houses the hotel's main lobby area. Behind this, away from the Bay, are the extensive meeting rooms and banquet halls; they are located in such a way that vacationers and convention-goers need seldom cross paths or rub shoulders, except perhaps in the restaurants. Jutting out from the West Wing is the Villa Wing offering larger rooms and easy access to the hotel's nicest pools and its spa facilities.

Rooms and Suites

One nice thing about staying in a hotel that aspires to five-star status is that even the most modest room is going to be pretty special. And even the "average" guest is going to be pampered by a level of service that the typical Orlando tourist never experiences.

All rooms have tall beds covered with Egyptian cotton linens and plush comforters. The bathrooms feature stone-like terra cotta tiles and a few are even tiled in marble. I especially appreciated the his-and-hers dual sinks. Also common to all rooms are such thoughtful touches as dual-line phones, so you can call home while surfing the 'Net, lavishly stocked mini-bars, bathrobes, an umbrella, an iron and ironing board, and a hair dryer. About nine percent of the rooms have balconies; most of them are quite small but a few are large enough to allow al fresco dining.

Standard rooms are a comfortable 400 square feet, while deluxe rooms are 600 square feet. Deluxe rooms have all the goodies found in standard rooms plus a fax machine, a CD player, and a video cassette player. Their bathrooms feature a separate shower stall, as well as the dual sinks, and have windows with louvered shutters over the tub that open onto the room. You may find the added perks well worth the added cost.

Beach Pool view rooms offer great views of the often dramatic Florida sunsets. Bay view rooms are ideal for those who want to feel as if they've been transported to the real Portofino. However, rooms in the Villa Wing that look out onto the Villa Pool offer a serenity that's hard to match.

At the rates charged at Portofino Bay you'll be relieved to know that kids under 18 stay free with a paying adult. Still, families with young children might want to consider a Kid's Suite that includes a separate, themed kid's bedroom that is accessible only through the parent's room. Other multi-room options include a one-bedroom suite with parlor and a two-bedroom suite. If you really want to treat yourself, consider the Presidente Suite. It has an outdoor terrace and goes for a mere $1,600 to $2,100 a night.

See *Room Rates At A Glance*, above, to get an idea of the price range at Portofino Bay and how it compares to the other on-site hotels.

Amenities

Perhaps the greatest amenity here is the easy access to the theme parks and CityWalk. Even so the amenities at the hotel itself are lavish in execution and may encourage you to linger in the lap of luxury with a masseuse and a poolside waiter at your beck and call.

Pools

There are three pools, ranging from the intimate to the lavish. The **Beach Pool** is the most extensive and, to my mind, the most fun. You find it nestled behind the West Wing. At one end it simulates a beach, with the ankle deep water surrounded by soft white sand; at the other end the pool is deeper, although never more than five feet. It surrounds a replica of the old lighthouse that stands along the Ligurian coast near Portofino. This crumbling ruin hides a very zippy water slide that is a favorite with kids and the young at heart.

Nearby, against walls that mimic ancient aqueducts, are two small secluded spa pools with hot bubbling water and warm waterfalls that provide a very nice shoulder massage. Also close at hand is a large, separate children's play area, with a pirate ship to climb in and over and a wading pool that is constantly spritzed by a trio of fountains. Campo Portofino, the children's program (described below), is close by.

The Beach Pool is near the Splendido Pizzeria and has its own poolside bar, so it's a great place to have a relaxed al fresco meal. Because of its popularity with kids, however, it can get noisy; so adults in search of peace and quiet might want to head elsewhere.

The **Villa Pool**, just a few steps from the Beach Pool and separated from it by a wing of the hotel, is much more elegant. The atmosphere is one of regal gentility. It's easy to imagine that you have your own palazzo or that you are a movie mogul cutting deals along the Italian Riviera. The layout of the pool is crisply formal with stately palm trees lining its borders and, at one end, an elaborate fountain backed by a raised balustrade.

The pool is ringed with "cabanas," canvas tents with overhead fans, electricity, phone lines, small refrigerators, even television sets. These can be rented for about $45 to $60 an eight-hour day and provide a modicum of privacy and a touch of class for your poolside lounging. All cabana rentals come with bottled water and include a selection of soft drinks and fruit. The more expensive ones include a TV and VCR. Make your reservations at the Beach Pool hut.

There is a heated jacuzzi–like pool too, of course, and attendants are on hand to take food and drink orders at poolside. Just for fun, try out the immaculately groomed bocce ball courts; a friendly attendant will explain the fine points of the game to the uninitiated.

On Saturday nights either the Villa or Beach Pool hosts a "Dive-In Movie." A huge screen is set up at poolside so guests can watch while floating on rented rafts. The films are family fare of fairly recent vintage, often with a tie-in to the theme parks, and never more racy than PG–13.

A good place to go for some real privacy is the **Hillside Pool** tucked away at the end of the East Wing. Much smaller than the Beach Pool, it has the virtue of seclusion and quiet and a view across the Bay.

Hours at the pools vary by season and occupancy. In summer, you will generally find the Beach Pool open 8:00 a.m. to 10:00 p.m. daily; the Villa Pool, 6:00 a.m. to 10:00 p.m., and the Hillside Pool 8:00 a.m. to 8:00 p.m. In winter, the pools usually close at 8:00 p.m.

The Greenhouse Spa at Portofino Bay Hotel

Near the Beach Pool is a state-of-the-art spa. This is your perfect chance to feel like an Italian movie star. Looking like an Italian movie star may be asking too much, but who knows.

You can get the full treatment of massages, mud wraps, and facials, all with the latest "all-natural" and "therapeutic" ointments, oils, and unguents, of course. Or you can simply have your hair and nails done in an elegant European salon setting. If you stroll in here and say, "Give me the works," be prepared to spend a bundle. The "Divine Day" package, which includes lunch and a free bathrobe in addition to a dizzying regimen of facial, massages, makeup, manicure, pedicure, hair styling, and aromatherapy, costs $1,000. Less lavish packages of pampering start at $195.

Campo Portofino

Located near the Beach Pool, this indoor play area houses Portofino's children's activities program. For more information about the services offered here, see *Good Things To Know About ...Kids' Activities* in the introductory section of this chapter. Make your reservations 24 hours in advance by calling 31200 on a hotel phone or (407) 503-1200 from outside.

Game Room

A small, unattended video arcade is located near the Beach Pool by the Splendido Pizzeria. The machines operate on quarters and a change machine is provided. The games, none of them terribly elaborate, cost between 50 cents and $1.

Fitness Center

Adjacent to the Greenhouse Spa is a sleek health club offering the very latest in pec-pumping paraphernalia. Here you can exhaust yourself on treadmills, recumbent and standing bicycle machines, or stair climbers. For the die-hard traditionalist, there are also free weights. Access to the fitness center costs $12 a day, which entitles you to use all the facilities of the Spa, including showers, saunas, and steam rooms. If you are a customer of the Spa, your access to the fitness center is free.

Many fitness-minded guests also use the paved walkway that surrounds the Bay as a handy jogging trail. The path to Universal Studios Florida and back also makes for a nice early morning jog.

Good Things To Know About. . .

Character Dining

Scooby Doo and Woody Woodpecker stop by to entertain diners in Trattoria del Porto on Friday nights from about 6:30 to 9:00 p.m. Double-check with the concierge on the schedule, since days and times are subject to change and during busier times of the year they may add nights.

Meetings and Banquets

The hotel has over 42,000 square feet of meeting space, ranging from the magnificent 15,000 square foot Tuscan Ballroom, which can accommodate 1,280 for a sit-down dinner to a sumptuous boardroom suite for 25. In addition to being beautifully appointed, with lavish hand-painted Italian murals, these facilities offer some of the most advanced telecommunications equipment available anywhere. That's made the Portofino Bay Hotel one of the most sought after meeting venues in Orlando. If you'd like to explore holding your next meeting at Portofino Bay, call Conference Management at (407) 503-1234.

Parking

The parking here is in a well-hidden and covered parking garage, making self-parking a more attractive option than at the other hotels, which have open lots.

Weddings

Looking for a very special place to tie the knot? Portofino Bay has quickly become a favorite spot for Orlando's discerning brides. There are two outdoor gazebos that, when adorned with flowers, make lovely wedding chapels. One is above the Villa Pool in a palazzo-like setting; the other is in a courtyard near the main ballrooms and just steps away from a majestic curving staircase that was seemingly custom-designed for bridal portraits. And Universal Orlando, with its panoply of diversions, makes a terrific honeymoon destination. Call (407) 503-1234 for more information.

Dining at Portofino Bay Hotel

Portofino Bay offers some superb gourmet dining, but reflecting the casual ambiance of its namesake, there are also casual, moderately priced eateries dotted around the property. Of course it's all Italian, in keeping with the hotel's theme. Unless you can be satisfied with a burger or a club sandwich, you'll have to travel to CityWalk or the parks for more varied fare.

Most of the hotel's eateries are positioned to take advantage of the piazza and the Bay. For this survey, I begin on the western side of the Bay and work my way around the piazza to the east, before describing two venues located elsewhere in the hotel.

Guests who just can't get it together to drag themselves to one of these restaurants can take advantage of the hotel's 24-hour room service.

Delfino Riviera

What:	Fine gourmet dining
Where:	On the third level overlooking the Bay
Price Range:	$$$$+
Hours:	Tuesday to Saturday, 6:00 p.m. to 10:00 p.m.
Reservations:	Not required, but strongly suggested
	(407) 503-1415

The very special experience offered here begins the moment you enter the restaurant. You pass down a narrow brick-arched passageway past a portion of the establishment's extensive wine cellar and emerge into a large high-ceilinged formal dining room that would not look out of place in a Roman palazzo. White columns set off a central atrium dominated by two large urns that almost explode with elaborate floral arrangements. Above, a mural of rural Italy rings the recessed Renascimento ceiling. Tall windows, set off with dramatic curtains, look out onto the Bay and the wall sconces are shrouded in fabric as they were in the time of the Borgias, lending the room a soothing candle-lit aura.

Atmosphere like this has a way of raising expectations and the chef rises to the challenge. Massimo Fedozzi hails from Portofino itself and he brings to the menu a light Ligurian touch that owes as much to Mama's kitchen as to the latest trends of haute cuisine. The dishes are subtle and rely more on the finest ingredients and exquisite technique than on assertive flavors and startling combinations. The presentations are artful yet subdued; only the desserts aspire to the theatrical. There is none of the over the top, food-as-artwork style that characterizes Emeril's at CityWalk or Mythos in Islands of Adventure. This is a restaurant for those who like fine food simply presented, and who don't blink at paying nearly $40 for a lobster entree.

The menu does not overwhelm but presents a manageable number of dishes in several courses: antipasti ($18 to $24), soups and salads ($8 to $14), primi piatti — pastas and risottos ($16 to $22), and secondi piatti — fish, poultry, and meat ($32 to $42). The dessert menu ($8) is presented at the end of the meal. Your server may encourage you to order a full-course meal in the Italian fashion, but I would urge caution. Although the portions are sensible, a four-course meal requires an extremely hearty appetite and you do want to leave room for dessert. If you want to sample more of the menu, however, they will be happy to split a single dish for two diners.

There is a large but not overwhelming wine list that concentrates on Italian and American wines. The only French wines on the list are a few champagnes. Wine prices are not outrageous as wine lists go but expect to pay over $30 for a modest bottle. A number of wines on the list are available by the glass at $6 to $12.

As you've no doubt noticed by now, this is an expensive restaurant. Given the pricing the five-course wine pairing menu, "Le Delizie di Delfino Riviera," represents something of a bargain. For about $100 you get five separate courses, all of them but the cheese course accompanied by a wine specially chosen by the chef. The dishes on this menu are specials not included on the regular menu. You can get this menu without the wines for about $70.

The menu changes roughly every quarter to take advantage of seasonal ingredients, so it will be impossible to predict what will be on offer at the time of your visit. However, a brief survey of some past selections will give an idea of what awaits you. Starters range from a simple yet exquisite minestrone (probably the best example of its kind you have ever tasted) to an elaborate braised stuffed breast of veal. Other starters have included a simple plate of vegetables stuffed with puffy ricotta and gently baked and a soulful saute of porcini mushrooms with potatoes and garlic. The primi piatti are equally inventive. They might range from a simple dish of gnocchi in a pesto sauce to a masterful risotto of lobster with artichoke hearts, and all of the pastas are handmade daily.

The entrees are hearty and flavorful. A veal chop was thick and perfectly cooked, garnished with strips of eggplant and zucchini on a bed of creamy mashed parsnips. Herb-roasted lobster was served out of the shell on a bed of sea bass chunks floating in a rich tomato cioppino sauce. Even a simple breaded chicken cutlet was made special with an intense balsamic reduction.

Chef Fedozzi is one of that rare breed of chefs who insist on creating their own desserts and he can certainly hold his own with any pastry chef. His panna cotta is simplicity itself, but when set off by an artful drizzle of reduced balsamic infusion and bits of fruit compote it rises well above the ordinary. My favorite dessert, however, was a warm mixed berry crumble set off by vanilla cream, homemade ice cream, and fresh berries.

This is one of Orlando's classiest restaurants. It isn't cheap and it doesn't deserve to be. A full meal with drinks and wine can easily top $100 per person. Still, this is the kind of food worth saving your pennies for. The service, too, is worth mentioning. There's none of that cheerfully familiar "Hi, my name is Giorgio" style that, while perfectly fine in its place, has become an instant cliché. The waiters here, in their suave white tuxedo jackets, remain blissfully anonymous and make no effort to become your best friend. They are expert advisors on the menu and wine list and smoothly efficient as each new course arrives on impeccable Donatella Versace china. It's nice to feel classy every now and again, even on vacation.

Tip: Here are some things that many first-time visitors miss: You can ask to have your dessert served on a terrace overlooking the main piazza. The view is unmatched and your cigar is welcome here. There is also a classy bar area where food is served. Feel free to stop in for a light meal of an appetizer or pasta, or drop by for a late-night dessert and cognac.

Delfino Riviera wins my vote for the most romantic restaurant in all of Universal Orlando. This is most definitely the place to come for that special anniversary celebration when price is no object and murmured conversation and long, loving looks are on the agenda. The tables are set far apart, assuring some intimacy. The refined atmosphere, the hushed professionalism of the staff, a strolling guitarist with a rich tenor voice, and the lovely views of Portofino's picturesque waterfront complete the menu for one very memorable evening.

The Thirsty Fish Bar

What:	Casual bar with snacks
Where:	Facing Portofino Bay, below Delfino Riviera
Price Range:	$ - $$
Hours:	5:00 p.m. to 2:00 a.m.; Saturday noon to 2:00 a.m., Sunday noon to midnight

One of the few spots in the hotel that doesn't have an immediate echo in Italy, this casual bar is just a bit too tidy to be called funky. It caters to bayside strollers in need of liquid refreshment. This is strictly a drinking establishment, no food is served here other than salty bar nibbles.

A small number of outdoor tables facing the Bay and the piazza make

The Thirsty Fish a great place to relax and survey the passing scene in the Italian fashion. Inside, a dart board and pool table set the laid back tone, and the two televisions tuned to the day's hot sporting event remind you that you're in the States.

Trattoria del Porto

What: Casual all-day dining
Where: Facing the Harbor Piazza
Price Range: $$ - $$$
Hours: 6:00 a.m. to 11:00 p.m.
Reservations: Not required but recommended during busier periods

This spacious 300-seat restaurant is the only eatery serving breakfast, lunch, and dinner. Large windows look out onto the piazza where there is plenty of al fresco seating. Should you care to eat outdoors, you'll be happily accommodated. The columns indoors are painted with fanciful scenes of commedia dell'arte figures cavorting under the sea with dolphins and seals. With its high ceilings, tile and mosaic accents in blue and gold , and polished wood trim, the Trattoria projects an air of laid back elegance.

At breakfast, the Trattoria lays on a sumptuous buffet that features made-to-order eggs and omelets ($15 for adults, $5 for kids). You can also order from a more traditional breakfast menu that features such favorites as eggs Benedict and waffles adorned with fresh fruit.

Lunch is on the light and casual side, with one half of the menu given over to a variety of soups, salads, and other starters. For the rest, there are sandwiches — both Italian panini and the American variety — "brick oven" pizzas, and simple pasta dishes. Starters run from about $5 to $12, sandwiches are $10 to $12, pizzas are $13 to $15, and pastas are $13 to $16. Specials may be priced slightly higher.

In the evening, prices rise slightly for pizzas and pastas and more interesting entrees ($18 to $24) are added. They range from salmon to a hearty New York steak with a wild mushroom demi-glace. A special kids' menu features simple dishes for less than $5. A dinner buffet Friday and Saturday is $20 for adults and $10 for kids.

If the weather's fine, the tables in the large al fresco dining area on the piazza offer the best seats in the house.

Note: Kids are specially welcomed. At the back of the restaurant there is a small dining area just for little ones, featuring brightly colored toddler-sized tables, a large-screen TV showing appropriate kiddie fare, and big pillows for comfy after-meal sprawling. On Thursday nights a magician performs, Friday nights feature Character Dining with Scooby Doo and Woody Woodpecker, and on Saturdays a clown drops by to create balloon animals.

Mama Della's Ristorante

What: Home-style Italian dinners

Where: Facing the Harbor Piazza, next to the Trattoria

Price Range: $$ - $$$

Hours: Open for dinner only

Reservations: Not required but recommended during busier periods

A lot of people will tell you this is their favorite Portofino Bay restaurant and it has attracted a dedicated local following. It isn't as fancy as Delfino Riviera and the cuisine is more comforting than intriguing, but perhaps that is the attraction. Then, too, Mama Della's comes complete with Mama, a perfectly cast woman of a certain age who greets you warmly at the door and makes you feel as if you never left the Old Neighborhood even if you were never there to begin with.

The decor evokes a large and comfortable country home with its beamed ceilings and colorful wallpaper. Vintage family photographs and gaudy gold-framed floral paintings line the walls of the various rooms. Colorful pitchers, bowls, and other folk ceramics are displayed in niches. Adding to the casual air is an open galley kitchen in the back room where you can see chefs in baseball caps dishing up their homey specialties. And a festive note is contributed by a strolling singer offering popular Italian songs to an accordion accompaniment.

Among the appetizers ($6 to $16), you'll find the tender fried calamari with both marinara and pesto dipping sauces and the Cozze Posillipo, mussels in a garlic infused sauce, especially noteworthy. The mixed antipasto of cured meats, cheeses, and marinated vegetables is also worth sampling.

The entrees ($17 to $27) can best be described as Italian comfort food: chicken cacciatore, chicken parmigiana, lasagna, and the like. The porcini mushroom risotto with a marvelous béchamel sauce is spectacular as is the sliced eye of sirloin served with rich caramelized onions and roasted potatoes. Another winner is the frutti di mare, grilled shrimp, scallops, and snapper with roasted tomatoes in a garlic sauce. Chicken cacciatore and veal scaloppini marsala are too often boring cliches, but here they are very toothsome indeed. In the same league is the rigatoni with spicy fennel sausage bits and broccoli rabe. Many of the dishes here can be served "family style" on large platters for a group. Family style service typically means a modest discount off the individual price for each additional person.

Vegetable side dishes are priced separately ($7 to $8) and include a very nice mixed salad, broccolini with lemon and olive oil, and spinach with roasted garlic and tomato. Desserts ($6 to $9) range from simple sorbets and tiramisu to a layered chocolate "lasagna" served with a blood orange sauce.

Sal's Market Deli

What:	Casual sandwiches and pizza
Where:	Facing the Harbor Piazza
Hours:	Varies with the seasons and occupancy level
Price Range:	$$

Sal's offers a casual atmosphere patterned on the famed Pecks of Milan but reminiscent of New York's Little Italy, with its marble topped cafe tables and arched ceiling. It's a nice place to stop for a quick bite. Panini (grilled Italian sandwiches, $11) are served at the deli-like counter along with cold antipasto-style salads ($4).

At the back is a sort of pizza bar where you can order one of five styles of pizzas (small $11 to $13, large $13 to $15) and sit on a stool along a marble counter and watch it baking in the open-doored oven. A small pie can feed two people generously. This ain't Domino's, either. The pizza chefs here make their own dough, using a mixture of high-gluten flour for toughness and durum semolina for taste and a rich yellow color. The oven is a true pizza oven, with the base kept at a steady 600 degrees. The result is a crisper and firmer crust than you'll find over at the Trattoria or the Splendido Pizzeria. Sal's version of Pizza Americana, with a generous topping of mushrooms, sausage, and pepperoni, is especially good.

Tip: You can have your pizza made to go, a good thing to know if you are not staying in the hotel.

If you like wine with your pizza, you can get it by the glass for $6 to $8. Sal's is also a good place to grab a cup of coffee. Espresso and cappuccino are available, as is regular coffee. For a stronger cup ask for a Caffe Americano, a shot of espresso with steaming hot water added.

Tip: Coffee is expensive here (over $3 for a large size serving), but if you hang on to your coffee container or your receipt, you can get free refills throughout the day.

Carrying the Italian deli theme to its logical conclusion, Sal's sells Italian specialties such as extra virgin olive oil, dry pasta, and Peroni beer. The attached Piccolo Forno ("Little Bakery") has been turned into a mini wine shop, with regularly scheduled tastings ($13 and up).

Gelateria Caffe Espresso

What:	Ice cream and coffee
Where:	In the East Wing facing the Harbor Piazza
Hours:	6:00 a.m to 11:00 a.m. and 4:00 p.m. to 10:00 p.m., but hours vary
Price Range:	$

This is two shops, really, each with its own entrance and specialty but joined at the hip so you can pass from one to the other. The gelateria side serves gelato, the creamy Italian ice cream, handmade daily on the premises. You can have it straight, in a sundae, or in a cream-topped milkshake. Sorbets and Italian ices are also served.

Pop next door for a coffee, espresso, cappuccino, or latte in any of their increasingly elaborate variations. A small selection of cookies, muffins, pastries, and cakes is also served here. In the mornings, croissants, muffins, and fresh fruit are laid out, making this a good serve-yourself alternative to a room service breakfast. There is both indoor and outdoor seating. In the Italian tradition, these establishments take a leisurely midday break.

Bar American

What:	Posh formal bar
Where:	Off the main lobby
Hours:	4:00 p.m. to midnight
Price Range:	$ - $$$$

There are vague echoes of Harry's Bar in Venice here, but this Bar American is very much its own room and in the fine tradition of upscale hotel bars where patrons signal their status in life by swirling $150 snifters of fine brandy.

Luckily you can enjoy a drink and the refined atmosphere for less than that. Specialty cocktails are in the $8 to $10 range, with appetizers like smoked salmon and shrimp cocktails available for under $20. Of course, if beluga caviar is your appetizer of choice, the cost soars to about $110. Other specialties here include single malt scotch ($8 to $11), grappa, an Italian fortified wine ($9 to $25), and the aforementioned cognacs ($7 to $175).

Splendido Pizzeria

What:	Pizzeria
Where:	Near the Beach Pool
Hours:	11:00 a.m. to 5:00 p.m., but hours vary
Price Range:	$$

The name is a nod to the exclusive hotel in the real Portofino, but the atmosphere is far from deluxe. This is a laid back and ultra-casual eatery whose small indoor and outdoor seating areas are supplemented by poolside service at both the Beach and Villa Pools.

Salads ($8 to $11) include mesclun, chicken Caesar, and an iced fruit coupe. Sandwiches ($9 to $10) are served with slaw, pasta salad, or French fries and include such standbys as cheeseburgers and ham along with hot dogs and grilled chicken.

The pizza you get here ($11 to $13) is much the same as that served up in the Trattoria del Porto. But here you can eat it poolside, which of course, makes it taste better. These are "personal pizzas" sized just right for lunch or a light supper and they are very good. Gelato, sorbet, and fruit smoothies round out the short menu. A kid's meal, including an entree, fries, and a beverage, is served in a little plastic bucket with shovel that can be taken poolside after the meal.

The Splendido also serves up some fancy cocktails (about $8) designed to produce that perfect poolside buzz. The Italian Ice Margarita, to cite just one example, is a creative blend of tequila and Amaretto with a splash of cream.

Shopping at Portofino Bay

Shopping is not the main focus at Portofino Bay Hotel. In fact, unlike many posh hotels I have had occasion to visit around the world, this one has remarkably few shops. The ones it has can be roughly divided between the practical and the posh.

On the practical side is **Le Memorie di Portofino**, or Memories of Portofino, where you can pick up a variety of sundries and magazines along with pricey polo shirts bearing the hotel's handsome logo. If you don't like the paper dropped outside your door, you can come here for *The New York Times* or the *Wall Street Journal*. Other reading matter includes glossy magazines and the latest thriller to take to the pool. There is also some posh Italian ceramic ware and resort wear with the Portofino Bay logo.

Another place to stop into to pick up the necessities of resort life is **L'Ancora** (The Anchor) located near the boat dock. It thoughtfully purveys sunscreen and other items you might need as you head for the parks. This shop also stocks chips, dips, and soft drinks to wash it all down with.

As you might have guessed, there is an outpost of the **Universal Studios Store** in Portofino Bay. It stocks plenty of t-shirts and polo shirts, some of them quite nice, along with silk pajamas in case you forgot to pack yours. You'll also find a small selection of toys and plush dolls for the kids.

The remaining shops are for pampering yourself or that special someone. Once you've taken in the luxurious atmosphere of the hotel, you might want to rush to **Alta Moda** (High Fashion) for something you'll feel comfortable being seen in. They have thoughtfully provided the best in contemporary resort wear, with everything from fashion accessories, to swimwear, to lingerie, to eveningwear for that special meal at Delfino Riviera.

Another place to spend the money you didn't spend on a ticket to Italy is **Galleria Portofino**. It features the work of contemporary artists. In addition to paintings, there is blown glass from Murano and jewelry from a variety of artisans. Hottest sellers: Paintings of Portofino's waterfront ($1,200 to $1,850).

HARD ROCK HOTEL

Imagine for a moment you are an aging rock star. Changing tastes and slumping record sales have reduced your income to pitiful new lows. Years of hard living and fiscal mismanagement have depleted your assets to the vanishing point. Your groupies have left you to your own devices in the palatial Beverly Hills mansion that you have filled with the memories and memorabilia of your high-flying years of hits and worldwide mega tours. Soon you will have to sell this last remnant of your once lavish lifestyle and move into a shabby condo. Then, inspiration strikes: you'll turn your mansion into a hotel and take in paying guests who will leap at the chance to experience, however vicariously, however briefly, what it must be like to live like a rock star.

That is the "backstory" of the Hard Rock Hotel. It's a story that will never be told in so many words to the guests who stay here, but it is the fanciful tale from which the architects and designers drew inspiration as they fashioned this flamboyant, flashy, and surprisingly elegant hostelry.

The 650-room Hard Rock Hotel draws on the architectural traditions of California's Spanish Mission style, with stucco arches and adobe-like touches, rising to seven stories at its highest point. With its gracious terraces and the towering palm trees that dot the 19 acres of manicured grounds, it looks more like the rambling mountain-top palaces of Hollywood's superstars than the well-appointed hotel it is.

Orientation

The Hard Rock Hotel is located on Universal Boulevard, just south of Vineland Road. It's huge front gates face the entrance to the Portofino Bay Hotel, just across the boulevard. For guests with hotel keys, there is also a side entrance near the dock where water taxis arrive from CityWalk.

The elegant main approach, an oval lawn flanked by stately palms, suggests pure luxury. The fountain out front, with its sculpture of spiraling guitars, adds a touch of whimsy. The pulsing rock music that subtly envelops guests as they walk over the marble-mosaic Hard Rock logo into the expansive lobby signals that a stay here is literally going to be an upbeat experience. The marble lobby gives way to a spacious sunken carpeted lounge overlooking the palm-dotted pool area out back.

The lobby lounge is decorated with the furniture and souvenirs that the unnamed rock star of our backstory has collected during his world tours. They range from the lavish to the funky, the tasteful to the bizarre, with coffee tables doubling as showcases for rare guitars once owned by rock masters. The effect is at once edgy and elegant and even the oddest looking furniture proves to be quite comfortable. Elaborate floral arrangements that are abstract art in their own right add the perfect finishing touch.

The public areas of the lobby level are dominated by large-scale art paying homage to some of rock's greatest stars. My favorite is the massive blowup of the cover photo from the Stones' *Beggars' Banquet* album. This is a Hard Rock property, of course, so as you might expect, the ample collection of rock memorabilia spills out into the public areas and down the hallways. In fact, more than $800,000 worth of rock memorabilia is scattered throughout the hotel, but judiciously so.

The lobby area, on the hotel's third level, features the Palm Restaurant, the Velvet Bar, the Hard Rock Store, and the hotel's small meetings areas. Two floors below, at ground level, is The Kitchen, the hotel's main restaurant, and the extensive pool area. Also on this level are the fitness center and Camp L'il Rock for kids. A single bank of elevators gives access to all the hotel's floors.

The hotel wraps itself around the pool area out back, so the hallways of the upper floors, beautifully carpeted in blue and tan, curve gracefully. Where wings meet, the halls are punctuated by circular mini-lobbies with carpet medallions on the floor and rock memorabilia or rock portraits on the wall. The overall effect is quite classy; the rocker who owned this place obviously had exquisite taste — or hired a decorator who did.

For most people, the Hard Rock Hotel's best feature is likely to be its "ground-zero" location, next to Universal Studios Florida. As noted above, the actual front entrance to the hotel faces Universal Boulevard, looking across to the Portofino Bay Hotel, but the hotel grounds nestle up against the theme park. A side entrance on the ground level leads to a boat dock where you can pick up a motor launch for the short ride to CityWalk. If you prefer to walk, out back, past the pool, is a path that will take you directly to the front gates of Universal Studios Florida. I've timed it and found that you can leave the hotel on foot and, walking at a liesurely pace, be inside Universal Studios Florida in less than six minutes. Nowhere else on earth can you come so close to staying inside a theme park.

Rooms and Suites

In general, the rooms are smaller than those at Portofino but just as nicely appointed. What you will find are beautifully designed and furnished rooms that would make the reputation of any big city "boutique" hotel. Most rooms avoid that boxy hotel room look with curved or angled walls and wavy accents in furniture that ranges from Deco to 50s retro. Most rooms are "standard" rooms, 375 square feet, while the deluxe rooms are 400 square feet and feature a larger sitting area. Pool view rooms, especially those on floors five through seven, are highly recommended. You can reserve either a pool view or garden view room, but if you choose a deluxe room, the hotel will not be able to guarantee the view.

There is no rock memorabilia in the rooms, but the walls are decorated with black and white photos of rock history, in artful black frames with plenty of white matting. Each room has a different selection of photos from the hotel's collection. There are no labels so your rock knowledge will be tested. If you get stuck, the management has thoughtfully provided each room with a guide to the photographs.

Every room boasts a compact but powerful CD-radio player. When you check in you will be given a sampler CD but you may want to bring along your favorites. It's hard to resist the temptation to slip in a Stones CD and crank up the volume. Otherwise, you can tune the player to the local classic rock station, 96.5 FM. Don't be surprised if you hear the dull throb of bass notes from other rooms lulling you to sleep and waking you up in the morning.

In what may be a subtle reference to a Beatles song, you'll even find a copy of Gideon's Bible. Gideon checked out and left it, no doubt, to help with some rocker's revival.

Hard Rock features a Club Level, with restricted access, on the seventh floor. For more on the Club Level, see *Amenities*, below. Kid's Suites, similar to those offered at Portofino, are also available, as are 685 square foot "King" Suites.

There is even a Graceland Suite, also named in honor of The King. But don't expect gaudy over the top furniture and pink Caddy fins on the bed. This is a beautifully appointed suite of rooms with Japanese antiques, abstract paintings, and beautiful furnishings. The master bedroom features a flat plasma screen TV hanging on the wall and a glass-fronted fireplace that also opens onto a lavish shower area with a jacuzzi that can hold several people. (Groupies not included, presumably.) Rates for the Graceland Suite range from $1,250 to $1,575 a night.

See *Room Rates At A Glance*, above, to get an idea of the price range at the Hard Rock and how it compares to the other on-site hotels.

Amenities

As a relatively small hotel on a smallish plot of land, the Hard Rock Hotel boasts fewer amenities than the nearby Portofino Bay, but what's here is choice.

The Pool

The Hard Rock's only pool, all 12,000 square feet of it, is like a jewel in a fine setting. The hotel itself almost completely encloses it. The open end looks out past a rocky hill topped by a thirty-foot guitar and a forest of palm trees toward Universal Studios Florida. The far side of the pool is an extensive sandy beach, dotted with lounge chairs and cabanas. The near side is dotted with more palm trees and still more lounge chairs. Two heated jacuzzi spas offer soothing massages. As a screenwriter might put it in a pitch meeting, "It's Bel Air meets Palm Springs."

Like the Beach Pool at Portofino, the Hard Rock pool features a water slide, this one a bit longer and a bit zippier. But the feature that will have everyone talking is the underwater sound system, which plays the same toe-tapping rock music you hear at poolside and throughout the hotel. It is possible to float lazily on your back, your ears below the water line, and groove to some of the greatest rock 'n roll ever recorded. And, yes, the sound quality is very good indeed. If you prefer, you can float on top of the water on one of the complimentary floats that have been thoughtfully provided or sit on underwater benches along the side where heated jets of water caress your back.

Near the pool, "interactive" fountains draw the kids, who can make the water splash higher the harder they jump. Farther back is a giant chess board, complete with waist-high pieces, for the more intellectually inclined. Near it is a concrete shuffleboard court, which struck me as a bit incongruous. I suppose even rockers grow old, but try as I might, I just couldn't picture Twisted Sister hanging out here.

A lot more "happening" is the Beach Club bar (reviewed below). Attractive young servers roam the pool area taking orders for exotic $8 drinks with names like Aldo's Passion and Hard Rockin' Lemonade.

Hollywood dealmakers can spread out in one of the private tent-like cabanas that can be rented by the day ($80) or half-day ($40); Club Level guests get a full day for just $40. All cabanas have a television, refrigerator, fresh water, newspaper, and a small selection of soft drinks.

On Friday nights the pool hosts a "Dive-In Movie." A huge screen is set up on the poolside beach so guests can watch while floating on rented rafts. The films are of fairly recent vintage, often with a tie-in to the theme parks, and never rated higher than PG-13. On Sunday night there is a "Dive-In Concert," the same concept with concert films.

The pool is open daily from 8:00 a.m. to midnight during warmer months. Access is through a gate that can be opened with your room key.

Club Level

The rooms and suites on the seventh floor have been set aside for those who insist on a little extra from their hotel stay. The concept is much like the Concierge Levels you may have encountered at those high-priced hotels that cater to business travelers.

For starters, access to the seventh floor is strictly limited. Just to make sure you are not bothered by the riffraff, you have to insert your room key into a slot in the elevator before it will take you to seven. Once there you can step into a spacious lounge staffed with friendly hosts and hostesses, who serve as your personal concierge from 7:30 a.m. to 11:00 p.m. This is where you come in the morning for a complimentary continental breakfast and to glance through the tony out of town papers high rollers insist upon. The lounge serves refreshments throughout the day; hors d'oeuvres, beer and wine in the evening; and cookies and milk before bedtime.

Club Level guests can borrow from the Club's collection of 400 rock CDs for private listening in their rooms. If they're feeling more sociable, the Club lounge offers a large screen TV with a DVD player in an area with very comfy seating. Club level guests also receive free access to the hotel's fitness center and discounts on poolside cabanas.

Camp L'il Rock

Hard Rock's kiddie club is located on the ground floor not far from the pool. For more information about the services offered here, see *Good Things To Know About ...Kids' Activities* in the introductory section of this chapter. Make your reservations 24 hours in advance by calling 32236 on a hotel phone or (407) 503-2236 from outside.

Workout Room

The compact fitness center on the ground floor has a small selection of treadmills and weight machines and even some free weights for purists. After your workout, you can relax in a steam room or sauna and then change in the locker room. Separate facilities are provided for men and women. There is an $8 a day fee for use of the facilities, $14 for two days, and $20 for three. Club Level guests and Loews First members get in free. Hours are 6:00 a.m. to 9:00 p.m. Kids 12 through 16 are allowed, but only if they have adult supervision.

Joggers can take off for a loop around either the Bay at Portofino Bay in one direction or City Walk in the other. A map of suggested jogging routes is available from the concierge.

Game Room

A small unattended video arcade is located under a sheltered portico between the Beach Club and The Kitchen. The machines operate on tokens dispensed by a machine that accepts $1, $5 and $20 bills. The games, none of them terribly elaborate, cost between 50 cents and $1.

Good Things To Know About...

Character Dining

Scooby Doo and Woody Woodpecker stop by to entertain diners in The Kitchen on Saturday nights from about 6:30 to 9:00 p.m. Double-check with the concierge on the schedule, since days and times are subject to change and during busier times of the year they may add nights.

Guest Laundry

The Hard Rock Hotel has small guest laundry rooms on the second and fourth floors near the elevators, each with two washers and two dryers. The cost is $1.75 to wash, $1.75 to dry.

Meetings and Banquets

There is very little meeting space at the Hard Rock. The largest space is the Avalon Ballroom, 3,000 square feet divisible into three separate sections, with a total capacity of 300 people. Two smaller rooms, the Apollo Board-room and the Fillmore Meeting Room are suitable for receptions or small meetings. There has been some speculation that the old Hard Rock Cafe building, which sits on a guitar-shaped platform just across a parking lot from the hotel, will be gutted, rehabbed, and used for additional meeting space. For more information, call (407) 224-6222.

Dining at the Hard Rock Hotel

There are just two full-service restaurants at Hard Rock, one offering gut- and wallet-busting steaks, the other serving up moderately priced casual fare. Guests who are too pooped to pop or too old to stroll can call on the hotel's 24-hour room service.

Palm Restaurant

What:	Steak house
Where:	On the lobby level, near Velvet; also has an outside entrance
Price Range:	$$$ - $$$$+
Hours:	Monday to Friday 11:30 a.m. to 11:00 p.m.; Saturday 5:00 p.m. to 11:00 p.m.; Sunday 5:00 p.m. to 10:00 p.m.
Reservations:	Not required but highly recommended, especially on weekends. Call (407) 503-7256

The original Palm opened in New York in 1926 and over the years developed a reputation as a place where movers and shakers gathered to devour mammoth steaks and cut big deals. The Palm has branched out to many other cities (26 at last count) and now, 77 years after its birth, it has arrived in Orlando. Those who know the original will find the Hard Rock incarnation familiar, if larger. Like the other branches, the walls of this one are filled with colorful caricatures of regular patrons and local celebrities from the business world and the media. The dark wooden wainscoting and room dividers evoke an earlier, male-dominated era when the steak house was something of a boy's club. The waiters in long white meat cutters' aprons complete the vintage picture.

This is a noisy boisterous steak house that fits in well with the spirit of Hard Rock and it should prove equally popular with tourists and high-rolling locals, which is probably the whole point. It's a great place to come in a celebratory mood with a bunch of friends who don't mind shouting to make themselves heard as they tuck into huge slabs of prime aged meat or crack open a five-pound lobster, all washed down with some pricey wines. Figure a bare minimum of $60 per person for the standard Palm blowout meal, much more with cocktails and wine. Those looking for a quiet table in the corner or a moderately priced meal should look elsewhere.

Steaks are the center of attention here and they are quite good. They range in price from $30 to $35, with a mammoth 36-ounce double steak for two going for $60. If you don't know exactly what you want, my advice would be to rely on the server's recommendation. Steak and lobsters at the Palm are traditionally accompanied by a number of side dishes served "family style for two or more" ($4 to $8). The creamed spinach is justly famous and the others are good, too.

For those not into thick slabs of steak or gargantuan crustaceans, the Palm offers a selection of fairly standard Italian veal dishes (about $20) as well as some pasta dishes ($15 to $26). For lighter appetites, two of the Palm's signature salads are worth recommending. The Gigi ($11) is a blend of tomatoes, bacon, onions, chopped shrimp, and green beans in a light vinaigrette and the Monday Night Salad ($9) is mixed greens, pimentos, onions, tomatoes, anchovies, and radishes.

Desserts ($6 to $8) are fairly pedestrian versions of old standbys and struck me as a tad overpriced. They include New York cheesecake, tiramisu, key lime pie, and creme brulee.

The Palm is open for lunch Mondays through Friday only. The lunch menu includes sandwiches ($9 to $14), a limited selection of fairly standard poultry and fish entrees ($11 to $18), and of course those steaks and lobsters.

Smoking is permitted in the bar and a small smoking section is provided in the restaurant. The Palm has two entrances. One leads from the hotel lobby down a stately corridor lined with psychedelic day-glo posters from the heyday of San Francisco acid rock; the other offers access from the hotel's front drive for those arriving by car.

Velvet

What:	Trendy watering hole
Where:	Off the main lobby lounge
Price Range:	$ - $$
Hours:	4:00 p.m. to 2:00 a.m. daily
Reservations:	None

Plasma TV screens on the wall provide a never ending flow of music videos for the crowds that gather in this intimate, postmodern lounge. It has quickly proved to be *the* place for groups of friends to meet before an evening at the hotel or CityWalk.

The decor relies on the same artfully mismatched furniture that fills the lobby. To this is added some wonderfully tacky faux zebra chairs, abstract art, and portraits of rock stars in a color-filled mish-mash that makes you feel like you've had a bit too much to drink before you take your first sip. A well-placed divider splits the room into a bar area and a more secluded lounge area and leggy girls in black leather mini skirts prowl the bar and the adjacent lobby lounge taking orders.

There are about a dozen specialty drinks ($8) on offer as well as an abbreviated menu ($7 to $14) of things to nibble on, including a number of mini-pizzas and a plate of "artisan" cheeses. Rockers with the midnight munchies will want to check out the dessert section of the menu ($6).

The Kitchen at Sunset Grill

What:	Casual all-day dining
Where:	On the ground floor overlooking the pool
Price Range:	$$ - $$$
Hours:	6:30 a.m. to 11:00 p.m. daily
Reservations:	Not required but accepted at (407) 503-2431

This artfully casual eatery features Southern-tinged comfort cuisine (if there is such a term) in a glamorous open setting that seems to run the length of the hotel. Near the entrance is Emack & Bolio's, a small ice cream parlor (reviewed below). The long main dining area features an open kitchen and a brick pizza oven. There is a separate, more intimate dining room at the far end. The furnishings and table settings follow the pattern of eclectic mismatching found throughout the hotel and the overall effect is delightful. The entire restaurant looks out through generous glass walls to the pool area and there is an outdoor seating area where the tables are shaded by snazzy square canvas umbrellas.

Breakfast is the most traditional meal, as the counters by the open kitchen are transformed into a sumptuous buffet. You can choose the full Breakfast Buffet (about $13), or you can order a la carte from a menu of standards, from bacon and eggs to waffles with fruit, all of them well executed.

Lunch is on the light side as is the service; a ten-minute wait for a table is not uncommon. Pizzas are $9 to $11, with the most interesting choice topped with ancho grilled chicken and roasted corn. Main dishes ($10 to $17) range from a simple Mac and Cheese to New York Steak and fries. Otherwise, there are salads and sandwiches ($7 to $12).

Dinner expands the lunch menu with straightforward interpretations of salmon, fish and chips, roasted chicken, and barbecued ribs. It's rather like what you'd expect to find over at the Hard Rock Cafe, and perhaps that's the point. The food is good without making an attempt to be exceptional. Salads are in the $9 to $14 range, pizzas $9 to $12, sandwiches and burgers $10 to $14. Heartier entrees range from the $10 Mac and Cheese to a $22 filet mignon and a $24 New York strip steak.

At press time, this restaurant seemed to be poised for a theme change, so by the time you visit things may have changed.

Emack and Bolio's

What:	Ice cream parlor
Where:	On the ground floor at the entrance to The Kitchen
Price Range:	$ -$$
Hours:	6:00 a.m. to 11:00 p.m. daily
Reservations:	None

In the morning, Emack and Bolio's serves up quick, easy to carry breakfast items like yogurt, fruit cups, and Starbucks coffee. It's main line of business, however, is upscale, high-fat, premium ice cream and fruit smoothies. The ice cream flavors have cutesy Ben & Jerry's style names, often with a rock and roll twist. A single scoop costs $3.25 and a pint goes for $7.50. Sundaes start at $4, but why not round up seven friends and splurge on a $22 Emack Attack?

Beach Club

What:	Bar and snacks al fresco
Where:	By the pool
Price Range:	$$
Hours:	11:00 a.m. to 10:00 p.m.

The pool enjoys its own **Beach Club**, a casual bar serving light fare, with optional poolside service. The circular bar is open to the pool and raffishly decorated with rusted metal sculptures of musicians. Tables spill out from under the conical roof, but roaming servers will take your order and fetch you food and drink anywhere in the pool area.

The abbreviated menu ranges from the sort of salty snacks that will encourage you to order another beer, to salads and sandwiches, to simple desserts. The sandwiches ($8 to $13) range from hot dogs and burgers (including veggie burgers) to more refined fare. Or you can build your own pizza ($9 and up). Salads ($9 to $13) range from a simple dish of mixed greens to Caesar salads with chicken or salmon. The desserts ($3 to $5) are basic affairs like ice cream bars and fruit pops, and the fruit cup is actually good for you.

Shopping at Hard Rock Hotel

"Love all. Serve all. Sell all a tchotchke." That's not *really* the Hard Rock motto, of course, but it's hard to escape noticing that the Hard Rock empire must make as much money selling branded clothing, souvenirs, and memorabilia as it does selling burgers, shakes, and booze. So it's fitting that the only shop in the hotel is the bluntly named **Hard Rock Store** just off the main lobby.

Most of the room in this spacious emporium is given over to souvenir clothing, from t-shirts to snazzy leather jackets with equally snazzy price tags. If you have arrived only to discover that your wardrobe isn't what it should be, you can remedy that here. There are some suitably slinky dresses and beachwear for women. Somehow, the men's clothing, while very nice, is rather staid, the kind of thing that wouldn't look out of place on the PGA tour.

There are some nice things for kids here, too, including a perfectly adorable teddy bear decked out in a Hard Rock t-shirt and black leather jacket (about $45). Almost as an afterthought, a corner of the shop is given over to a small selection of the sort of sundries you usually find in a hotel gift shop. You will have to head to Le Memorie di Portofino shop in Portofino Bay's lobby for a larger selection.

ROYAL PACIFIC RESORT

Like the Hard Rock, the Royal Pacific Resort has a "backstory" that subtly informed the design of the hotel and the themes of its restaurants. This one involves the Royal Pacific family of companies, a made-up travel and transportation conglomerate that flourished in the 1930s, the "Golden Age of Travel." It's holdings included Royal Pacific Airways, a fleet of dashing sea planes that linked the sprawling island chains of the South Pacific, and Royal Pacific Steamship Lines, a fleet of luxury ocean liners that plied the tropical seas. The Royal Pacific Resort, it would seem, is the latest jewel in the Royal

Pacific crown, a luxury getaway located somewhere in Bali. Of course, none of this is terribly overt. It's a muted story, told with subtlety — a welcome message in the in-room hotel directory, the 30s-style jazz that plays throughout the property, the retro-art on the travel posters in your room, and the occasional display case of memorabilia dotted around the property, not to mention the Royal Pacific Airways Grumman Albatross sea plane floating near the water taxi dock. Everything here has been inspired by, rather than copied from, Indonesia and Fiji, so the hotel reminds you of the South Seas while remaining very much its own place.

If the fictional Royal Pacific was a company of the 30s, the present seven-story hotel is very much of the twenty-first century. Its public spaces are expansive, airy and luxurious, tastefully decorated with genuine Indonesian woodcarvings and other art works. Its amenities are state of the art and the dining venues, including a new restaurant by Emeril Legasse, are a cut or three above standard hotel fare.

The architecture reflects its Balinese inspiration. The facade is rather flat and featureless, a mustard-colored slab in the Florida sun. The exterior looks far better at night, when artfully placed spotlights and the shadows cast by palm trees add texture and depth to the building's flat surfaces.

While the other hotels have meeting space — Hard Rock a little, Portofino Bay somewhat more — the Royal Pacific was designed as a full-fledged convention hotel. The attached convention center is vast. In fact, all of Portofino Bay's meeting space could fit into Royal Pacific's Grand Ballroom with enough space left over to swing quite a few cats. Of course, with its fabulous and fun pool and its proximity to two great theme parks, the Royal Pacific has drawn a large leisure and family business as well.

Note: The Royal Pacific is the newest of the resort hotels, so there will be an inevitable period of experimentation, as the hotel discovers which elements are a big hit with guests and which elements need to be tweaked or even eliminated. Consequently, the descriptions in this section are subject to change without notice. If something is particularly important to you, make sure to check with the hotel before arrival.

Orientation

Your Royal Pacific Resort experience begins when you cross a broad, thatched-roofed, bamboo-accented bridge over an artificial river. Step into the massive rectangular lobby and you enter a Balinese demi-paradise. Pause to admire the intricately carved Indonesian wood panels hanging on the walls on either side of the entrance. The lobby completely surrounds a glassed-in, orchard-accented courtyard pool. Statuary elephants cavort in its shallow depths while fountains in the form of Southeast Asian temple statuary constantly replenish its waters. At night, with a crescent moon high overhead, this courtyard is ravishingly romantic.

To the left of the courtyard pool is the reception area, to the right an elegant staircase that descends two stories to the hotel's main restaurant and the swimming pool area. Also to the right, just around the corner and past the staircase is a spacious seating area complete with expansive views and the elegant Orchid Court Lounge bar. The floor to ceiling windows here evoke the open-air pavilion architecture that represents the finest in Balinese living.

The hotel's 1,000 rooms are arrayed off the lobby in three Y-shaped, seven-story wings, called Towers. Tower 1, The Windward, is to your right as you enter, Tower 2, The Leeward, is to your left, and Tower 3, The Royal, which houses the hotel's Club Level rooms on its seventh floor, is directly opposite the main entrance. (In your four-digit room number the first digit indicates which tower you're in and the second digit denotes the floor.)

The swimming pool is located between the Windward and Royal Towers, and beyond the pool the rides and attractions of Islands of Adventure form an antic skyline. The space between the Leeward and Royal Towers, in contrast, is given over to a quiet putting green and open spaces, such as the Wantilan Terrace, designed for outdoor events. The Leeward and Windward Towers frame the main entrance.

The lobby is on the third level. Most of the dining and other amenities will be found two floors below. From the Islands Dining Room, the hotel's main restaurant, a covered walkway hugs the building as it makes it way past the pool to Tchoup Chop, Emeril Legasse's latest splashy restaurant, and the vast convention center beyond that is attached to the hotel.

The water taxi dock is near Tchoup Chop, most convenient to rooms in the Royal Tower and a longish walk past the pool from the lobby area. From the water taxi stop, the "Garden Walkway" runs along the shore of the Bali Sea, past the pool and on to CityWalk. It takes less than ten minutes to stroll there at a leisurely pace. The main entrance is not recommended for pedestrian traffic and is most conveniently reached by car.

Rooms and Suites

Compared to the wide-open public spaces, the rooms seem small. They are decorated in tones of burgundy red and muted gold with dark wood furniture and carved wooden lamps echoing Indonesian influences. The pictures on the walls, also framed in dark wood from the islands, are often fanciful 30s-style travel posters or paintings of cruise ships of the Royal Pacific Steamship Lines. Some find the decor "dark," but I find it rather soothing.

There is a compact vanity area with a sink just outside the bathroom (which has no sink). All rooms have coffee makers for that morning jolt of java, as well as the usual blow dryer for damp hair and iron and ironing board.

Since the Royal Pacific was designed as a convention hotel, there is one distinct difference from the other hotels: all rooms are standard rooms. There are no slightly larger rooms designated as "deluxe rooms" as there are at Portofino and the Hard Rock. The next step up from a standard room is a suite. Like the standard rooms, the suites were designed with the convention trade in mind. They are the nicely appointed two-room suites you would expect in any business hotel; they feature a small microwave, CD/DVD players, and video games for the kids. The Royal Pacific does not have gaily decorated "Kids' Suites" such as those at the other resort hotels. The hotel does, however, feature a Club Level with restricted access in the Royal Tower. For more on the Club Level, see *Amenities*, below.

For high rollers, I would strongly recommend The Captain's Suite, located on the seventh floor Club Level of the Royal Tower. It is exquisitely decorated with Indonesian art and fabrics and features a full kitchen and a guest bathroom off the entry foyer. All the super luxury suites at the resort hotels are grand and splashy, but to my taste this one is the most quietly elegant, the kind of place you could imagine yourself having as a permanent residence. It also has the best view in the hotel, a sweeping vista of the pool area and Islands of Adventure. Compared to the suite rates charged at the other resort hotels the $1,000 or $1,200 it will cost to book the Captain's Suite is a positive bargain.

Pool view rooms are obviously much sought after. Unfortunately, the hotel has just 173 such rooms, so your odds of getting one are approximately one in six. The hotel will try to honor requests for a specific view but they cannot guarantee them.

See *Room Rates at a Glance*, at the beginning of this chapter, to get an idea of the price range at Royal Pacific and how it compares to the other on-site hotels.

Amenities

One thing you might expect of a hotel with "resort" in its name is a spa, but Royal Pacific lacks this amenity, directing its guests to the Greenhouse Spa at the Portofino Bay Hotel. For the rest, the choices are limited but well executed.

Lagoon Pool

The Royal Pacific may have only one pool, but it's the largest in the city of Orlando (although not, it should be noted, in the greater Orlando area). It sprawls languorously between the Windward and Royal Towers beside the

Bali Sea end of the winding waterway that links all the resort hotels with CityWalk. The heated pool is like a small tropical sea itself, with an irregular, sinuous shape and even a tiny palm-dotted island. It's shallow, too, designed more for playing than serious swimming, with no spot deeper than about four feet seven inches.

One side is dominated by the superstructure of the Royal Bali Sea, a ship of the Royal Pacific line that seems to have run aground and buried itself in the sand. Actually it's an elaborate water play area (think *Curious George* over at Universal Studios) that gushes cold, bracing water from every conceivable orifice, while kids man a battery of water cannons, never seeming to tire of squirting each other and unsuspecting swimmers who venture too close to shore. This is Royal Pacific's answer to the water slides at the other resorts and kids love it.

On this side, the pool bottom slopes gently up to water's edge, affording little ones easy entry. Nearby is a white sandy beach area and a fenced children's play area complete with wading pool and sandbox (pails included).

Near the middle, the pool narrows to accommodate a volleyball net strung from shore to shore and an impromptu game between former strangers always seems to be in progress. The opposite side is more adult-oriented. Here you will find the Bula Bar and Grill, three cabanas, a red-topped pool table, and two hot tubs — one somewhat larger than the other. Between the pool and the hotel is a concrete shuffleboard court; you will often see a ping pong table in this area when the weather cooperates.

Cabanas are small (two lounge chairs fill them up), canvas-sided shelters with a TV, ceiling fan, and a small fridge. Full day rentals (8:00 a.m. to pool closing) are $75 with half-day rentals (3:00 p.m. to pool closing) at $35. Club Level guests get full day rentals for just $40. Rentals are handled by the staff at The Gymnasium (see below) and cabanas can be reserved weeks or months in advance, just like rooms.

Each night at sunset, near the Bula Bar end of the pool, the wail of conch shells and the sonorous singing of a Samoan chieftain signal the start of a brief "torch lighting ceremony." Many people drift over to watch from the shallow water.

Just outside the fenced-in pool area is the "Garden Walkway" that takes you to CityWalk. The gates are usually open during the day, but in the evening you will need your room key to gain entry.

Volleyball Court

Also just outside the pool, on the very edge of the Bali Sea, is a splendidly inviting, white sand regulation volleyball court. Reserve the court and borrow a ball at The Gymnasium (see below). It's **free**.

Club Level

The rooms and suites on the seventh floor of the Royal Tower have been set aside for those who enjoy that extra little bit of pampering. The concept is much like that used at the Hard Rock, and if you've enjoyed Club Level service there, you'll no doubt want to see how the Royal Pacific compares.

As at the Hard Rock, access is strictly limited; a slot in the elevator reads your room key before it will take you to seven. At the end of the corridor, you will find a spacious V-shaped lounge with picture windows looking out across Interstate Four to the International Drive area. It is staffed with friendly hosts and hostesses, who serve as your personal concierges from 7:30 a.m. to 11:00 p.m. This is where you come in the morning for a complimentary continental breakfast and to glance through the tony out of town newspapers high rollers insist upon. The lounge serves refreshments throughout the day; hors d'oeuvres, beer and wine in the evening; and "Something Sweet" before bedtime.

Club Level guests can borrow from the Club's collection of DVDs for viewing on the large screen TVs at either end of the lounge. Club Level guests also receive free access to the hotel's fitness center and discounts on poolside cabanas.

Game Room

A small unattended video arcade is located along the sheltered walkway that leads from the Islands Dining Room to Tchoup Chop and the convention center. The machines operate on tokens dispensed by a machine that accepts $1, $5, $10, and $20 bills. The games, none of them terribly elaborate, cost between 50 cents and $1.

The Mariners' Club

Just past the Game Room is Royal Pacific's children's playroom. For more information about the services offered here, see *Good Things To Know About . . . Kids' Activities* in the introductory section of this chapter. Make your reservations 24 hours in advance by calling 33235 on a hotel phone or (407) 503-3235 from outside.

The Gymnasium

This sleek, modern, but rather spartan fitness room is close by the Lagoon Pool, just past the Treasures of Bali shop as you head to the convention center. The equipment is state-of-the-art but free weights are also available for the old-fashioned pumping iron crowd. The fee is $8 per day, $12 for two days, and $20 for three; it includes use of the sauna, steam bath, and a unisex whirlpool room, which is a particularly lovely place to hang out and relax. Club Level guests and Loews First members receive complimentary use of the fitness facilities. Kids 12 through 16 are allowed, but only if they have adult supervision. The Gymnasium is open from 6:00 a.m. to 9:00 p.m.

Putting Green

Far from the frenzied activity of the pool area, on the other side of the Royal Tower wing, is a meticulously groomed six-hole putting green, where the harried executive can come to unwind and practice those elusive double birdie putts. If you didn't bring your own, you can pick up a **free** putter and a ball at The Gymnasium.

Good Things To Know About. . .

Character Dining

Scooby Doo, Curious George, and Woody Woodpecker stop by to entertain diners in the Islands Dining Room on Monday and Tuesday nights from about 6:30 to 9:00 p.m. Double-check with the concierge on the schedule, since days and times are subject to change.

Guest Laundry

Each Tower has a guest laundry room. In the Royal Tower, it is on the second level. In the other two towers, it is on the bottom floor with an outside entrance. There are three washers and three dryers in each room. The cost is $2 per load to wash and the same to dry.

Meetings and Banquets

The Royal Pacific was designed as a convention hotel, with some 75,000 square feet of meeting space. The Grand Ballroom alone is 41,500 square feet. The convention area, which is adjacent to but quite separate from the hotel itself, is spacious and airy and decorated with a South Seas nostalgia theme. The walls are dotted with fanciful 1930s-style travel posters and memorabilia. If you'd like more information about how your company might take advantage of all this, call (407) 503-3100.

Parking

As with the other hotels there is a $6 per day fee for self-parking and $12 a day (plus tips, of course) for valet parking. There is less guest parking available at the Royal Pacific than at the other resort hotels, which means that if you are self-parking, finding an empty space can be a challenge. One choice is to park at the rear of the hotel in the convention center parking area. Or you might want to consider paying the extra money for valet parking to avoid the hassle. If you fly into Orlando and plan to spend most of your time at the major attractions, you might want to consider foregoing a rental car during your Royal Pacific stay and using shuttles and other options to get around. (See *Good Things To Know About... Transportation Elsewhere* at the beginning of this chapter.)

Dining at Royal Pacific Resort

The food at Royal Pacific tends to be of the sit-down variety and on the pricey side. The good news is that the food served here is worth the premium prices charged. Those looking for a quick bite or more moderately priced fare will have to travel to City Walk.

Orchid Court Lounge

What:	Lounge bar with continental breakfast and appetizers
Where:	In the main lobby
Hours:	6:00 a.m. to midnight
Price Range:	$$ - $$$

This elegant lobby bar and lounge area is awash in the gorgeous orchids from which it takes its name. It serves up exotic drinks ($9) along with a short menu of elegant appetizers ($9 to $21). Among the latter, the lobster martini is nicely spicy with a soothing touch of avocado and the spring roll, served in a deep bowl in a mild broth, is stuffed with rich snow crab meat. A sampler platter unites sushi and sashimi to delicious effect.

The potables range from martinis, to frozen drinks, to elaborate "South Seas" concoctions like Mai Tais and the signature Pacific Passion that arrive garnished with colorful little umbrellas or enormous tropical palm leaves. Wine is available by the glass.

You can sit in the small tiled area near the bar, but I prefer the expansive lobby seating area looking out over the Lagoon Pool across to Islands of Adventure. Here you can sink into a wicker chair or sit on a beautiful Chinese-style bed that has been converted into a settee. Waitresses in smart silk trousers with contrasting tops will take your order.

In the morning, from 6:00 a.m. to 11:00 a.m., the bar at the Orchid Court turns into a cafeteria line serving an a la carte continental breakfast featuring cereal, fruit, and a variety of breakfast breads and pastries. It has proven to be a popular option and the lines are frequently quite long. Careful! If you have a hearty appetite the cost can quickly approach that of the buffet breakfast downstairs at the Islands Dining Room. One saving grace is that coffee refills are free and unlimited until 11:00 a.m.

Islands Dining Room

What: Full-service all-day dining
Where: Directly below the lobby overlooking the pool
Hours: 7:00 a.m. to 2:30 p.m. and 5:00 p.m. to 11:00 p.m.
Price Range: $$$ - $$$$+

The hotel's main dining room is a real winner, one that may give Emeril a run for his money in the gourmet dining sweepstakes at Royal Pacific.

The large dining area (the restaurant seats 380) is styled in the Indonesian fashion with louvered walls and ceiling fans hand-fashioned from silken hand fans. A service station takes the form of a fanciful Balinese hut, while Indonesian carved wooden panels divide the room into separate seating areas. Floor to ceiling windows seem to bring the pool area indoors and huge carved frogs from Indonesia stand sentinel-like, adding a whimsical touch. Alcoves along one side of the room serve as added dining space, or buffet lines, one of them set aside for the special evening kids' buffet ($4), complete with kiddie-sized tables and chairs, a great way to give the grown-ups a mealtime break.

Most breakfast tastes can be accommodated — there's even a Japanese breakfast option — with the typical a la carte breakfast running just over $10. Unless, of course, you order something like Roasted Chicken Egg Foo Yong or Guava Bar-B-Q Shredded Pork on Goat Cheese Grits (topped with fried eggs and very good indeed), in which case your bill could easily reach $15, the price of the sumptuous, all-you-can-eat breakfast buffet that includes made-to-order eggs and omelettes. The children's version of the breakfast buffet is $7.50 with a la carte children's dishes about $3.

The lunch menu is an abbreviated version of the dinner menu, with more moderate prices. For example, Jake's New York Strip Steak (very good, by the way) is $19.50 at lunch, $24 at dinner. Sandwiches ($9 to $12) are also available and include South Seas versions of the standard burger and the traditional club sandwich.

Dinner is where the kitchen at Islands Dining Room comes into its own. Islands turns out some of the best dinner entrees at any of the resort hotels, with prices to match. It is easy to spend $30 to $40 or more per person on food alone, without drinks, tax, or tip. For many people that will put dinner here in the "special occasion" category, although the aforementioned $4 kids' buffet may lessen the impact on the old wallet. That being said, I don't think you will leave the table disappointed.

The appetizers ($9 to $21) are those served upstairs in the Orchid Court Lounge and they are very good indeed. Salads ($8 to $10) include a wonderfully simple "Seven Leaf" with lemon-soy vinaigrette.

Entrees ($12 to $26) range from upscale versions of homey dishes like udon noodles and fried rice to a buttery filet mignon ($26) served over creamed spinach with a yuca goat cheese puree on the side. Among the seafood choices, the Pistachio Crusted Pacific Sea Bass ($22) and the Black Cod in Sake-Miso ($20) are especially good.

Desserts (just over $6) are superb. The serving sizes are modest with presentation every bit as important as taste. The consensus is that the Dark Chocolate Souffle and the Trio of Pacific Fruit Creme Brulee (a mini-masterpiece of Japanese-style minimalist art) are the best.

The Islands Dining Room features Character Dining (I've spotted Curious George and Woody Woodpecker) and strolling entertainers. Several nights a week a themed buffet is offered for $24. Australian, Balinese, and Hawaiian have been among the themes featured, with entertainment to match. You may also see a strolling witch-doctor magician or hear strolling Pacific-islands musicians.

Jake's American Bar

What:	Bar and light meals
Where:	Downstairs, near Islands Dining Room
Hours:	2:00 p.m. to 2:00 a.m., kitchen closes at 11:00 p.m.
Price Range:	$$

Jake McNally was quite a guy, a sea plane pilot for Royal Pacific Airways who won the "World Series of sea plane racing" in 1927. Jake's exploits in love were as dismal as his airborne feats were glorious. Dumped by the love of his life, Jake disappeared and is rumored to be flying from one backwater dive to another trying to forget. This bar is a tribute to his memory by his friends, who have donated memorabilia to help decorate the joint. It's all made up, of course, but this fanciful story forms the basis for one of the most successful themed restaurants in all of Universal Orlando.

The decor is clubby and casual, echoing the open architecture of the South Seas, where any breeze is welcome. In fact, it's worth peeking into Jake's just to marvel at the ceiling fans. Also a great deal of fun is the Jake McNally memorabilia and the framed love letters that grace the walls. There is something ever so slightly mysterious about Jake's that I can't quite put my finger on, but it makes you feel like a minor — but dashing — character in *Casablanca*, not a bad feeling at all.

The food is as jaunty as the decor with the accent on casual bar fare that won't overly tax the wallet, another reason Jake's has become so popular with guests. The "From The Hangar" section of the menu ($8 to $11) consists of appetizer-like nibbles such as "peel n' eat" shrimp and plantain nachos, a nice take on a familiar favorite. The Royal Pu Pu Platter is well worth sampling, certainly not the cliche its name might suggest. For veggie lovers there are salads like Caesar and Cobb, with the mixed garden greens a light-bite winner, especially with the ginger soy dressing.

Slightly more substantial are the club sandwiches and burgers, with the most expensive item on the menu ($20) Brandi's Baby Back Ribs, melt in your mouth guava glazed ribs served with baked potato and steamed corn. Yum!

Of course, Jake's *is* a bar and dining is not mandatory. Jake's would make an excellent choice for drinks before (or after) dining at Islands. Along with the usual, the bartenders here whip up a variety of lethal "South Seas" concoctions with don't-tell-me-I-didn't-warn-you names like Tsunami. Setting new heights for exotic concoctions is the flaming Mt. Kumuneyewana-drinkya, a 32-ounce behemoth with at least eight ounces of rum and other booze lurking in its depths.

If you stop by for a nightcap, I recommend the small outside seating area under the bridge that forms the entrance to the hotel. Here you can enjoy the lingering warmth of a summer night with a waterfall providing a romantic soundtrack.

Bula Bar and Grille

What:	Casual poolside dining
Where:	By the pool, near the Royal Tower
Hours:	11:00 a.m. to 10:00 p.m., kitchen closes at 8:00 p.m.
Price Range:	$$ - $$$

An inviting palapa-like bar beckons thirsty swimmers with exotic drink concoctions (a bit over $8) ranging from Mai Tais to less well-known potions with names like "Witch Doctor," whose lengthy list of ingredients might give even the heartiest boozer pause. Other drinks are available as well, of course, with beers going for $4 to $5. Non-alcoholic Tropical Smoothies in strawberry, mango and passion fruit flavors are also on tap for those who want to get into the South Seas swing of things and still walk.

Light meals, snacks really, are available from the Grille part of the establishment, cooked up in a small kitchen a few paces away. They range in price from $8 to $12 and include plantain chips with a roasted poblano cheese dip, a shrimp cocktail, the "Hang-Ten" hot dog, and (at about $10) the "famous" Bula Burger. More adult choices include seafood skewers and a cilantro marinated grouper wrap.

Tchoup Chop

What:	Another Emeril's extravaganza
Where:	Near the convention center

Hours: To be announced
Price Range: $$$$+

Tchoup Chop (pronounced "chop-chop") was not open at press time. When it does open, it promises to be to Royal Pacific what Delfino Riviera is to Portofino Bay, the signature restaurant for the hotel and a destination in its own right. And being an Emeril Legasse restaurant, the cooking should be as bold as the pricing.

Emeril has apparently been nurturing this concept for some time and originally planned it for New Orleans. (The Tchoup in Tchoup Chop is a reference to Tchoupitoulas Street where the original Emeril's restaurant is located.) The cuisine is inspired both by the Polynesian islands of the South Pacific and Asian cooking techniques, with the fresh seafood of the Gulf of Mexico and the nearby Atlantic playing a strong supporting role. But don't expect a re-run of Trader Vic's, which is the stereotype of a Polynesian restaurant. Emeril is promising what he calls "the real deal," an authentic menu that is true to its culinary inspiration.

The restaurant is located at the point where the Royal Pacific Resort meets the massive convention center attached to the hotel, and guests arriving from CityWalk will find it wonderfully convenient to the boat dock. Tchoup Chop will be pretty massive itself. Over 6,200 square feet, the space will be surrounded by a terrarium of tropical plants, waterfalls, and elaborate gardens.

Guests will pass through a carved wooden moon gate into dining areas accented with soft wooden grilles, batik canopies, pierced metal light fixtures, and cast-glass chandeliers, all of which will be offset by bright tropical flowers. An outdoor dining terrace will seat 160.

The open kitchen will add drama to a meal at Tchoup Chop and provide an opportunity for what is being billed as "interactive" experiences between chefs and diners. Sake and tea will feature in the culinary concept here, much as wine would in a fine French restaurant. Tchoup Chop is destined to become instantly popular and the odds are that the Legasse touch will keep the place booked up well after the initial curiosity has been satisfied. So if you plan to dine here, book your dining reservation when you book your hotel room.

Wantilan Luau

What: Hawaiian-themed dinner show
Where: On the Wantilan Terrace
Hours: Saturday nights at 7:30 p.m.
Price Range: Adults $50, children under 13 $29

Wantilan is Indonesian for "gathering place" and at the outdoor

Wantilan Terrace, on Saturday nights, the hotel gathers its guests together with that tried-and-true staple of warm weather tourism, a Hawaiian luau complete with roast suckling pig on your plate and Hawaiian hams on stage, but thankfully no poi.

The generous buffet meal starts with fruits and salads, continues with Lomi Lomi Chicken Salad, Roasted Pacific Wahoo, and the aforementioned Pit-Roasted Suckling Pig, before wrapping up with a dessert station with goodies like White Chocolate Macadamia Nut Pie and Chocolate Banana Cake. Wine, beer, and soft drinks are included in the price and a cash bar is available. The entertainment is as rich and filling as the meal, featuring a medley of Polynesian song stylings and hula dancing.

This sort of thing is not to everyone's taste, but there's no denying its popularity. By my count, this makes the third luau-style dinner show in the Orlando area. Reservations are required and are open to non-guests. Call (407) 503-3463 to make your arrangements.

Shopping at Royal Pacific Resort

Shopping here is muted and low key. Off the lobby, you will find **Toko Gifts**, a small shop that at first glance seems entirely devoted to casual clothing and souvenirs, all with Royal Pacific and Universal logos. Peek around the corner at the back and you will find magazines and sundries of the sort you'd expect at any hotel lobby store.

More elaborate is **Treasures of Bali**, located near the pool on the way to the convention wing. This is the place to come if you forgot to pack your swim gear. Swimsuits for men and women are stocked here, along with a variety of balls and toys suitable for pool play. You will find some very nice resort wear for after-pool occasions, much of it with a South Seas flavor. A small selection of Indonesian crafts can be found here and, if you poke around in the back of the shop, you'll discover some magazines and popular novels for poolside reading.

CHAPTER SEVEN:

Staying Near The Parks

If you aren't staying at one of Universal Orlando's on-property hotels, you may want to consider staying close by. The following hotels are located along Major Boulevard, just opposite the Kirkman Road entrance to the Universal Orlando property. They are listed below in order of their distance to CityWalk. It is actually possible to walk into the parks from these hotels, although it can be an uncomfortably warm walk on hot days. Major Boulevard is also served by the Super Star Shuttle (see *Chapter One*) which stops at the Radisson Twin Towers, the Holiday Inn, and the Sleep Inn. Guests staying at adjacent hotels often avail themselves of this service, which at press time was free to all.

The price range refers to the cost of a standard double room, from low season to high, as follows:

$	Under $50
$$	$50 – $100
$$$	$100 – $150
$$$$	Over $150

Be aware that at particularly busy times the cost of a room can soar to astronomical levels, regardless of what it says here.

Radisson Twin Towers
5780 Major Boulevard
Orlando, FL 32819
(800) 333-3333; (407) 351-1000; fax (407) 363-0106

www.radisson.com

A sleek corporate-style hotel (there's a convention center attached) that is a favorite with upscale overseas visitors.

Price Range: $$ – $$$$

Amenities: Large pool, five restaurants, playground, exercise room, business center, shops

Holiday Inn

5905 South Kirkman Road
Orlando, FL 32819
(800) 327-1364; (407) 351-3333; fax (407) 351-3577
www.basshotels.com/holiday-inn

Standard mid-range hotel with ten-story all-suite tower.

Price Range: $$ – $$$$

Amenities: Pool, volleyball, TGI Friday's restaurant, fitness center, business center

Amerisuites

5895 Caravan Court
Orlando, FL 32819
(800) 833-1516; (407) 351-0627; fax (407) 351-3317
www.amerisuites.com

Mid-range all-suite hotel chain.

Price Range: $$ – $$$

Amenities: Outdoor pool, fitness center, complimentary breakfast buffet

Days Inn

5827 Caravan Court
Orlando, FL 32819
(800) 329-7466; (407) 351-3800; fax (407) 363-0907
www.daysinn.com

Typical budget-class motel.

Price Range: $ – $$

Amenities: Pools, in-room movies, game rooms

Ramada Limited

5652 Major Boulevard
Orlando, FL 32819
(800) 228-2828; (407) 354-3996; fax (407) 354-3299
www.ramada-hotels.com

Spartan budget motel.
Price Range: $ - $$
Amenities: Pool, continental breakfast

Comfort Suites
5617 Major Boulevard
Orlando, FL 32819
(800) 424-6423; (407) 363-1967; fax (407) 363-6873
www.choicehotels.com
All-suite hotel.
Price Range: $$ - $$$
Amenities: Pool, continental breakfast

Red Roof Inn
5621 Major Boulevard
Orlando, FL 32819
(800) 843-7663; (407) 313-3100
www.redroof.com
Standard budget motel.
Price Range: $$ - $$$
Amenities: Pool, HBO, continental breakfast

Suburban Lodge
5615 Major Boulevard
Orlando, FL 32819
(800) 951-7829; (407) 313-2000; fax (407) 313-2010
www.suburbanlodge.com
Mid-range all-suite property with kitchenettes.
Price Range: $$ - $$$
Amenities: Pool, HBO

Extended Stay America
5620 Major Boulevard
Orlando, FL 32819
(800) 398-7829; (407) 351-1788; fax (407) 351-7899
www.extstay.com
Budget-priced all-suite property with well-equipped kitchenettes, including pots, pans, dishes, a microwave, and a coffee maker.
Price Range: $ - $$
Amenities: Laundry room, three Showtime channels, use of pool at StudioPLUS

StudioPLUS
5610 Vineland Road
Orlando, FL 32819
(888) 788-3467; (407) 370-4428; fax (407) 370-9456
www.extstay.com
Mid-range all-suite property, a slightly more upscale variant of the Extended Stay America formula.
Price Range: $ - $$
Amenities: Laundry room, Showtime, pool

Sleep Inn & Suites
5605 Major Boulevard
Orlando, FL 32819
(800) 7533-3746; (407) 363-1333; fax (407) 363-4510
www.sleepinn.com
Eleven-story hotel with both standard rooms and suites.
Price Range: $$ - $$$
Amenities: Outdoor pool, exercise room, continental breakfast

Fairfield Inn & Suites
5614 Vineland Road
Orlando, FL 32819
(800) 826-7045; (407) 581-5600; fax (407) 581-5601
www.avistahotels.com
Standard budget hotel with some suites.
Price Range: $$ - $$$
Amenities: Outdoor whirlpool, exercise room, breakfast

Best Western Universal Inn
5618 Vineland Road
Orlando, FL 32819
(800) 780-7234; (407) 226-9119
www.bestwestern.com
Standard mid-range motel chain.
Price Range: $$ - $$$$
Amenities: Pool, continental breakfast

Index to Rides & Attractions

This Index lists (mostly) rides, attractions, and restaurants mentioned in the text. The location of each entry is indicated by the following abbreviations: (CW) - CityWalk; (HR) - Hard Rock Hotel; (IOA) - Islands of Adventure; (PB) - Portofino Bay Hotel; (RP) - Royal Pacific Resort; (USF) - Universal Studios Florida.

Updates

For updates to this book or information about its two companion volumes, *The Other Orlando: What To Do When You've Done Disney & Universal,* by Kelly Monaghan, and *The Hassle-Free Walt Disney World Vacation*, by Steven M. Barrett, please visit:

http://www.TheOtherOrlando.com

Other Books from The Intrepid Traveler

The Intrepid Traveler publishes money-saving, horizon expanding travel how-to and guidebooks dedicated to helping its readers make world travel an integral part of their everyday life.

In addition, we offer hard-to-find specialty books from other publishers. For more information visit our web site, where you will find a complete catalog, frequent updates to this and other of our books, travel articles from around the world, Internet travel resources, and more:

http://www.IntrepidTraveler.com

If you are interested in becoming a home-based travel agent, visit the Home-Based Travel Agent Resource Center at:

http://www.HomeTravelAgency.com

For this book's companion volumes, *The Other Orlando: What To Do When You've Done Disney & Universal* and *The Hassle-Free Walt Disney World Vacation,* plus updates to all our Orlando guidebooks, visit:

http://www.TheOtherOrlando.com